DUE PROCESS
IN THE ADMINISTRATIVE STATE

Due Process in the Administrative State

JERRY L. MASHAW

YALE UNIVERSITY PRESS
New Haven   London

Published with assistance from the foundation
established in memory of Amasa Stone Mather
of the class of 1907, Yale College.

Designed by Margaret E.B. Joyner
and set in Baskerville type by Eastern Graphics.
Printed in the United States of America by
Edwards Brothers Inc., Ann Arbor, Michigan.

Library of Congress Cataloging in Publication Data

Mashaw, Jerry L.
   Due process in the administrative state.

   Includes index.
      1. Due process of law—United States.
   2. Administrative procedure—United States.
   I. Title.
   KF5407.M37   1985   347.73   84-20948
   ISBN 0–300–03258–7   347.307

The paper in this book meets the guidelines for
permanence and durability of the Committee on
Production Guidelines for Book Longevity of the
Council on Library Resources.

10   9   8   7   6   5   4   3   2   1

For

A.U.M.

If you are a man who leads,
Listen calmly to the speech of one who pleads;
Don't stop him from purging his body
Of that which he planned to tell.
A man in distress wants to pour out his heart
More than that his case be won.
About him who stops a plea
One says: "Why does he reject it?"
Not all one pleads for can be granted,
But a good hearing soothes the heart.

The Instruction of Ptahhotep
(Egyptian, 6th Dynasty,
2300–2150 B.C.)

I have always thought that one of this Court's most important roles is to [protect] the legitimate expectations of every person to innate human dignity and a sense of self worth.

Justice William Brennan, dissenting
in *Paul v. Davis*,
424 U.S. 693, 734–35 (1976).

Contents

ix

Preface

I have been writing on aspects of this topic for longer than I like to remember, and I have not addressed the subject again, and at length, merely to retract all my former views. Those conversant with the literature of administrative due process will therefore find much in chapters 3 through 5 that is familiar. Nevertheless, I invite even those who know this field and my prior efforts well to think it through with me once again. For as I have tried to make sense of what I and others have been saying over the past decade, I have rather substantially reoriented by ideas. This book is in some sense an integration of earlier views, but the whole has turned out to be surprisingly different from what I anticipated when contemplating earlier versions of its parts.

To a degree this sense of novelty emerges from a shift in perspective. I attempt here to think about administrative due process in terms of the demands of constitutional adjudication—to develop a theory that is at once continuous with our constitutional history, consistent with our peculiar liberal-democratic political philosophy, appropriate for a modern administrative state, and yet usable in the context of appellate litigation. This aspiration, at once theoretical and practical, has led me to consider anew some old questions and to address some new ones. Chief among the latter are (1) an assessment of the *Goldberg v. Kelly* "due process revolution" and its meaning for contemporary political organization, (2) an appreciation of ordinary legal discourse and its implications for the structure of due process adjudication, and (3) an analysis of the appropriate allocation of power to design administrative processes among legal institutions. Reflections on these issues make up the bulk of chapters 1, 2, 6, and 7.

Taken together, the old and the new are meant to represent an integrated theory of administrative due process adjudication. But the reader should be warned that this is a theory that combines many awkward components. It insists simultaneously on judicial value creation and on judicial restraint; on the necessity of philosophical inquiry and on the utility of ordinary legal reasoning; on the fundamental value of individual dignity and on the competence of institutions of collective choice (legislatures and administrative agencies) to make virtually all judgments about the design of public decision processes affecting individuals. My readers must determine whether an integration, rather than a mere pastiche, of these apparently conflicting features has been presented—and, if so, whether the discussion also provides a convincing argument for the theory's adoption.

Whatever the success of the enterprise from the reader's perspective, it has been made possible, and on occasion joyous, for its author by the contributions of many. Crucial research support was provided by the Russell Sage Foundation. Commentary both critical and encouraging has been lavished on the project by so many colleagues, students, and friends, over such an extended period, that to mention any would (given my feeble memory) risk omitting others whose contributions were surely as great. The Yale Law School has provided, as usual, an environment that not only supports, but indeed demands, one's best efforts. Lorraine Nagle has deciphered tapes and scrawls, kept drafts in order, and suffered through endless revisions while maintaining both her efficiency and her good humor. To these and others I acknowledge a debt that is no less real because it entails no burden.

DUE PROCESS
IN THE ADMINISTRATIVE STATE

1 / *Was the Revolution a Success?*

That persons should not be deprived of "life, liberty, or property without due process of law" perhaps seemed, when that language was formulated, as noncontroversial as it was nonproblematic. Clearly security of person and property was
essential to the realization of the basic goals of the Revolution,
and security, at a minimum, required that government officials
be restricted to the ordinary forms of law. In England and the
colonies it was well understood that "due process of law" meant
according to the "common law " (which included legislation),
and that, as "life, liberty, or property" suggest, both criminal
and civil processes were subject to the due process constraint.

From the perspective of two centuries this original understanding, however correct in outline, seems bucolic, if not primi-
tive. If our forefathers failed to anticipate that due process of
law would come to mean that *no* legal intervention is permissible
in the case of a woman's "liberty" to abort a fetus during the first
trimester of pregnancy[1] or that welfare recipients would someday hold property interests in the public treasury, [2] they may
certainly be excused. The redefinition of American constitutionalism in these two hundred years has been remarkable —indeed
fantastic. And, as a government of limited purposes and insignif-
icant means was transformed into the modern administrative

1. Roe v. Wade, 410 U.S. 113, 164 (1973).
2. Goldberg v. Kelly, 397 U.S. 254, 262 (1970).

state, the elaboration of the notion of due process of law has been a primary mechanism for that redefinition. If habeas corpus is the "Great Writ," due process must surely be the "Great Clause."

It is not, however, the purpose of this book to follow the career of the due process clause as it charts the development of administrative government. This is not a constitutional history. It is instead an attempt to specify how we *ought* to think about due process questions in a bureaucratic state dedicated to liberal-democratic ideals. Yet, because "ought" implies "can," the normative presumes the empirical. Some history is not only relevant, it is inevitable. "[H]istoric continuity with the past is not a duty," Holmes reminds us, "it is only a necessity."[3] And although our history will be developed here interstitially, in pursuit of an understanding of normative concepts, rather than linearly, as a primary principle of organization, we must begin with at least a sketch of the historical significance of administrative due process questions and of the path of American administrative law. Without such a sketch we cannot hope to appreciate the domain of administrative due process issues and the way in which those issues relate to contemporary concerns about due process adjudication and administrative governance.

THE CAREER OF A CLAUSE

The emergence of due process litigation as an important category of constitutional claims seems to have been directly related to the increasing activism of government. Simple statistics provide a prima facie case. Between 1787 and 1866 only one due process case was decided by the Supreme Court. For the next sixty-five years, until the New Deal, virtually all of the Supreme Court's due process jurisprudence was concerned with the activities of state government. Why? Because prior to 1933 governmental activity directly affecting individual citizens and enterprises was carried on primarily by states and localities. Before the ratification of the Civil War amendments state and local activity was not subject to due process review under the federal

3. O.W. Holmes, *Learning and Science*, in COLLECTED LEGAL PAPERS 139 (1920).

constitution. Thereafter such review was possible and increasingly was sought with respect to these relatively activist levels of government.

The New Deal reversed the situation. Whereas four out of five due process claims reaching the Supreme Court between 1866 and 1933 had concerned state action, four out of five of such decisions in the period from the New Deal to the Great Society involved the federal government. Thereafter, however, the proportions were again reversed. One might well wonder why, for surely the conventional wisdom is that the shift from state and local toward national administrative activity has continued almost unabated. Yet since the 1950s there has also been another discernible trend in American administrative governance. While federal programs and budgets have grown, the number of federal employees has not expanded at nearly the same rate, because much of the implementation of federal programs is carried out by state and local personnel.[4] Thus when new or expanded federal programs generate lawsuits demanding due process, that litigation is often directed at state or local officials and state or local statutes, ordinances, and regulations that complete statutory schemes now generically known as programs in "cooperative federalism."[5]

This association of due process litigation and governmental activism can be explained relatively easily. As government began to act in new areas or to expand activity in older ones, it adopted new forms. While tradition has a strong hold on the legal imagination, legislation is an empiric business and experimentation is constant. This has been true throughout our history but is surely most perceptible in this century. Within the lifetime of many still living there has been a shift in the paradigmatic legal techniques of social control. Legislative rules of conduct enforceable by criminal sanction in the courts have been replaced by the more flexible techniques of regulatory commissions. Post hoc regula-

4. Mosher, *The Changing Tactics and Responsibilities of the Federal Government*, in AMERICAN PUBLIC ADMINISTRATION: PATTERNS OF THE PAST (J. Fessler ed. 1982).

5. *See generally* Mashaw and Rose-Ackerman, *Federalism and Regulation*, in THE REAGAN ADMINISTRATION'S REGULATORY RELIEF EFFORT 1 (G. Eads & M. Fix eds. 1984).

tion through liability rules has given way to ex ante intervention, either to regulate harmful or to subsidize useful activities. Legislative grants of individual licenses, charters, or subsidies were replaced by legislative programs administered by specialized agencies. Because these forms of governmental operation did not fully conform to the nineteenth-century common law model—a model that seemed to presume that government functioned through executive enforcement of legislative policy in the courts—they were viewed by some as constitutionally suspect.

Over the years the litigants who have raised these constitutional suspicions as due process claims have all been in some sense correct. Something new was afoot. Administrative action was replacing legislative enactment and judicial adjudication as the primary means for creating legal rules and resolving legal disputes. The question was whether the administrative state was constitutional. Was administrative process also due process?

The answer, of course, had to be sometimes "yes" and sometimes "no." A general negative was impossible. A realistic appraisal of judicial and legislative activity revealed that each had always carried out functions that abstract models assigned to the other.[6] Judicial rejection of the legislature's novel techniques for accomplishing permissible, and sometimes urgent, social objectives could hardly be premised on a demand for conceptual tidiness that neither the legislature nor the courts could meet. On the other hand, a general affirmative seemed to read the due process clause out of the Constitution. Surely there would be occasions on which legislative experiments went too far.

PROCESS AS PROCEDURE AND SUBSTANCE

The way the constitutional issue has just been described should not mislead. The question of governmental forms is *the* due process question, but it is not one purely of form or procedure. Due process claims are asserted as claims of constitutional

6. L. K. Davis, Administrative Law Treatise §2:4 (2d ed. 1978). *See also* Rugg, *The General Court of Massachusetts*, 11 Boston U.L. Rev. 1 (1931). For a historical review of the problem of separation of powers, see Atkins v. United States, 556 F.2d 1028, 1066–67 (Ct. Cl. 1977) *cert. denied*, 434 U.S. 1009 (1978) and Chadha v. Imm. and Nat. Serv., 634 U.S. 408, 420–25 (9th Cir. 1980), *aff'd on other grounds, Imm. and Nat. Serv. v. Chadha* 103 S. Ct. 2764 (1983).

right, as limits on the permissible activities of government. The part of the citizen's bundle of constitutional rights that has developed under the due process clause is and always has been[7] both substantive and procedural. Although much ink has been spilled by courts and commentators in the attempt to separate questions of substance and process, the attempt can never be wholly successful because the questions are functionally inseparable.

Many procedural rights do not stop the government in its tracks but rather require that decisions be made or actions taken by certain governmental institutions or through particular decisional processes. The right to a hearing, ubiquitously claimed in contemporary due process litigation, is a primary example. Yet clearly the right to a hearing involves more than process. It is often a right to change *who* decides[8] and is always an attempt to change *what* is decided. Rights to trial-type hearings may ultimately empower citizens or groups to impose costs on government that result in the transformation, even the abandonment, of governmental activities.[9] Process rights affect substantive outcomes.

Similarly, there is both an institutional and a process side to substantive due process rights, such as the contemporary freedom to abort or the one-time freedom of contract. To say that government may not decide when women will carry fetuses to term or what hours bakers will work is to say that some other person or institution has the right to decide. The exclusion of the government leaves decisions to individuals, families, and social or market processes and institutions. As a society we agree in such circumstances to be governed by the decisions that emerge from this decentralized, bottom-up decision making rather than by decisions, however democratic, that take a collective, top-down form. Whether the substantive results (decisions to abort or contract terms, in our examples) that will emerge over time from these allocations will differ from those attempted to be imposed by government remains speculative at the time these due process rights are adjudicated. The only clear outcome of the

7. *See, e.g.,* pp. 71–81 *infra.*
8. *See, e.g.,* Gibson v. Berryhill, 411 U.S. 564, 578–79 (1973).
9. *See* pp. 261–63 *infra.*

supposedly substantive constitutional interpretation is that the decision process has been constitutionally prescribed.

DUE PROCESS AS A RESIDUAL AND GENERATIVE TEXT

All constitutional constraints, of course, function in much the same manner. Constitutions are preeminently about the structure of decision making. Yet in our particular constitution the due process clause plays a peculiarly extensive role in moderating the conflict between the demands of individual and of public welfare. The clause has become a residual shield which, along with its cousin the equal protection clause, has to some degree replaced other, atrophied, constitutional protections, such as the nondelegation doctrine,[10] the limitations of the privileges and immunities,[11] and contracts[12] clauses. Due process has also

10. U.S. CONST. art. 1, §l. *See* Yakus v. United States, 321 U.S. 414, 425–26 (1944); Amalgamated Meat Cutters & Butcher Work. v. Connally, 337 F. Supp. 737, 744–63 (D.C. Cir. 1971); L. K. DAVIS, ADMINISTRATIVE LAW TREATISE §§3:1–16 (1978 & Supp. 1982). For recent examples of application of the nondelegation doctrine, see Nat'l Ass'n of Property Owners v. United States, 499 F. Supp. 1223, 1239–40, 1247 (D.Minn. 1980), *aff'd sub nom.* State of Minnesota by Alexander v. Block, 660 F.2d 1240, 1256–57 (8th Cir. 1981). Cf. Eastlake v. Forest City Enterprises, Inc., 426 U.S. 668, 675–80 (1976) (discussing delegation in the context of the referendum power of the people in zoning classification). *But see* Am. Textile Mfrs. Inst. Inc. v. Donovan, 452 U.S. 490, 543 *et. seq.* (1981) (dissenting opinion by Justice Rehnquist joined by Chief Justice Burger); Indus. Union Dep't, AFL-CIO v. Am. Petroleum Inst., 448 U.S. 607, 671 *et seq.* (1980) (concurring opinion by Justice Rehnquist).

11. U.S. CONST. amend. XIV; Slaughter-House Cases, 83 U.S. (16 Wall.) 36, 77–78 (1982). *But cf.* Twining v. New Jersey, 211 U.S. 78, 96–99 (1908) (overruled on other grounds in Malloy v. Hogan, 378 U.S. 1 [1964]) (listing rights within the Privileges and Immunities Clause, including the right to travel). *Compare* the uncertain basis for decision in Shapiro v. Thompson, 394 U.S. 618 (1969). *And see* Benoit, *The Privileges or Immunities Clause of the Fourteenth Amendment: Can There Be Life after Death?* 11 SUFFOLK U.L. REV. 61 (1976); Kurland, *The Privileges or Immunities Clause: "Its Hour Come Round at Last"?* 1972 WASH U.L.O. 405.

12. U.S. CONST. art. 1, §10, cl. 1. *Compare* Trustees of Dartmouth College v. Woodward, 17 U.S. (4 Wheat.) 518 (1819); Fletcher v. Peck, 10 U.S. (6 Cranch.) 87 (1910) *with* Home Bldg. & Loan Ass'n v. Blaisdell, 290 U.S. 398, 427–44 (1934). *And see* Allied Structural Steel Co. v. Spannaus, 438 U.S. 234, 240–51 (1978); El Paso v. Simmons, 379 U.S. 497, 517 (1965) (dissent by Black); Note, *A Process-Oriented Approach to the Contract Clause,* 89 YALE L.J. 1623 (1980); Hale, *The Supreme Court and the Contract Clause,* 57 HARV. L. REV. 512, 621, 852 (1944) (a three-part article charting the early history of the contract clause).

provided a means for applying the original Bill of Rights to state action[13]; and, as the contract and abortion cases suggest, it has also been a testing ground for those substantive, structural, or procedural initiatives that adversely affect private interests but seem to escape more specific constitutional proscription. One reason for this extensive domain is precisely the substance/procedure ambiguity that surrounds the due process clause. Due process claims cast in procedural terms invite the interposition of constraints on governmental action in circumstances where a direct confrontation with the substantive power of the states or of coordinate federal branches would excite concern about the judiciary's constitutional mandate.[14] That framing claims in process terms should somehow solve or avoid separation of powers problems is of course also an artifact of our peculiar constitutional and political history, to which we shall shortly return.

A second reason for the extensive domain of due process adjudication is that the clause is not just ambiguous (substance/procedure); it is wonderfully vague. Any issue that can be captured by an anguished, "But what sort of government is this anyway?" can be reformulated in due process terms. In his penetrating text on American constitutional law,[15] Lawrence Tribe describes various portions of the constitutional text as embodying different ideals or models of constitutionalism. Interestingly, the due process clause, alone among constitutional texts, refuses to remain cabined—indeed cannot be captured or rendered—within the confines of a single model. The substantive economic aspects inform one model,[16] procedural regularity[17] another, and what Tribe has come to call "structural due process" seems to infuse or perhaps synthesize his analysis of the whole Constitution.[18] Indeed, one does find due process cases in virtually every arena of constitutional conflict. The great political issues of the times, certainly those of post–Civil War America—immigration, state economic regulation, communist

13. See discussion *infra* at 160.
14. *E.g.,* Stanley v. Illinois, 405 U.S. 645 (1972) (fitness of unwed father).
15. L. TRIBE, AMERICAN CONSTITUTIONAL LAW (1978).
16. *Id.* §8–1, at 427 *et seq.*
17. *Id.* §10–7, at 501 *et seq.*
18. *Id.* §17–1, at 1137 *et seq.*

subversion, abortion, welfare rights, the treatment of social deviance and criminality, to name but a few—converge on the federal courts with due process claims leading the charge.

The vagueness and ambiguity that have promoted the invocation of due process as a residual shield could have been interpretatively debilitating. The text of the clause seems to excite conflict without providing a means for resolving it. If the clause is empty, to what should courts make reference when filling it in? The answer is certainly not obvious. Why then has due process not been consigned to the scrap heap of unusable constitutional texts, like the guarantee of a republican form of government; or given the narrowest possible construction, like the privileges and immunities clause?[19]

My own guess begins with the recognition that constitutional adjudication is a value-affirming exercise as well as a conflict-resolving one. We need some interpretive placeholder around which or within which to structure our most general constitutional conversations about the evolution of American government. That the due process clause should have become the occasion for much of the conversation about the administrative or welfare state—the constitutional focal point for synthesizing political values and governmental technique—is in some sense a historical accident, a function of the way American administrative law and American constitutional history happened to develop.

CONTEMPORARY DUE PROCESS CONCERNS IN LEGAL AND HISTORICAL PERSPECTIVE

If these suggestions concerning the historical significance of due process adjudication approximate the reality, then we should hardly be surprised that due process cases and due process decisions have been a constant, certainly a recurrent, source of legal and public concern. What then is singular about the current period? What should interest us now about the due process clause? A first answer is the perception, I think widely shared, that since the early 1970s we have been in the grip of a "process

19. *But, cf.* United Bldg. & Constr. Trades Council v. Mayor & Council of Camden, 104 S. Ct. 1020 (1984).

explosion,"[20] a "due process revolution"[21] that has inundated the courts with claims of procedural deprivation. Given that we are a conservative folk, not comfortable with revolutionary change, these characterizations also suggest that something has gone wrong—that due process litigation is currently out of hand.

Determining whether this flood of due process litigation has actually occurred is not a simple matter. Even with the electronic marvels of LEXIS and WESTLAW a fully accurate count of the cases cannot be offered with confidence. Yet several techniques of electronic search[22] have suggested remarkably similar trends in the litigation. It seems, for example, that federal court complaints of procedural due process deprivation in the 1970s showed a 350 percent increase over the 1960s.[23] The increase

20. Friendly, *Some Kind of Hearing*, 123 U. PA. L. REV. 1267, 1268 (1975).

21. F. GRAHAM, THE DUE PROCESS REVOLUTION: THE WARREN COURT'S IMPACT ON CRIMINAL LAW (1971); Griswold, *The Due Process Revolution and Confrontation*, 119 U. PA. L. REV. 711 (1971). *See also* Rendleman, *The New Due Process: Rights and Remedies*, 63 KY. L.J. 531 (1975).

22. LEXIS queries for cases involving procedural due process were limited to library: GENFED, file: CASES. Searches were: (a) Due process w/10 procedure and date aft 1969 and date bef 1980; (b) Due process w/10 procedure and date aft 1959 and date bef 1970; (c) Due process w/10 procedur** and date aft 1969 and date bef 1980; (d) Due process w/10 procedur** and date aft 1959 and date bef 1970. Our actual reading of all United States Supreme Court cases using the term "due process" in 1971, 1975, and 1979 (192 cases) indicated that in any single year, 55 percent to 70 percent of the cases using the term might actually involve an issue which the due process clause did some work to resolve. We assume that this variation from year to year would not be significant to figures encompassing and comparing entire decades. *See* n. 25, *infra*. WESTLAW's division of libraries and more complex search logic in use at the time this research was done made it inconvenient, indeed impossible, to run a really similar search. We did run a key number search using topics and key numbers typically producing relevant cases. Using the breakdown: Constitutional Law—***—XI Due Process of Law—318 Administrative Proceedings—(1) General and Social Security and Public Welfare—I In General—***—8 Administrative Proceedings, we ran the following searches: (a) topickey (92k318 92k318(*) & date (after 1969 and before 1980); (b) topickey (92k318 92k318(*) & date (after 1959 and before 1970); (c) topickey (92k318 92k318(1)) & date (after 1969 and before 1980); (d) topickey (92k318 92k318(1)) & date (after 1959 and before 1970); (e) topickey (356ak8) & date (after 1969 and before 1980); (f) topickey (356ak8) & date (after 1959 and before 1970). Each inquiry had to be run separately in files for Supreme Court Reporter, Federal Reporter, and Federal Supplement and then totalled.

23. The LEXIS searches described in n. 22, *supra*, yielded the following results: (a) 2,893 cases; (b) 639 cases—an increase of 352.7%; (c) 5,106 cases; (d) 1,153 cases—an increase of 342.8%. The WESTLAW searches described in n. 22,

in litigation of all kinds was only 70 percent.[24] Procedural due process cases were increasing five times as fast as litigation generally.

Moreover, a significant portion of this litigation challenges the activities and procedures of administrative agencies.[25] In

---

supra, yielded the following results: (a) 1,328 cases; (b) 333 cases—an increase of 298.8%; (c) 193 cases; (d) 46 cases—an increase of 319.56%; (e) 42 cases; (f) 9 cases—an increase of 366.67%.

24. Court	1960s	1970s
U.S. Supreme Court	26,388[a]	42,307[b]
U.S. Circuit Court	65,602[c]	164,371[c]
U.S. District Court		
civil	668,160[c]	1,150,900[c]
criminal	301,804[c]	390,884[c]
Totals	1,061,954	1,748,462

[a]*Bureau of the Census, U.S. Dept. of Commerce, Historical Statistics of the United States, Colonial Times to 1970 Part I* (1975).

[b]*Bureau of the Census, U.S. Dept. of Commerce, Statistical Abstract of the United States 1980* (1981).

[c]*Reports of the Proceedings of the Judicial Conference of the United States; Annual Report of the Director of the Administrative Office of the Director of the Administrative Office of the United States Courts* (hereafter, *Annual Report*) *1979* table 1, at 190–91; table 15, at 212, 213; tables 20–22, at 220–25; table 45, at 266–67 (1980); *Annual Report 1961*, 61 (1962); *Annual Report 1960*, 69 (1961).

These figures show a 64.6% increase in cases filed in the 1970s over cases filed in the 1960s. If one were to eliminate district court criminal cases, one would obtain a 78.6% increase with the caution that criminal cases in the appellate courts would remain in the figures.

See also Clark, *Adjudication to Administration: A Statistical Analysis of Federal District Courts in the Twentieth Century*, 55 So. Cal. L. Rev. 65 (1981). Professor Clark cites a 71% increase in civil filings between 1973 and 1980. *Id.* at 144.

25. A LEXIS inquiry in library: GENFED, file: SUP in the form: (a) Due process and date aft 1970 and date bef 1972; (b) Due process and date aft 1974 and date bef 1976; (c) Due process and date aft 1978 and date bef 1980; will yield a list of 193 cases, one of them (Standard Oil Co. v. City of Marysville, 278 U.S. 596 [1929]) generated by a LEXIS error. If each is scanned for its treatment of due process and with an expansive concept of when due process is helping to resolve an issue in the case, the results are:

	1971		1975		1979	
Total Cases	64		69		59	
Relevant use of due process	36		37		41	
crim:	16	44.44%	17	45.95%	13	31.71%
civ:	6	16.67%	4	10.82%	13	31.71%
admin:	14	38.89%	16	43.24%	15	36.58%

the 1970s and early 1980s the Supreme Court of the United States has reviewed the activities of officials administering programs and institutions for state and local public assistance,[26] unemployment insurance,[27] medical[28] and disability insurance[29] under the Social Security system, licensing of drivers,[30] public education in schools[31] and colleges,[32] transfer and discipline of prison inmates,[33] custody and rehabilitation of the emotionally disturbed and mentally incompetent,[34] restricting access to alcoholic beverages,[35] public safety,[36] public employment,[37] denial or revocation of parole,[38] publicly owned utilities,[39] tax collection,[40] railroad rate regulation,[41] licensing of nursing homes,[42] and construction and operation of nuclear reactors.[43] And that list names but some of the administrative due

26. Goldberg v. Kelly, 397 U.S. 254 (1970).

27. *Cf.* California Human Resources Dep't v. Java, 402 U.S. 121 (1971) (avoids the due process issue in the majority opinion, discussed in concurring opinion).

28. Schweiker v. McClure, 456 U.S. 188 (1982). *Cf.* Usery v. Turner Elkhorn Mining Co., 428 U.S. 1 (1976) (discusses due process problem in ordering black lung benefits for previous employees); Mathews v. Diaz, 426 U.S. 67 (1976) (aliens' rights to supplemental medical insurance).

29. Mathews v. Eldridge, 424 U.S. 319 (1976); Richardson v. Perales, 402 U.S. 389 (1971).

30. Mackey v. Montrym, 443 U.S. 319 (1976); Dixon v. Love, 431 U.S. 105 (1977); Bell v. Burson, 402 U.S. 535 (1971).

31. Goss v. Lopez, 419 U.S. 565 (1975).

32. Bd. of Curators of the Univ. of Mo. v. Horowitz, 435 U.S. 78 (1978).

33. Meachum v. Fano, 427 U.S. 215 (1976); Baxter v. Palmigiano, 425 U.S. 308 (1976); Wolff v. McDonnell, 418 U.S. 539 (1974).

34. Vitek v. Jones, 445 U.S. 480 (1980); Parham v. J.R., 442 U.S. 584 (1979).

35. Wisconsin v. Constantineau, 400 U.S. 433 (1971).

36. Paul v. Davis, 424 U.S. 693 (1976).

37. Bishop v. Wood, 426 U.S. 341 (1976); Arnett v. Kennedy, 416 U.S. 134 (1974); Perry v. Sindermann, 408 U.S. 593 (1972); Bd. of Regents v. Roth, 408 U.S. 564 (1972).

38. Jago v. Van Curen, 454 U.S. 14 (1981); Greenholtz v. Nebraska Penal Inmates, 442 U.S. 1 (1979); Gagnon v. Scarpelli, 411 U.S. 778 (1973); Morrissey v. Brewer, 408 U.S. 471 (1972).

39. Memphis Light, Gas, and Water Div. v. Craft, 436 U.S. 1 (1978).

40. Comm'r v. Shapiro, 424 U.S. 614 (1976). *Cf.* Bob Jones Univ. v. Simon, 416 U.S. 725 (1974) (discussing the due process problem in imposing the Anti-Injunction Act on nonprofit entities).

41. United States v. Florida East Coast Ry. Co., 410 U.S. 224 (1973).

42. O'Bannon v. Town Court Nursing Center, 447 U.S. 773 (1980).

43. Vermont Yankee Nuclear Power Corp. v. Natural Resources Defense Council, Inc., 435 U.S. 519 (1978).

process business that has been presented to the combined state and federal judiciaries.

But so what? The pervasiveness of administrative due process litigation in the 1970s is not necessarily a problem. It may merely signal a period of transition from one acceptable and understandable set of legal rules to another—the necessary working out of the forms of access, participation, and decision making for the modern administrative state. Litigation about administrative due process may be pervasive in the recent past simply because it is in that period that administrative governance became pervasive. And, if that is true, then the fact that constitutional adjudication involves the courts in the creative process of evaluating, synthesizing, and legitimating the structure of the new administrative state is not itself a cause for alarm.

A TALE OF THE "ADMINISTERED" LIFE

It is not only trite, it is no longer sufficient to say that we have a cradle-to-grave administrative, welfare state. Administrators make decisions that affect us from *before* the cradle to *beyond* the grave. The Secretary of Health and Human Services, in developing the regulations governing public financing of abortions, may influence or even determine whether we are born. The decision of a county welfare official concerning our mothers' access to prenatal medical care or to income support or to food stamps, and the decisions of a state health planning agency concerning the location of special postnatal care facilities, may critically affect the physical and mental resources with which we begin our lives.

During our years of dependency we are surrounded by a supportive and regulative administrative structure. Our basic support may depend on the favorable determination of administrators in a host of programs providing income maintenance and in-kind distribution of essential goods and services. The types of educational experiences available to us are often determined by the general policies of the administrators of a multilevel educational bureaucracy or by the classifications assigned to us ("good student," "troublemaker," "college-bound," "vocational aptitude") by the administrators with whom we come in contact. The degree to which we are raised in a family situation or an institution, protected from or subjected to parental abuse, placed under behavioral restrictions for misconduct, or allowed to engage in particular part-time or full-time occupations, is regulated by yet another class of administrators.

As we emerge from the semiprivacy of family dependency to take up our more public producer and consumer roles, the network of administrative supports, protections, and regulations becomes even more ubiquitous. Entry into an occupation may depend upon an administrative grant of a license, enforcement of nondiscrimination requirements, or provision of a subsidized training slot. Conditions on the job will be determined in part by regulatory action purporting to ensure the fairness of employer-employee relations, the adequacy of compensation and benefits, the safety of processes and equipment, and the healthfulness of the working environment.

Less directly, but often more critically, the existence and character of employment may depend upon the economic conditions generated by the combined activities of administrators (1) who determine the availability and terms of a locality's access to transportation services, energy resources, and investment capital; (2) who make government contracts, grants, or loans; (3) who determine the tax treatment of various productive activities; (4) who oversee the structural characteristics of numerous markets; and (5) who decide where and how much industries may pollute, whether their products are sufficiently safe or effective for sale, and what advertising and marketing techniques can fairly be used in the products' distribution.

Lurking within each worker-as-producer is, of course, a worker (and perhaps a worker's family) who consumes. The flip side of administrative activity that regulates, taxes, or subsidizes production is administrative activity that protects consumer health, safety, or access to amenities and expands or contracts the range of consumer choice. The decisions of administrators will substantially affect the safety and efficacy of our automobiles, the availability and price of our foods and drugs, the density and architectural character of our neighborhoods, the price and form of our housing, how we get to work in the morning, and what we watch on television at night.

The possibilities for prolonging this litany of administrative contacts are virtually endless, and the rich possibilities of retirement years have not even been mentioned. Nor have we departed from the "normal" life to inquire into the administration of prisons, mental health facilities, drug rehabilitation programs, parole systems, and a host of other programs and institutions for the "deviant." To observe administration beyond the grave, we might merely note that how, where, and at what price we are finally laid to rest will be influenced by the decisions of several administrative agencies. And whether our physical remains "rest in peace" may depend on the decisions of highway, water project, or other public works administrators concerning the use of our final resting place for some public purpose.

Moreover, if one thinks back on the programs or activities that the litany mentions, most of them either were created or experienced geometric growth in the 1960s and 1970s. Public budgets, the number of civilian governmental employees, every indicator of the size and extent of government was literally rocketing off the charts during this period. Increased collective action almost inevitably leads to dissatisfaction focused on the collectivity's agents. The pronouncements of administrators are hardly greeted with universal acclaim. Saccharin and laetrile users protest that they do not want the protection of the Food and Drug Administration. On the other hand, residents of Queens want more protection from sonic booms and engine noise than the secretary of transportation and the New York Port Authority are willing to provide. Environmentalists are appalled by the licensing of any additional nuclear power plants, and industry is equally appalled at the length and cost of the approval process at the Nuclear Regulatory Commission.

We obviously have many interests and we are many publics. That is not all. As individuals we play many roles. Conflict over public policy is not only between those who represent industry and environment, residents and travelers, safety and freedom of choice. The conflict is also within ourselves as we pursue the competing values that individually we hold. The decisions of administrators cannot hope to reflect the same priorities of the majority, perhaps any, of the affected citizens.[44] If we add to this scenario the simple fact that litigation has increasingly become the vehicle for expressing social or personal dissatisfactions of all sorts, then the geometric growth of administrative due process litigation is not terribly surprising.

Yet these explanations surely are not a complete answer to those who believe that litigation about due process is a cause for concern. If administration is ubiquitous, why have we not made peace with it? And why are the cases primarily about *procedure*? If the suggestion is that escalating litigation merely reflects escalating enforcement of rights to welfare state benefits or conflict about welfare state policies, why are the cases not about substantive claims to those benefits and substantive challenges to those policies, rather than about the decisional processes through which benefits are allocated and policies chosen?

THE PROBLEM OF ADMINISTRATIVE DISCRETION

Explaining why contemporary litigation should take the form of incessant complaints about administrative process requires a slight historical digression into administrative law. Administrative law has always been concerned with constraints on administrative power, and it has often been concerned with procedure. But there are features of the legal landscape of the 1960s and 1970s, reflecting the political and social landscape of the same period, that have combined to produce a peculiarly intense focus on the idea of legitimating administrative power through controlling administrative process.

Consider first what the legitimation of administrative power is fundamentally about. The basic question is this: What makes an administrative decision legitimate? If the decision of an administrator is not the one we would have made—that is, if it limits our freedom of action or fails to limit those whom we want constrained—what, beyond realpolitik, can make it acceptable? What perception of collective action will support the legitimacy of an exercise of administrative discretion with which we intensely disagree? Or, put in terms that recognize that some ad-

44. *See, e.g.,* K. ARROW, SOCIAL CHOICE AND INDIVIDUAL VALUES (1951).

ministrative action is indeed illegitimate, what separates that latter category of administrative decisions from those that are legitimate, however erroneous or disagreeable?

Three Models of Administrative Legitimacy

According to the now-conventional story American administrative law has been characterized by three different models of legitimation.[45] The first approach attempts to integrate administrative discretion into conventional democratic theory. This view, which Stewart calls the "transmission belt" model of administration, holds that administrative discretion does not really pose a problem for democratic theory; rather, it merely poses the usual problems of a republican form of government. As the citizen controls the legislature through electoral politics, so elected representatives control the activities of administrators. The latter are merely the ultimate effectuators of popular sentiment as mediated through the legislative process. Because administrators implement policies previously established by the accepted mode of collective choice in a representative democracy, the legitimacy of their decisions is established by determining whether they in fact carry forward legislative prescriptions.

The transmission belt explanation of administrative legitimacy will leave the observer of the modern administrative state at least vaguely dissatisfied. Although there is certainly some validity to the search for an electoral connection as a basis for administrative legitimacy, the transmission belt approach fails to account for much of the reality of public administration. When the Congress instructs the Federal Communications Commission to issue broadcast licenses in "the public interest," it has been less than crystal clear concerning the approach the commission should take to sex and violence on television, Anglo-Saxon expletives on the radio, equal access by opposing viewpoints to commercial air time, local and minority programming, and a host of other issues both large and small. Nor is the vagueness of the FCC's mandate singular. Most federal and state administrators operate over some substantial portion of their do-

45. *See* Stewart, *The Reformation of American Administrative Law*, 88 HARV. L. REV. 1667 (1975).

mains with instructions that may be formulated differently, but that are similarly capacious. Clearly, administrators exercise more than a mere implementing discretion. A search for the relationship between their exercise of discretion and the democratic expression of public policy in a statute can begin and end in a verbal haze.[46]

More specific legislative instructions may enhance democratic control, but the transmission belt seems to retain substantial slack in the face of increasing statutory particularity. The Food and Drug Administration, for example, is required to ban all food additives that are carcinogenic[47]—a relatively straightforward and absolute legislative instruction. But between that legislative statement of policy and its effectuation lies significant administrative discretion. Does the statute require banning the use of water in food processing in New Orleans and Duluth, where water supplies are contaminated with known carcinogens? Should the FDA consider the economic and social dislocations that such a definition of "additive" would entail? Or, to take another exemplary issue, must additives that may be converted into carcinogens by combination with other chemicals be proscribed? Should the FDA in considering this last question be influenced by the knowledge that such a definition of "carcinogen" might eliminate the use of food preservatives, which have enormously reduced the incidence of botulism?[48]

These examples are not meant to suggest that the transmission belt model is weak only at a few critical points where high-level policy choices are confronted. Choices at the point of individualized administrative implementation may be similarly uncontrolled. When evaluating their nearly 1.5 million disability claims each year, the Social Security Administration's thousands of claims examiners have been guided, historically, by quite

46. For a recent instructive example, see Indus. Union Dep't, AFL-CIO v. Am. Petroleum Inst., 448 U.S. 607 (1980).

47. More precisely, the Delaney Amendment bans the use of additives found to induce cancer in man or in laboratory animals. 21 U.S.C. §§348(c)(3)(A); 360b(3)(1)(H); 376(b)(5)(B) (1976).

48. For a general discussion of the FDA's exercise of discretion concerning carcinogens in food, see Merrill, *Regulating Carcinogens in Food: A Legislator's Guide to the Food Safety Provisions of the Federal Food, Drug, and Cosmetic Act*, 77 Mich. L. Rev. 171 (1978).

amorphous statutory standards. A substantial category of disability decisions might be aptly characterized as moral judgments concerning whether a particular person *should* be expected to work. Given the breadth of the discretion conferred, it is hardly surprising that congressional studies find the likelihood that two disability adjudicators will agree concerning the appropriate disposition of a claim to be only marginally more likely than that two tosses of a coin will produce two "heads."[49]

In short, much administrative decision making, at the micro as well as the macro level, involves the exercise of judgment concerning not only the technical means of implementing policy, but also the priorities to be accorded relevant and competing social values. Even a more elaborate account of the electoral connection — an account that considers the effects of the power of appointments, the budgetary review process, and congressional oversight activities — leaves the transmission belt model's invocation of democratic control over administrative judgments rather ragged and worn. "What the administrator decided, we decided through our elected representatives" is to some an engaging statement, but it poorly describes the realities of the administrative state.

The exercise of administrative power need not be rationalized as an instance of democratic decision making in order to make it acceptable. We are often prepared to yield a certain amount of our freedom of choice to persons whose training or experience makes them better decision makers concerning our affairs than we are. The role of the expert or professional thus can be made the second model for the administrator. From this perspective administrative decision making might be viewed as a science, or perhaps as an arcane art. Administrative governance is then an organizational form that recognizes the necessity for combining the locus of decision with appropriate expertise. The expertise model of legitimacy would, therefore, premise the ac-

49. STAFF OF THE SUBCOMM. ON SOCIAL SECURITY, DISABILITY INSURANCE — LEGISLATIVE ISSUE PAPER, PREPARED FOR SUBCOMM. ON SOCIAL SECURITY, COMM. ON WAYS AND MEANS, HOUSE OF REPRESENTATIVES, 94TH CONG. 2ND SESS. 31 (Comm. Print 1976); *and see* COMM. STAFF REPORT, DISABILITY INSURANCE PROGRAM, COMM. ON WAYS AND MEANS, HOUSE OF REPRESENTATIVES, 93RD CONG., 2ND SESS. 1, 5, 77 (1974).

ceptability of any particular administrative structure or decision on its correspondence with the appropriate form of scientific or professional methodology.

Certainly much of the impetus for the creation of many prominent administrative agencies can be traced to a desire for the exercise of an expert rather than a lay or political judgment.[50] During the vast majority of American political history, the common law courts, informed occasionally by legislative amendment to the common law rules, were the principal, official actors on questions as diverse as the reasonableness of carrier and utility rates, the cleanliness of the environment, the appropriate relationship between investors and corporate management, and the whole range of employer-employee relations. The legislative decision to transfer major responsibility for these (and many other) areas of substantive regulation from judges to administrators depended on the notion of a need for the application of continuous, specialized intelligence to underlying issues of policy. By virtue of constant exposure to a single type of problem, as well as by selection of personnel with specialized training, the administrative agency could bring to bear an expertise that generalist courts and generalist legislatures could rarely hope to match. Although the agency may not have the requisite scientific knowledge or technical expertise to effect final solutions at the inception of its operations, the expertise model of administration imagines that over time experience and research will produce increasingly sound administrative judgments.

Yet for a number of reasons the expertise model of administrative legitimacy is also unsatisfactory. First, the expertise approach must rely on continuous achievement to sustain acceptability. But the result of much administrative activity cannot be measured. Administrative success stories are always open to revisionist interpretation. Have the utilities commissions tamed the trusts, or have they instead merely legalized monopoly and participated in the creation of the high prices, limited service, and shortages that are characteristic of monopolistic production?[51] Is the Interstate Commerce Commission doing more

50. *See, e.g.,* J. LANDIS, THE ADMINISTRATIVE PROCESS (1938).
51. *See, e.g.,* CRISIS OF THE REGULATORY COMMISSIONS (P. Macavoy ed. 1970).

than protecting inefficient railroads from more efficient truck lines and presiding over the demise of the passenger train?[52] Why has an interstate airplane trip on a CAB-regulated carrier historically cost three times the unregulated intrastate fare for a similar distance?[53] Does the FTC's activity have any substantial impact on the fairness of trade practices?[54]

The problematic character of any evaluation of administrative performance also lends credence to behavioral hypotheses that directly challenge the capacity of expert agencies to serve the goals that purportedly informed their creation. Commentators argue that time increases not expertise, but rigidity and inertia. The natural affinity of regulatory experts and industry experts (a common technical language and professional culture) is thought to lead to a symbiotic relationship in which the regulators and the regulated support their common interests at the expense of the public.[55] Both free market and Marxist theorists have transformed this "capture theory" into a conspiracy scenario by suggesting that expert regulation was always a front for cartelization with government support.[56] Others link agencies to their relevant constituencies and to legislative oversight and appropriations committees in an "iron triangle" of micropolitics

52. *See, e.g.*, T. MOORE, FREIGHT TRANSPORTATION REGULATION: SURFACE FREIGHT & THE INTERSTATE COMMERCE COMMISSION (1972).

53. *See, e.g.*, Note, *Is Regulation Necessary? California Air Transportation and National Regulatory Policy*, 74 YALE L.J. 1416 (1965).

54. *See, e.g.*, RALPH NADER'S CENTER FOR STUDY OF RESPONSIVE LAW, WORKING ON THE SYSTEM: A COMPREHENSIVE MANUAL FOR CITIZEN ACCESS TO FEDERAL AGENCIES, chap. 5 (J. Michael ed. 1974); REPORT OF THE AMERICAN BAR ASSOCIATION COMMISSION TO STUDY THE FEDERAL TRADE COMMISSION (1969). *See* history and current operation of the Magnuson-Moss Warranty—Federal Trade Commission Improvement Act, Pub. L. No. 93–637, 88 Stat. 2183 (1975); Pub. L. No. 94–299, 90 Stat. 588 (1976); Pub. L. No. 95–558, 92 Stat. 2130 (1978); *Hearings before the Subcomm. on Oversight and Investigations of the Comm. on Interstate and Foreign Commerce, House of Representatives*, 94th Cong., 2nd Sess. 543–51 (Serial No. 94–83 1976).

55. M. BERNSTEIN, REGULATING BUSINESS BY INDEPENDENT COMMISSION (1955).

56. *See* G. KOLKO, RAILROADS AND REGULATION, 1877–1916 (1965); G. KOLKO, THE TRIUMPH OF CONSERVATISM: A REINTERPRETATION OF AMERICAN HISTORY, 1900–1916 (1963); Peltzman, *Toward a More General Theory of Regulation*, 19 J. OF LAW & ECON. 211 (1976); Stigler, *The Theory of Economic Regulation*, 2 BELL J. OF ECON. & MGT. SCI. 3 (1971).

that serves the special interests of this limited set of actors.[57] Another view predicts administrative failure simply by denying the very possibility of the supposed administrative expertise. From this perspective agencies are attempting to manage markets or social processes whose structures and operations are simply too complex for effective planning.[58] Administration, therefore, is bound to fail because its vision of expertise promises more than it can deliver.

Administrative expertise also has unfortunate antiegalitarian connotations. For example, arguments for the necessity of leaving the pursuit of quality education in the hands of educators have come to be regarded as a cover for resistance to school integration. The war on poverty and the welfare rights movement have cast an often harshly critical light on the intrusive and paternalistic policies of public assistance, housing, and medical care institutions—policies that were derived from the basic concepts of social work and other "helping" professions—supposedly the experts in this area.[59]

Finally, expertise seems almost necessarily to imply tunnel vision. Experts tend to translate their capacity into policy imperatives. Dissatisfaction with the results of this approach to policy certainly stimulates distrust of expertise. Well-known examples abound. The Federal Highway Administration and the Corps of Engineers employ increasingly sophisticated engineering techniques to transform the rural and urban landscape in ways that are intensely displeasing to affected local interests. The Department of Housing and Urban Development has aided the development and execution of vast urban renewal and public housing plans which have too often destroyed neighborhoods or recreated slums. Some would even argue that the Kennedy–

57. This view owes much to A. Downs, Inside Bureaucracy (1967) but has recently taken a variety of forms, *e.g.*, D. Arnold, Congress and the Bureaucracy: A Theory of Influence (1979); M. Fiorina, Congress—Keystone of the Washington Establishment (1977); W. Niskanen, Bureaucracy and Representative Government (1971).

58. F. Hayek, The Constitution of Liberty (1960).

59. *See, e.g.*, F. Piven & R. Cloward, Regulating the Poor: The Functions of Public Relief (1972); Handler, *Controlling Official Behavior in Welfare Administration*, 54 Cal. L. Rev. 479 (1966).

McNamara Defense Department used its planning and management expertise to rationalize our military posture, which gave us
a capacity to intervene in localized conflicts, which in turn made
the Vietnam War seem feasible.

The solution to the problem of tunnel vision (or what others
have called "trained incompetence") is not obvious, at least not if
the idea of expertise is expected to retain substantial legitimating force. The more administrators have been driven to move
outside their traditional ambit of expert judgment, in order to
address questions of the impact of their decisions on other societal values, the more their judgments seem nonexpert or political. When Congress instructs the Federal Highway Administration or the Corps of Engineers to consider environmental and
cultural values, it has instructed the experts to abandon their expertise. When Congress requires the newer administrative agencies, under statutes such as the Water Quality Act, the Air Quality Act, the Consumer Product Safety Act, the Occupational
Safety and Health Act, the Motor Vehicle Safety Act, or the
Toxic Substances Act, to make trade-offs between the need for
public health or safety and the need for employment, product
diversity, and a vibrant economy, it seems clear that administrators must make value choices that outrun any definition of technical or professional competence. Administrative discretion to
choose among competing social values thus undermines both
the transmission belt and the expertise models of administrative
legitimacy.[60]

The difficulties with the transmission belt and expertise justifications for the exercise of administrative authority might, however, be ameliorated by the third model of administrative legitimacy—a model that concentrates on the administrative process
itself. If administrative decision making is too divorced from the
macropolitics of legislative action to satisfy democratic ideals,
those ideals might be embodied, at least partially, in administra-

60. For an instructive example of technocratic decision making combined
with explicit political considerations of acceptability and implicit moral judgments on the sanctity of life and the appropriate place for paternalism in public
policy, see the Department of Transportation's *Notice of Proposed Rulemaking and
Public Hearing on Motor Vehicle Occupant Crash Protection*, 41 Fed. Reg. 24070–79
(June 14, 1976).

tive procedures that ensure the participation of affected interests in the process of administrative policy formation. Similarly, if rational analysis is inadequate to justify choices among competing values, those values might be represented in a pluralist, bargaining approach to administration. Presumably the outcomes of that process would combine administrative expertise with the political legitimacy of the traditional legislative compromise. Attempts to overcome the limitations of either the transmission belt or the expertise models thus suggest a participatory approach. Moreover, the notion of direct participation in administrative governance responds to deep strains of individualism and political egalitarianism in the American character. It rekindles the nostalgic image of the town meeting.

On closer examination, however, the participatory approach also has serious limitations. For one thing the micropolitics of a participatory administrative structure may undermine rather than support what remains of the attachment to legislative control or to rational decision making. There is no obvious reason to expect that the outcome of pluralist bargaining at the micropolitical, administrative level should reproduce the results of bargaining in the macropolitical, legislative process. And a participatory, bargaining process will complicate, perhaps stifle, the application of those rational modes of thought that are necessary for the solution of many of our more complex and subtle problems.[61]

Participation might, of course, be urged on other grounds. It might, for example, be argued that administration that cannot be shown to be democratically controlled or expert should at least be "fair," in the sense of providing equal opportunities to affected parties to influence the ultimate administrative judgment. But even were this principle accepted, it is not at all clear what a fair structure would look like. The immediately appealing analogy is to a judicial trial—open, neutral, and with strict equality of participation. Yet for questions that are broad and complex, such procedure is terribly cumbersome. Moreover, although the participatory approach seems to presume that the

61. *See generally* Mashaw, *The Legal Structure of Frustration: Alternative Strategies for Public Choice Concerning Federally Aided Highway Construction*, 122 U. Pa. L. Rev. 1, 54–70 (1973).

process of decision can be made open and neutral, it seems rather more likely that, with respect to many areas of administrative policy formation, certain interests, because of their intensity, resources, and organization, will come to dominate even an open decision-making process. Or, to put the point somewhat differently, interests that are substantially affected might, because of lack of resources or organization, fail to participate effectively in administrative forums. Any attempt to prevent these inequalities from skewing policy in "unfair" directions, by fine-tailoring the decision processes through the use of evidentiary presumptions, burdens of proof, required disclosure of information, and the like, reveals the need for some criteria for determining the importance of the interests represented by the various potential participants. The participatory model itself provides no such guidelines.

THE PATH OF ADMINISTRATIVE LAW

Although it is an obvious oversimplification, the development of American administrative law can be pictured as having three overlapping phases that mirror the approaches of the three models of administrative legitimacy set out above. Administrative law is, and has been, concerned with protecting the transmission belt. There is continuing attention to the limits of administrative action, that is, to whether action is within the bounds of authority conferred by the legislature.[62] Other approaches to policing the transmission belt have also been a prominent part of the legal landscape. Where legislation leaves administrative discretion too much at large, the courts have, infrequently, annulled that legislation under the constitutional doctrine prohibiting the delegation of the legislative functions.[63] More commonly, they have trimmed the legislative

62. *See, e.g.,* Indus. Union Dep't, AFL-CIO v. Am. Petroleum Inst., 448 U.S. 607, 639–46 (1980); Citizens to Preserve Overton Park, Inc. v. Volpe, 401 U.S. 402, 410–12 (1971); NLRB v. Brown, 380 U.S. 278, 291–92 (1965); Colorado Interstate Gas Co. v. FPC, 324 U.S. 581, 589, 602–04 (1945); Stark v. Wickard, 321 U.S. 288, 307–10 (1944); Waite v. Macy, 246 U.S. 606, 610 (1918); ICC v. Chicago, R.I. & P. Ry., 218 U.S. 88, 101–03 (1910).
63. Schechter Poultry Corp. v. United States, 295 U.S. 495, 537–42 (1935); Panama Refining Co. v. Ryan, 293 U.S. 388, 421–30 (1935); *and cf.* Indus. Un-

grant of discretion down to instructions sufficiently clear to permit a court to determine whether they are being implemented.[64] These devices were often utilized in an era generally hostile to social and economic regulation. Indeed, in that era, many statutes establishing new forms of administrative activity, such as workers' compensation commissions, were annulled by reviewing courts under federal and state due process on the simple ground that the necessity for subjecting private relationships to public oversight had not been established.[65]

As the political ideals of the progressive movement replaced the ideology of laissez-faire, administrative law, without abandoning its prior verbal formulas, entered a much more generous phase. The mere perception by legislatures that a problem existed began to provide the necessary predicate for social legislation empowering administrators to act. Delegations of power to administrators were upheld which were bounded by little more than an admonition to pursue the public interest, and administrative jurisdiction was expansively interpreted (indeed sometimes thrust on reluctant administrators) in order to further the broad remedial purposes of legislation. Doctrines emphasizing judicial self-restraint—the limited scope of judicial review, restrictive criteria for party standing, the requirements of ripeness and exhaustion of administrative remedies, and the doctrine of nonreviewability—were pressed into service by progressive courts that sought to protect legislative experiments with scientific, administrative problem solving from the intrusive and episodic oversight of lay judges.[66] Administrative law became in substantial part law describing the barriers to judicial review of administrative action.

ion Dep't, AFL-CIO v. Am. Petroleum Inst., 448 U.S. 607, 646 (1980) (indicating continuing availability of this limitation). *See also* Annot., 92 A.L.R. 400 (1934): L. K. Davis, Administrative Law Treatise §3:14 (2d ed. 1978); *and cf.* Annot., 3 A.L.R.2d 188 (1949).

64. Kent v. Dulles, 357 U.S. 116, 129 (1958); *see also* Hampton v. Mow Sun Wong, 426 U.S. 88, 116 (1976); L. K. Davis, Administrative Law Treatise §3:13 (2d ed. 1978).

65. *See* E. Corwin, The Constitution and What It Means Today 462–66 (14th ed., H. Chase & C. Ducat rev. 1978).

66. *See generally* L. Tribe, American Constitutional Law §8–7 (1978); L. K. Davis, Administrative Law Treatise §3:5 (2d ed. 1978); *see also* Ferguson v. Skrupa, 372 U.S. 726 (1963).

Having lost the substantive battle against an activist state that increasingly acted through administrative bodies, the forces of reaction counterattacked on procedural grounds. Orderly procedure, a right to be heard, so the argument went, is as important in the administrative as in the judicial forum. A partial victory for the rule of law so conceived was won in the Federal Administrative Procedure Act (APA) of 1946.[67] Moreover, as bright new social experiments came to be perceived as creaky bureaucracies, and the dominant vision of social process shifted from social engineering to interest balancing,[68] the APA model of administrative law *as* administrative process suggested a vehicle for a more searching judicial scrutiny, a scrutiny that could at the same time pay homage to established doctrines protecting the substantive discretion of the legislature and the administrator.

A procedurally oriented judicial review seemed to have at its command a range of techniques for intruding without deciding. Instead of addressing the issue of whether the administrator was wrong, courts could remand administrative decisions for more complete findings[69] or for a testing of the evidence in a more adversary administrative proceeding.[70] Instead of determining by proofs in court whether an agency had deprived the plaintiff of a statutory entitlement,[71] the courts required that such action be preceded by an administrative hearing that would elicit the relevant facts.[72] Rather than imposing new decisional criteria or priorities on administrators, courts required that decisions be taken only after listening to the views or evidence presented by interests that traditionally had not been represented in the

67. ATTORNEY GENERAL'S COMMITTEE ON ADMINISTRATIVE PROCEDURE, ADMINISTRATIVE PROCEDURE IN GOVERNMENT AGENCIES: REPORT OF THE COMMITTEE ON GOVERNMENT AGENCIES v–viii (C. Woltz ed. 1968).

68. *See generally* T. LOWI, THE END OF LIBERALISM: THE SECOND REPUBLIC OF THE UNITED STATES (2d ed. 1979).

69. Indus. Union Dep't, AFL-CIO v. Am. Petroleum Inst., 448 U.S. 607, 642–45, 654–62 (1980); United States v. Nova Scotia Food Prod. Corp., 568 F.2d 240, 251–52 (2nd Cir. 1977).

70. Mobil Oil Corp. v. FPC, 483 F.2d 1238,1264 (D.C. Cir. 1973).

71. *Cf.* Crowell v. Benson, 285 U.S. 22 (1932).

72. *Cf.* Goldberg v. Kelly, 397 U.S. 254 (1970); Friendly, *Some Kind of Hearing*, 123 U. PA. L. REV. 1267 (1975); Rendleman, *The New Due Process: Rights and Remedies*, 63 KY. L.J. 531 (1975).

administrative process.[73] All of these techniques tended to
broaden, intensify, or redefine the participation of affected parties in the administrative process.

The courts have not acted alone in this regard. Building on
the structure of the Administrative Procedure Act, the Congress
has opened up the administrative process by means of general
reforms such as the Freedom of Information Act,[74] the Sunshine Act,[75] the Federal Advisory Committee Act,[76] and by
more specific statutory provisions guaranteeing participation, of
hearing rights with respect to the operations of particular agencies.[77] In addition, the agencies themselves, sometimes prodded
by Congress or the courts, sometimes on their own, have increasingly sought to broaden and improve participation in their
proceedings.[78] As a result the question of the adequacy of participation, whether in adjudicating or in rulemaking proceedings, has for nearly two decades dominated legal discussion of
the legitimacy of administrative decision making.

This contemporary notion, that disagreement with the outcome of administrative action should be reformulated as a disagreement with administrative decision processes, has a strong
ideological foundation. It satisfies simultaneously a craving for

73. *See* J. Vining, Legal Identity: The Coming of Age of Public Law
(1978); Stewart, *The Reformation of American Administrative Law,* 88 Harv. L. Rev.
1667 (1975).

74. Freedom of Information Act, Pub. L. No. 93–502, §§1–3, 88 Stat. 1561
(1974).

75. Government in the Sunshine Act, Pub. L. No. 94–409, §4(a), 90 Stat.
1241 (1976).

76. Federal Advisory Committee Act, Pub. L. No. 92–463, 86 Stat. 770
(1972); Pub. L. No. 94–409, §5(c), 90 Stat. 1247 (1976); Pub. L. No. 96–523 §2,
94 Stat. 3040 (1980).

77. *See, e.g.,* Occupational Safety and Health Administration, 29 U.S.C. §659
(1976); Consumer Product Safety Commission, 14 U.S.C. §§2058 (a)(2), 2059,
2061(d), 2064(f), 2076 (1976); Magnuson-Moss Warranty—Federal Trade
Commission Improvement Act, 15 U.S.C. §§57a, 2309 (1976 & Supp. IV 1980).

78. *See, e.g.,* Joseph v. United States Civil Serv. Comm., 554 F.2d 1140, 1152–
54 (D.C. Cir. 1977) (suggesting that courts can order public participation even in
situations exempt under 5 U.S.C. 553); Greene County Planning Bd. v. FPC, 559
F.2d 1227, 1234–35 (2d Cir. 1976), *cert. denied* 434 U.S. 1086 (1978) (noting FPC
authority to pay intervenors' expenses); 15 U.S.C. §57 a (h) (1976 & Supp. IV
1980) (an FTC provision authorizing the agency to compensate people
participating in the rulemaking process); Exec. Order No. 12,160, 3 C.F.R. 430–
34 (1980) (Paragraph 1–4 (e) of this order requires agencies to establish procedures for responding to consumer complaints).

direct democratic participation in an increasingly bureaucratic public life and the demand for equality before the law. There may be winners and losers in bureaucratic politics, but the game should be fair. *Access* to the seat of power—now the bureau rather than the legislature or court—should be open to all. Moreover, framing legal claims as demands for access rather than for outcomes invites judicial response while protecting the constitutional position of a judiciary that has spent nearly fifty years recovering from the traumatic conflict between the legal and political processes during the progressive era. New Deal policies vanquished a vision of judicial legality tied too closely to the prevailing substantive outcomes permitted by the common law, and the courts are not likely to forget it. But, that victory in no way impugned the integrity of judicial *process* or the expertise of judges as the architects of fair procedural systems.

The Path of the Law Revisited

The foregoing section presents an Olympian view of the path of the law. Law does not, in the normal case, self-consciously define social roles or develop techniques for the elaboration or protection of dominant political theories. Rather, the law does these things incidentally as legal institutions go about the empiric business of resolving particular disputes or particular social problems and then explaining why they resolved that dispute or problem in that fashion. Theory and generalization are sometimes important, but legal discourse usually proceeds at the level of assertions about rights.

The question of appropriate forms of participation in administrative proceedings does not present itself to a court (or to a legislative committee or to an administrator) as a question of competing theoretical models of administrative due process. Instead, a court will confront a claim by a particular party that it has a right to participate, or to participate in a particular way at a particular time, in an agency decision process. In making that process claim the suitor may well advance arguments that relate to all three of the models of administrative legitimacy discussed here. Indeed, it is commonplace to find litigants urging: (1) that faithful implementation of the statute requires that the administrator attend to their evidence and arguments; (2) that decision making absent their contribution is unreliable, uninformed, and therefore inexpert; and (3) that, given the impact of the decision on their interests, the agency process excluding their participation is unfair.

These arguments demand some reformulation or reinterpretation of the transmission belt and expertise models. The legislature must be viewed as both initiating a policy *and* creating or recognizing the interests that will be benefited or constrained by the policy. The transmission belt is thus seen as carrying both policies and rights. Expertise must also be extended or generalized to imply rationality as its goal. Participants are then viewed as increasing the stock of information and analysis available to an expert agency that is not omniscient, merely skilled. Yet, given the intuitive appeal of these reinterpretations—their tighter fit with contemporary conceptions of pluralistic politics and bounded rationality—the process lens through which claims are refracted increases the power and appeal of the due process paradigm that such claims invoke. Such a paradigm synthesizes the historic foundations of administrative legitimacy into an ideal of delegated, rational, and fair administration, realizable through decision processes designed to guarantee appropriate participation. It is this "access," "participation," "some kind of hearing," that the plaintiffs in thousands of administrative due process cases demand.

An Emerging Counterrevolution?

The attractiveness of this vision notwithstanding, a contemporary countertendency is discernible. Participation has costs as well as benefits. As recognition of those costs mounts, particularly the costs of intense participation by affected interests via trial-type procedures, the political appeal of participatory legitimation has declined.[79] The Supreme Court has begun, directly and indirectly, to discourage the procedurally revisionist stance of the lower federal courts that provided much of the legal un-

---

79. *See, e.g.,* D. Moynihan, Maximum Feasible Misunderstanding: Community Action in the War on Poverty (1969).

derpinning for the participatory approach.[80] Both at the legislative and judicial levels there is in a sense a turning back to
reexplore the possibilities of substantive legitimation either
through legislative review of the transmission belt[81] or through
rational discourse.[82] This return to a substantive focus increasingly features flirtation with the contemporary incarnations of
rationality, cost-benefit and risk-benefit analysis.[83]

In a sense, as administrative law has muddled its way from a
dim recognition of the problem of administrative legality to the
present, still process-oriented, jurisprudence, it has recognized
three different social functions for administrators. Initially
theirs was to implement, not to choose. Then, in response to
growing political unrest, theirs was the expert task of rationalizing the market forces that had created great economic power
combined with great social insecurity. More recently, the task of
administrators seems to have been to provide a specialized forum within which major issues of public policy can be addressed

80. *See, e.g.,* Vermont Yankee Nuclear Power Corp. v. Natural Resources
Defense Council, Inc., 435 U.S. 519 (1978); Mathews v. Eldridge, 424 U.S. 319
(1976). Indeed, just looking at the numbers the Supreme Court seems to be attempting to dampen plaintiffs' enthusiasm. From 1970 to 1975 the Court ruled
favorably on administrative due process claims 56 percent of the time. From
1976 to 1982 that percentage was cut almost exactly in half to 29 percent.

81. *See, e.g.,* Scalia, *The Legislative Veto: A False Remedy for System Overload,* 3
REGULATION 19 (Nov/Dec 1979); Bruff & Gellhorn, *Congressional Control of Administrative Regulation: A Study of Legislative Vetoes,* 90 HARV. L. REV. 1369 (1977).

82. *See, e.g.,* Ethyl Corp. v. EPA, 541 F.2d 1 (D.C. Cir. 1976), *cert. denied,*
426 U.S. 941 (1976) (a 118-page opinion by the court sitting en banc, and including two concurring and two dissenting opinions and several appendices); *and see*
Polsby, *FCC v. National Citizens Committee for Broadcasting and the Judicious Uses of
Administrative Discretion,* 1978 SUPREME COURT REVIEW 1; Wright, *The Courts and
the Rulemaking Process: The Limits of Judicial Review,* 59 CORNELL L. REV. 375 (1974).

83. *See, e.g.,* Exec. Order No. 12,044, 3 C.F.R. 152 (1979) as amended in
Exec. Order No. 12,221, 45 Fed. Reg. 44,249 (1980) and revoked by Exec. Order
No. 12,291, 46 Fed. Reg. 13,193 (1981). *See* opinions in the plurality decision in
Indus. Union Dep't, AFL-CIO v. Am. Petroleum Inst., 448 U.S. 607, 644–53
(1980) (a benzene case from the 5th Circuit). *Cf.* Texas Independent Ginners
Ass'n v. Marshall, 630 F.2d 398, 410–11 (5th Cir. 1980) (cotton dust) *and* Aqua
Slide 'N' Dive v. Consumer Prod. Safety Comm., 569 F.2d 831, 839–40 (5th Cir.
1978) (pool slides) *with* Am. Iron & Steel Inst. v. OSHA, 477 F.2d 825, 235–36
(3rd Cir. 1978) (coke ovens) (adopting the approach of Indus. Union Dep't v.
Hodgson, 499 F.2d 467, 477–78 (D.C. Cir. 1974) (asbestos dust). The place of
cost-benefit and risk-benefit analysis in OSHA regulation has been resolved, at
least for the moment, in Am. Textile Mfrs. Inst. v. Donovan, 452 U.S. 511 (1981)
(a cotton dust case from the D.C. Circuit).

and resolved, either at the level of general policy or on the level of individualized implementation. And, in the contemporary era, concern with administrative decision processes has begun to focus on how to make those processes rational rather than merely participatorily fair. Substantive rationality seems to be waxing, pure proceduralism waning. Yet, given the durability of the twin engines that fired the modern due process revolution —participatory ideology and the strategic virtues of proceduralist claims for preserving the political capital of the judiciary— this retrenchment need not so much dampen enthusiasm for procedural reform as slightly refocus the direction of reformist energies. For, as we have seen, rationality also can be interpreted as a procedural demand.

THE CONTEMPORARY CONCERN RESTATED

So where are we? We now know something about the extensive domain of the due process clause: its peculiar significance in American constitutional history. Moreover, we now have a firmer notion of why administrative due process has been a particularly salient issue for the past two decades and how the general history of administrative law, along with the political and social history of which it is a part, has conditioned us to talking about procedure when discussing issues of administrative legitimacy. Should we not conclude that due process adjudication has merely continued, albeit in a somewhat expanded fashion, its historic role of mediating conflict about the appropriate forms of American government?

The answer, of course, is "yes." But it is "yes, but." For the recognition that we will muddle on, that we will apparently survive, that there are no wholly novel problems, that our condition is neither unique nor terribly opaque, is not an answer that exhausts our interest. To survive is not necessarily to prosper. Moreover, there are concerns about contemporary due process adjudication that cannot be dismissed so easily. Stated generally, they are that the law of administrative due process is performing neither its regulative (conflict-resolving) nor its symbolic (value-creating) functions well. Indeed, ever clamorous as we are, we seem almost as dissatisfied with administrative due process litigation as we are with administrative action. Complaints take a number of general forms. Some decry the sheer level of litigation that has been spawned by judicial receptiveness to process-based complaints. Others complain that judicially imposed (or suggested) procedural formalities have been usually costly, often irrelevant, and sometimes seriously dysfunctional. Others object that the courts have intervened too little to maintain the position of individual rights and democratic participation in the face of a rampant bureaucratization of public life. Still another group of critics maintains that whatever its empirical effects, much of the major Supreme Court jurisprudence is both incoherent and inconsistent with our constitutional traditions.

The Tale That Follows

All of the critics are in some sense correct. But it is the last group that will hold our principal attention, for I want to argue that the basic methodology of administrative due process adjudication has gone awry. Moreover, I will maintain that the questions whether there is too much or too little due process litigation and whether its results are irrelevant or dysfunctional or underprotective cannot be answered except from some starting point that defines the way that due process adjudication should be approached. Indeed, I think many of the results merely *look* wrong and the level of litigation merely *looks* excessive because the constitutional conversation has been misdirected and trivialized.

But reaching that conclusion will take us many pages. Let me begin by elaborating a bit on two radically different types of complaints that contribute to the contemporary sense of malaise. I hope in that way to convince you both that there is something interesting here to talk about and that the fruitful way to talk about it is to reexamine our methodological premises.

The first type of complaint is functionally oriented. It suggests that recent due process litigation and the ubiquitous hearing rights that it has spawned have produced costly and dysfunctional consequences that far outweigh any benefits that may have accrued to those who obtained those due process rights. Indeed, it is often suggested that the recipients of these rights have themselves been made worse off by becoming rights bearers.

This complaint sees due process adjudication primarily as a reckless intrusion by courts and litigants into domains much better understood by administrators.

The second type of complaint concerns the failure of administrative due process doctrine to provide a means for addressing some of the critical issues of contemporary administrative governance. The concern is that the Court is stifling the due process dialogue just at the points where it is needed most. From this perspective the jurisprudence has failed to maintain basic values of individual autonomy and democratic governance. Together these criticisms suggest that the due process jurisprudence has managed somehow to become simultaneously overintrusive and underprotective.

Since by most accounts the due process revolution began with the Supreme Court's opinion in *Goldberg v. Kelly*,[84] the effects of hearing rights on welfare administration may provide a particularly apt example of both types of complaints. The overintrusiveness charge takes the form of an allegation that *Goldberg* radically altered the substance rather than the process of welfare administration. The dynamics of this transformation are fairly straightforward.

Goldberg required that recipients be provided a relatively full trial-type hearing (timely and specific notice, oral presentation of evidence and cross-examination, a neutral hearing officer, assistance of counsel, and a decision based wholly on the evidence produced at the hearing) before benefits could be terminated. The ruling presented welfare administrators with a significant problem.[85] First, if a substantial percentage of the recipients no-

84. 397 U.S. 254 (1970).

85. The impact of *Goldberg* has been analyzed extensively. The description in the text is based on a number of sources, including: SUBCOMMITTEE ON PUBLIC ASSISTANCE, SENATE FINANCE COMMITTEE, STATISTICAL DATA RELATED TO PUBLIC ASSISTANCE PROGRAMS, 96TH CONG., 2D SESS. (1980); COMMITTEE ON GOVERNMENT OPERATIONS, HOUSE OF REPRESENTATIVES, ADMINISTRATION OF THE AFDC PROGRAM, 95TH CONG., 1ST SESS. (1977); Office of Research and Statistics, Social Security Administration, *Requests for AFDC Hearings in Public Assistance* (Fiscal Years 1970–79); D. Baum, The Welfare Family and Mass Administrative Justice (1974); J. HANDLER, PROTECTING THE SOCIAL SERVICE CLIENT (1979); Note, *Procedural Due Process and the Welfare Recipient: A Statistical Study of Fair Hearings in Wisconsin*, 1978 WIS. L. REV. 145; Cooper, *Goldberg's Forgotten Footnote*, 64 MINN. L. REV. 1107 (1980); Simon, *Legality, Bureaucracy, and Class in the Welfare System*, 92 YALE L.J. 1198 (1983).

ticed for termination exercised their appeal rights, the welfare departments would simply be unable to process the cases without a large infusion of funds for administration. Because of the complexity of welfare decision making, adequate preparation of cases to prove the correctness of termination decisions was likely to be quite costly. But the alternative would be even more expensive—leaving substantial numbers of ineligible persons on the rolls.

These administrative difficulties reinforced a political difficulty. Welfare rolls were already increasing rapidly. State legislators were unwilling to provide more funds either for well-constructed hearings or for welfare benefits. A strategy was needed that would preserve fiscal integrity and produce defensible decisions.

A number of tactical moves ultimately comprised the grand design. One was to tighten up and slow down the initial eligibility determination process. Another was to generalize and objectify the substantive eligibility criteria so that messy subjective judgments about individual cases would not have to be made and defended. This move led to the realization that professional social welfare workers were no longer needed. Costs could be reduced further by lowering the quality of the staff and by depersonalizing staff-claimant encounters. If these reactions were not sufficient to restore fiscal balance, then payment levels could be reduced or allowed to remain stable in the face of rising prices. A tougher stance was also to be taken with respect to work requirements and prosecution of absent parents. Moreover, because hearings presumably protected the claimants' interests, internal audit procedures were skewed to ignore nonpayment and underpayment problems and concentrate on preventing overpayments and payments to ineligibles.

If this story of welfare since *Goldberg v. Kelly* is generally accurate, then the legal reconceptualization of welfare recipients as rights-bearing citizens entitled to quasi-judicial processes for the protection of their rights has had very substantial effects. Programs that were avowedly paternalistic, discretionary, and individualized have been transferred into semiadversary, impersonal, property-rights regimes. There are surely some gains from such a transformation. But do the benefits exceed the costs? Are welfare claimants as a class better off? Does the administrative reality reflect the true political underpinnings of welfare? Is the society well served by the elimination of the historic connection between income support and social services that attempted to ameliorate nonpecuniary sources of distress and to promote development toward self-reliance?

I do not know the answers to these questions. But it is surely plausible, and increasingly popular, to answer them all in the negative. The attitudes such answers reflect might be applied equally to the impact of process rights across a whole range of social service and social welfare programs—public schools, public hospitals, homes for the aged—the multitudinous ameliorative efforts of the welfare state. For the basic idea that anyone seriously affected by governmental action should have a right to be heard is as general as it is intuitively appealing. Indeed, if one directs attention away from "welfare state" and toward public regulatory activity, one finds the effects of the due process revolution primarily in statutes, rules, and judicial opinions that carry forward the basic thrust of the quasi-judicial model for administrative decision making, a model that seems to provide the core of the constitutional due process ideal. But in these areas too the dynamic effects of quasi-judicial procedural protections are both unpredictable and problematic.[86] All, or even most, litigated process claims need not be successful for these effects to be felt. The ease with which procedural claims can be stated can so overload the legal and administrative resources of states and localities, even federal agencies, that compromise verging on concession is the only feasible course of action.

Whereas the overintrusiveness critic makes a case for institutional dysfunction, the underprotectionist critic may claim that the due process revolution has stopped short of its essential goals: building legal security and democratic control into the administrative state. Legal security for the welfare claimant, for example, would at a minimum require that the hearing right be oriented to the issues that produce erroneous deprivations and that the recipient class has the necessary resources to make use of hearings to protect its interests. Yet neither condition seems

86. See discussion in the text *supra* at nn. 67–83.

to obtain. A careful study of errors suggests that they occur at least as often through misinterpretation of policy as through mistakes on questions of fact. The *Goldberg* decision limits due process hearings to facts. Moreover, welfare recipients generally lack the human or material resources to make use of the hearings *Goldberg* provided. Except for an occasional flurry of political activism expressed through appeals requests, hearings have been utilized about as infrequently after *Goldberg* as before.

This sort of criticism may be pressed further to suggest that the hearing technique—the demand for individualized and detailed attention through quasi-judicial process—simply misses the point of the welfare state. The problem has become one of mass, not individual, justice. Legal security for the class of welfare claimants lies, not in hearings, but in good management. Unless due process, therefore, comes to terms with administration, becomes systems- rather than case-oriented, it will be irrelevant.

The underprotectionist case goes further. *Goldberg*'s hearing rights extend only to the protection of what can be termed "positive entitlements," substantive interests already enjoying common law or statutory legal significance. Due process hearings are thus only an addition to the legal security of existing rights. They provide no access to the administrative forums in which rights are being created and no opportunity to avoid the application of general rules on the basis of individual circumstances. *Goldberg*'s hearing rights thus leave untouched the contemporary concern with (1) the remoteness of administrative policy making from immediate participation by affected interests and (2) the unfairness and irrationality that seem to attend bureaucratic implementation of general rules.

Consider, for example, a slightly different form of welfare case, *O'Bannon v. Town Court Nursing Home, Inc.*[87] There patients in the respondent institution objected to the decertification of their place of residence as a qualified nursing home under the Medicare and Medicaid statutes without affording them an opportunity to participate in the decertification process. Their claim to involvement in the decertification decision was circumstantially appealing. The legal effect of decertification

87. 447 U.S. 773 (1980).

would be to make the patients' Medicare and Medicaid benefits unavailable for continued care at Town Court and thereby, in effect, to force them to seek care elsewhere. The limited availability of nursing home beds would almost certainly mean that the residents would be separated from each other and that they might have to relocate away from their friends and families. Evidence was introduced demonstrating the general pattern of extraordinary deterioration in nursing home residents' conditions and the associated rise in their death rates, which tended to follow such institutional transfers. In short, given the potentially devastating effects of decertification, the residents wanted an opportunity to demonstrate that their care was adequate and that their home should remain a qualified provider.

The Supreme Court's response was that the residents had failed to make the threshold showing of liberty or property interests necessary to activate due process concern. The residents had a legal property interest, the Court reasoned, in the Medicare/Medicaid benefits that supported their institutional care. That interest was limited, however, by the proviso that care be received from a qualified provider. The decertification of any *particular* provider did not, therefore, alter the beneficiaries' statutory entitlement to have payments made to *some* qualified provider. Although disqualification of a particular home might put the residents to the choice of remaining there without Medicare or Medicaid assistance or of moving to a qualified home, that choice was integral to the type of legal interest that they held.

The Supreme Court's analysis is in one sense flawless. If hearings are required by due process only for the protection of existing property rights, and the hearing to which entrance is requested is not one that would in any way alter those rights, then to provide a hearing would be an exercise in futility. *O'Bannon* is, moreover, consistent with a long line of Supreme Court cases that make a connected and fundamental point: when general rules foreclose particular issues to which hearings might otherwise have been addressed, a hearing on those now-irrelevant issues will not be required.[88] This result holds notwithstanding

---

88. *E.g.*, United States v. Storer Broadcasting Co., 351 U.S. 192 (1956); FPC v. Texaco, Inc., 377 U.S. 33 (1964).

the existence of a recognized legal entitlement that is, in appropriate circumstances, protected both by statutory and by constitutional procedural requirements. Indeed, the jurisprudence legitimating the central technique of bureaucratic governance—
general rules—is sufficiently clear, constant, and substantial
that one might wonder why the *O'Bannon* plaintiffs thought they
might avoid it.

The answer is, I suspect, part desperation and part faint
hope. The two types of due process claims that really fit their
case are even more firmly foreclosed by the Court's precedents.
A claim that state legislative and regulatory criteria permitting
decertification without resident participation are irrational confronts the massive post–New Deal jurisprudence that retreats
from substantive rationality review of the legislature's "social
and economic" judgments.[89] However appealing the residents'
complaint that a program purportedly designed to help them is
hurting them instead, their lament will not be heard as a legal
objection to the state's power to act legislatively. Nor will the
Court require, as a matter of due process, that nursing home
residents be given any role in the legislative or administrative design of the regulatory scheme that certifies and decertifies qualified providers.[90] The residents' only hope was that the Court,
seeing the poignancy of their plight, would tack a hearing onto the paternalistic legislative-administrative machinery that
threatened to destroy them by the clumsiness of its protection.

The hope was not born, however, merely of desperation. Although it was clear from the jurisprudence that the residents
would not be afforded a hearing on the qualifications of a decer-
tified provider were they to remain in the home and have their
individual benefits withdrawn, it was not *quite* so clear that a
collateral approach via the decertification hearing itself was
doomed. The Court has not always approved the application of
general rules to individual cases where the possibility of injustice

89. *See, e.g.*, Williamson v. Lee Optical Co., 348 U.S. 483 (1955); Dandridge
v. Williams, 397 U.S. 471 (1970).
90. *See, e.g.*, Pac. States Box & Basket Co. v. White, 296 U.S. 176 (1935);
Florida East Coast Ry. Co. v. United States, 410 U.S. 224 (1973); Vermont Yankee Nuclear Power Corp. v. Natural Resources Defense Council, Inc., 435 U.S.
519 (1978).

and the prospects for substantial harm loomed large. Sometimes it has demanded individualized hearings.

The seemingly eclectic series of cases that have provided an escape route from legislative-administrative generalization enunciate the so-called irrebuttable presumption doctrine. These cases occurred in two flurries,[91] emerging and disappearing like a recurrent plague of locusts—for the irrebuttable presumption doctrine has a voracious appetite for statutes.[92] It states that statutes (or administrative rules) may employ no proxy categories. Every statutory classification equating some objective characteristic of persons with some goal of public policy must choose objective characteristics that are precisely coextensive with that goal. If there are real world exceptions that would, under the challenged statutory scheme, be treated like the rule, the statute establishes an illicit, irrebuttable presumption—a violation of due process of law.[93] That violation is remediable only by the provision of hearings permitting discretionary mediation between specific persons or occasions and the general goals of public policy.[94]

This doctrine fits the *O'Bannon* situation perfectly. If the goal of federal medical benefits and state regulation of nursing homes is to make nursing home residents better off, then surely those beneficiaries must have a hearing which will permit them to demonstrate that refusal to pay benefits for them to a particular home makes them worse off. Otherwise, the Social Security Administration would be using the state decertification judgment as an irrebuttable presumption that payments to a particu-

91. The first flurry includes Heiner v. Donnan, 285 U.S. 312 (1932); Hoeper v. Tax Comm'n, 284 U.S. 206 (1931); Schlesinger v. Wisconsin, 270 U.S. 230 (1926). Among the cases in the second flurry are Cleveland Bd. of Educ. v. LaFleur, 414 U.S. 632 (1974); United States Dep't of Agriculture v. Murry, 413 U.S. 508 (1973); Vlandis v. Kline, 412 U.S. 441 (1973); Stanley v. Illinois, 405 U.S. 645 (1972); Bell v. Burson, 402 U.S. 535 (1971). For recent cases upholding general uniform administrative rules, see Mathews v. Lucas, 427 U.S. 495 (1976); Mourning v. Family Publications Serv., Inc., 411 U.S. 356 (1973).

92. *See* Note, *The Irrebuttable Presumption Doctrine in the Supreme Court,* 87 HARV. L. REV. 1534, 1548–49 (1974).

93. Vlandis v. Kline, 412 U.S. 441, 446–54 (1973).

94. That is the strict view. In at least one irrebuttable presumption case, however, the Court allowed that a more limited presumption than the one at bar might have been permissible, even without providing for individualized determinations. Cleveland Bd. of Educ. v. LaFleur, 414 U.S. 632, 647 n.13 (1974).

lar provider will not further the welfare purpose of the medical assistance programs. And if the residents would be entitled under the irrebuttable presumption jurisprudence to a hearing when confronted with a termination of third-party payments to a particular home, how much more sensible it would be to provide access for them to address this general question in the decertification proceeding. Indeed, returning to the *O'Bannon* opinion's logic, the residents' property right in the third-party payments can be viewed as including the right to continued payments to a particular provider where, under the particular circumstances of the case, the chosen provider is the best available and should, therefore, remain qualified.

To say this is, of course, to reveal the problem at the heart of the irrebuttable presumption doctrine. Its application in *O'Bannon*—indeed, anywhere—changes the substantive criterion for judgment. The irrebuttable presumption doctrine is substantive due process in procedural disguise. Once that is recognized, we can understand both its attraction and its impossibility. The concern that the irrebuttable presumption doctrine represents is after all not trivial: legislative or administrative generalizations that ignore personal and situational differences, that tend to stamp out individuality, may be harmful indeed. The question is, "How much of this kind of assault on individual personality is bearable?" Sidestepping that substantive question, the formalistic irrebuttable presumption doctrine has been invoked to respond in terms of fits between evidentiary presumptions and adjudicatory facts. Yet behind the fancy footwork it is clear that the doctrine implicitly answers, "None." It thereby signals the practical necessity for its periodic return to dormancy. For, left long at large, the doctrine will gnaw its way through most of the Statutes-at-Large, the Code of Federal Regulations, and the legislation and regulations of all subnational governmental units. It will solve the problem of the administrative state by abolishing the use of legal rules.

The underprotectionist thesis, then, comes down to this: as administrative activity moves increasingly toward the use of generally applicable rules, [95] a due process jurisprudence oriented

---

95. *See generally* Fuchs, *Development and Diversification in Administrative Rulemaking*, 72 Nw. U.L. Rev. 83 (1977).

solely to the protection of individual rights through adjudication, rather than toward the ways in which rights are created by quasi-legislative processes, is impoverished. If the Court is to have anything constitutionally significant to say about the shape of modern administrative processes, an approach focused on accurate application of existing legal rules will not suffice. The underprotectionist presents us with an unsettling image of the modern administrative state: an efficient machine for generating increasing numbers of inevitably arbitrary general rules, unconstrained by any operationally relevant constitutional limitation that might preserve the values of either democracy or individualism.

At its most pessimistic, then, our contemporary concern is that the demand for due process of law has managed to become simultaneously underprotective and overintrusive. It is underprotective because it fails effectively to mediate our love-hate relationship with the administrative state; to provide a sense of personal security, understanding, and legitimacy for contemporary forms of government. It is overintrusive because it imposes or induces inefficient processes and leads to ineffective or unwanted public policies. In both its symbolic and regulative aspects the law of due process has become dysfunctional.

This indictment is surely overdrawn. But it makes at least a prima facie case for further inquiry. If the history of constitutional adjudication is any guide, we need an ideal of due process of law that can mediate social conflict, inform effctive public action, and legitimate government. In the present moment the challenge is to come to terms with our liberal, individualist aspirations in the context of a collectivized, bureaucratic public life; to develop an approach to administrative due process that preserves our ideals and our institutions.

AN OVERVIEW OF THE ARGUMENT TO COME

SYMBOLISM AND EFFICIENCY

I believe the question of functional adequacy can be answered only by addressing the issue of symbolic appropriateness. The functionally oriented empirical literature that seeks to evaluate the effects of due process adjudication on particular administrative systems is hopelessly muddled and often contradictory. This situation reflects more than the usual difficulty with constructing good empirical studies of the impact of legal rules. Such efforts are undermined at the outset by their failure to specify and defend a set of criteria by which to evaluate the goodness of the effects that they find. To discover that due process adjudication has added costs, delayed implementation, shifted power, changed substantive criteria, protected rights, or disappointed expectations provides only a minor premise for some ultimate conclusion about the goodness or badness of these effects. What is the major premise that will permit convincing evaluative conclusions to be deduced?

No satisfactory major premises for evaluating the concrete social effects of due process litigation can be provided at the level of functionally oriented policy analysis. Whether due process doctrine has made welfare, prisons, energy regulation, or some other administrative function better (assuming that causality has been established) depends in the first instance upon one's vision of the social function of the program affected. Even if we were to assume that evaluators could agree on a *single* legislative or social purpose for one or another of these complex distributive or regulatory schemes, there seems no reason to limit evaluation of the effects of due process doctrine to the pursuit of legislative purposes. Judicial review for constitutionality presumes that legislative purposes may be improper or impossible to effectuate as the legislature intended without too great a loss of other constitutional purposes having a higher, and therefore legally protected, political value.

When addressing the so-called due process revolution we thus are pressed relentlessly toward an attempt to formulate basic political principles. What indeed are the values that due process adjudication should support? What are the ideological symbols of legitimate governance that our particular liberal-democratic constitutional order affirms? More pointedly for this discussion, what interpretive methodology—what means of approaching—administrative due process questions is likely to focus on symbolically relevant questions of procedural adequacy?

To put the question in this way does not abandon the notion that due process adjudication *has* a social function. We have already suggested that, historically, litigation about administrative due process is a means for absorbing political conflict about the forms of governance. But all criteria for adjudication can play this role. Unless due process adjudication structures the constitutional conversation about administrative legitimacy in a fashion that reveals shared ideological bases for resolving disputes, the mediating function of judicial pronouncement will fail. Constitutional adjudication can resolve our political disputes successfully only as it instructs us in our shared political principles. For decision making to be functionally adequate at the level of constitutional adjudication it must be symbolically appropriate.

The argument that we will make is thus methodological and normative. Our search is for a means of approaching due process. We need some way to analyze administrative due process questions, some methodology that is at once feasible for the relevant legal institutions (courts, legislatures, and administrative agencies) and consistent with our normative constitutional aspirations. In seeking to provide that methodology we will obviously want to try to understand how such questions have been approached in the past. But the analysis in these pages is at best quasi-historical. The jurisprudential history is mined for its methodological and normative insights, not to provide a fully textured understanding of the role of administrative due process in American constitutional history. Ours is an argument about the strengths and weaknesses of competing methodologies and, ultimately, about the normative superiority of one.

A First Cut at an Interpretive Approach

The meaning of "due process of law" can be approached from several directions. Literal interpretation, a concentration on the ordinary meaning of the words, has little to offer the scholar or the courts. The clause is obviously designed to be open textured. It is a question in the form of an answer. Of course due process is due. But what is that? The approach of courts and commentators has varied, both over time and at any one time. The variations are clustered, however, around three central themes: tradition, natural rights, and interest balancing. Each theme is complex and richly embellished in the due process jurisprudence. We will state here only the core ideas and hint at their difficulties and limitations.

TRADITION

A tradition-based approach to due process analysis asks whether the procedures under consideration conform to the usual processes of law. As a historical matter, this way of putting the due process question has much to recommend it. The original understanding of the due process constraint may have been that it provided protection against oppressive governmental action enforced through special proceedings. The due process clause is thus constitutional heir to English concerns with Star Chamber proceedings and to the American revolutionary concern with an arbitrary colonial magistracy.

But tradition has serious limitations. As a jurisprudential technique, tradition's weakness lies in the difficulty of identifying a single appropriate tradition. When, for example, the Supreme Court for the first time confronted the question of an appropriate process for terminating welfare benefits, it was required to choose from among competing traditions. The long tradition of nonenforcement of gratuitous promises, including promises of continuous income support, suggested that there was no legal interest involved sufficient to actuate due process concern. The tradition of commercial law remedies suggested that the welfare recipient (creditor) should have posttermination recourse to ordinary civil process to determine the legality of the government's (debtor) failure to perform. The tradition of governmental cancellation of other valuable privileges, such as common carrier certificates or professional licenses, suggested that some form of pretermination proceeding was necessary. By what jurisprudential technique does a court decide which tradition should have the greatest claims of relevance?

The implicit values of a traditional approach to due process protection are also troublesome. If tradition implies adherence to the original understanding of "life, liberty, or property," then many governmental activities that encroach on modern notions of humane values (for example, privacy, beneficial social and economic relations, opportunities for education or for artistic and professional self-realization) evade the constraints of due process. And, on one original understanding of due process—meaning the processes of the ordinary courts or of the legislature—much of the regulatory apparatus of the welfare state applicable to property interests would be unconstitutional (the National Labor Relations acts, all federal environmental quality legislation, most safety legislation, the antifraud activities of the Federal Trade Commission and the Securities and Exchange Commission, to name a few). By modern standards the process constraints of such a traditional approach to due process (a choice limited to representative assemblies and judicial trials) are as overprotective as that traditional view's substantive values (protection only against death, incarceration, or invasion of common law property) are underinclusive.

But a tradition-based approach need not be synonymous with a conceptually static jurisprudence. Analogical development is the principal mode of judicial law reform; thus tradition evolves. The question for contemporary scholarship is how the traditional approach actually works. What are the rules of recognition for new substantive values worthy of due process concern? What are the models and metaphors of process that have informed the comparisons that an analogical method requires? What is the continued role and relevance of traditional values and techniques in the modern administrative state? What are the normative propositions that give tradition legitimating force?

NATURAL RIGHTS

A natural rights analysis takes a quite different view of the due process problem. It begins not with the historical contingencies of tradition, but with a basic moral premise concerning individual autonomy. Each citizen is an end in himself, not merely a means for the attainment of collective ends. The government cannot, therefore, pursue its purposes through processes which ignore the independent status and purposes of the individual. From the natural rights perspective this dignitary principle is what the due process clause, like other portions of the Bill of Rights, protects.

Although this secular formulation of the natural rights approach has substantial support in liberal political theory and clear connections with the individualistic ethos of ordinary political discourse, it also raises some obvious problems of application. The set of procedural rights necessary to preserve individual dignity seems infinitely expansive. Any governmentally imposed disappointment provides an occasion for invocation of the principle. And the principle implies that due process should be defined as that set of processes freely accepted by affected individuals. Because such a principle forecloses governance, limitations must be imposed. But what are the principles of limitation? Where is the objective set of *truly important* human values and *sufficiently dignified* procedures for making collective decisions about them?

The judicial dilemma is apparent. Questions of value are crucial to the application of the due process clause. The constitutional formulation requires that human interests be characterized as life, liberty, or property concerns that either have or do not have sufficient status to trigger due process protection. And, the substantive stake in decisional outcomes aside, it is surely not irrelevant to the adequacy of governmental processes that they do or do not respect individual interests in autonomy. Yet, in an increasingly secular and scientific society, confronting questions of moral value directly and in an authoritative context is embarrassing. Because they have no attachment to revealed truth and no underpinning of scientific expertise, moral pronouncements as constitutional interpretations appear radically subjective.

INTEREST BALANCING

The functional criteria so conspicuously absent from natural rights propositions are promised by the dominant contemporary mode of due process analysis—interest balancing. Under the current Supreme Court formulation, the constitutional judgment concerning process adequacy includes consideration of (1) the magnitude of the interests of private parties, (2) the governmental interest in procedural expedition, and (3) the likely contribution of various procedural ingredients to the correct resolution of disputes. In short, the Court does a social welfare calculation to determine whether society will be better or worse off should it honor the due process claim.

The great advantages of the interest balancing approach are its adaptability to any question of procedural adequacy and its recognition that judgments about process adequacy necessarily involve trade-offs between collective and individual ends. But, as a constitutional theory, this brand of utilitarianism has the defects of its virtues. For one thing, interest balancing suggests that, given a good enough reason, the government can use any process it pleases. The Bill of Rights is, however, not meant only to facilitate adaptation of constitutional constraints to changing governmental forms. Rather, its most obvious function is to protect against encroachments on individual liberty. The interest balancing methodology seems to contradict the basic libertarian presuppositions of the text that it would implement. Moreover, the information demands of a thoroughgoing utilitarian calculus may be excessive. Can the dignitary costs of individuals and the administrative costs of government, for example, be measured in the same currency? Is it possible to predict the effect of any discrete change in the decision process on the accuracy of decision making?

The questions posed by the interest balancing approach are, again, questions both of technique and of value. Can the technique deliver what it promises? Do information demands always defeat analysis, or are there acceptable strategies for dealing with uncertainties and discontinuities? Does the approach, by posing its questions in social welfare terms, misconceive the basic purposes of due process protection? Finally, does the utilitarian focus on the relationship of process to the attainment of collective ends systematically ignore or undervalue concerns that relate, not to the attainment of specific individual or collective goals, but to the place of the individual in the structure of governmental process?

A LITTLE SOPHISTICATION

These notions of tradition, natural rights, and interest balancing are quite familiar to American lawyers. Methodological examples of each could be found in any area of constitutional, and much common law, jurisprudence. Yet, as they have just been described, they do not really do justice to the ideas that have informed American legal reasoning. Tradition fails to capture the dynamism of a technique that is metaphorical and functional, as well as empirical and historical. Natural rights suggests a deductive, philosophical, perhaps transcendental approach that misses historical reliance on pure intuition and the possibility for a pragmatic and prudential jurisprudence anchored in fundamental, secular conceptions of human dignity. Interest balancing suggests a flexibility that is often belied by a positivist conceptualism that excludes some interests from the balance and by a hierarchy of constitutional values that gives special weight to others.

The discussion that follows will, therefore, proceed under different labels. I shall elaborate three related, but somewhat different, models: the models of appropriateness, competence, and dignitary interests. The model of appropriateness begins with tradition but then seeks to account for precedent and metaphor as integral elements of what might be called ordinary legal reasoning. The model of competence adds to interest balancing its historic and contemporary companions positivism and instrumentalism. The model of dignitary interests seeks to devise and explicate ideas about the place of the individual in collective decision processes that are barely visible in a natural rights jurisprudence justly excoriated for its intuitive assertions of fundamental fairness.

In developing these models I shall be concerned first to understand the techniques and dynamics of the methodology. In some cases this alone is no easy task. Second, I shall try to keep my eyes on the subtle relationships between substance and procedure—between issues of the constitutional legitimacy of *what* was done and of *how* it was done—that are established by a commitment to one or another interpretive approach. Third, I shall be concerned with the political implications or political foundations of each methodology. Constitutional reasoning is, after all, reasoning about the structure of politics. My question is whether the underlying political norms that inform a particular methodology are acceptable bases for constitutional adjudication.

JUDICIAL REVIEW IN AN ADMINISTRATIVE STATE

Closely connected to the question of political acceptability is the question of institutional role. To what sort of role in political life does a particular method commit the judiciary, and what roles does it leave to the overtly political branches? Are these roles acceptable ones? I shall be concerned also with the practicalities of judicial analysis of due process questions in one or another methodological form. Does the method ask questions that courts can answer convincingly? Does it structure communication about due process issues through constitutional adjudication in ways that permit public understanding, institutional dialogue, and self-application of principle by nonjudicial actors?

We shall find that each methodology has both strengths and weaknesses. Each responds to relevant demands for collective decision making. What after all is to be said for procedures that are inappropriate or incompetent or that violate human dignity? I shall argue, in the end, that a reinterpretation of the natural rights approach is best able to integrate procedural and substantive concerns, to mediate conflict over process rights, to elaborate an acceptable constitutional politics, to define appropriate institutional roles within that politics, and to operate simultaneously at the level of constitutional ideal and practical implementation. The dignitary approach has these strengths in part because it has the capacity to incorporate elements from the competing methodologies, while giving them a firmer theoretical foundation and a more determinate meaning.

More important, and somewhat ironically, I shall argue that, in the end, a well-considered natural rights methodology—the methodology that asks the most open-textured question (what is fundamental fairness?) and gives the judiciary the broadest possible decisional discretion—produces at once the most restrained judicial posture vis-à-vis coordinate institutions and the greatest protection for essential liberal-democratic values.

2 / *The Model of Appropriateness*

ORDINARY PROCESS

One linguistically plausible approach to the constitutional requirement of due process is that "due" means "ordinary." "The letter will arrive in due course," we say (or, in a happier era of postal service, might have said). The constitutional instruction, then, is to provide the ordinary process; to avoid special processes for special persons or for particular actions having legal consequences for any person's life, liberty, or property. Such a construction has much to commend it. It is an interpretation that is consistent with the apparent Magna Charta roots of our due process provision.[1] It generalizes the notions embodied in the Constitution's bills of attainder and ex post facto prohibitions and restrictions on the suspension of habeas corpus. The due process clause might thus be elaborated by analogy to those provisions[2] as pursuing the themes of equality, impersonality, and prospectivity that constitute our most fundamental ideas of the rule of law.

---

1. *See* J. Holt, Magna Charta 327 n. 39 (1965) ("No free man shall be taken or imprisoned or designed or outlawed, or exiled or in any way ruined, nor will we go or send against him, except by the Law of the land.") The term "due process of law"—which meant procedure by original writ or by an indicting jury— first appeared in place of "the law of the land" in the 1354 statutory interpretation of Magna Charta by Parliament, under Edward III. *Id.* at 9. *See also* R. Mott, Due Process of Law 4–5 n. 52 (1926).

2. *See, e.g.,* L. Tribe, American Constitutional Law 474–501 (1978).

Perhaps most important, a demand for ordinary process refers judicial decision making to its primary mode of reasoning —a search for concrete analogies to the challenged procedure and a comparison of the case at hand with the way the legal system ordinarily deals with similar matters. As Martin Shapiro has argued in his work on stare decisis, the basic technique has useful communication and coordination properties for a legal system that is rather loosely organized institutionally and that values both stability and the possibility of change.[3] Given these virtues, it is hardly surprising that the question "What process is due?" has been put and decided throughout much of our constitutional history on the basis of the appropriateness of a challenged process, viewed against the background of the legal system's customary ways of making decisions.

APPROPRIATE PROCESS

An attentive reader may have noted that in the preceding sentence the language of "ordinariness" was shifted to the language of "appropriateness." The shift was not accidental. For in our catalogue of the virtues of policing for process ordinariness there are several different ideas of ordinary, not all of which are captured by the notion of judgment based on a broad consideration of customary methods of operation.

The Magna Charta meaning of ordinary process, as interpreted by post-seventeenth-century British courts, was rejected early[4] in the history of judicial review under the due process clause of the U.S. Constitution. Having no power to declare legislation invalid, British courts take the "usual course of the law" to mean that course or process specified by statute, regulation, or common law. They enforce process requirements from these various sources, thereby securing equality before the law. But they do not, at least ostensibly, void or supplant them in the process of interpretation and enforcement.[5] The situation for

3. Shapiro, *Toward a Theory of Stare Decisis*, 1 J. LEGAL STUD. 125 (1972); Shapiro, *Decentralized Decision Making in the Law of Torts*, in POLITICAL DECISION MAKING (S. Ulman ed. 1970).
4. Davidson v. New Orleans, 96 U.S. 97, 102 (1877).
5. *See generally* E. WADE & A. BRADLEY, CONSTITUTIONAL LAW 46–47, 54–56, 62–78 (8th ed. 1970).

American courts is, of course, different. Stated more accurately it became different in 1877, when the Supreme Court decided that the power of judicial review, combined with the due process clause, implied a judicial duty to determine the adequacy of process, not merely an investigation into whether administrative practices were consistent with positive law.[6]

Judicial technique can all but erase the line between interpretation and review. British courts will not find that Parliament intended to violate "natural justice,"[7] and American courts avoid constitutional questions by finding that agencies have failed to follow their own procedures or the procedures legislatively specified or authorized.[8] Moreover, American courts do so in circumstances demanding substantial creativity in the construction of the applicable text.[9] Nevertheless, the point remains: due process means something more in American jurisprudence than the right to equal application of positive law. "Ordinary" or "customary" has a normative loading that is not exhausted by determining that the procedure utilized was the one specified and that it was consistently applied.

Nor is the normative premise for judgment of process appropriateness captured by the straightforward prohibition of certain processes or their close analogues. The question put to a court is not just whether official action has avoided the use of some set of extraordinary processes recognized by the Constitution as bad, or a process that might be viewed, in Justice Douglas's melifluous phrase, in *Griswold v. Connecticut*,[10] as an "emanation from the penumbra"[11] of such processes. Rather,

6. Davidson v. New Orleans, 96 U.S. 97, 104–05 (1877).
7. E. WADE & A. BRADLEY, *supra* 646–48. "The requirements of natural justice are essentially unwritten rules of the common law, and foremost among these rules is the right to a hearing. Although the courts will not question the supremacy of Parliament, there is a presumption that Parliament does not intend to deprive a subject of his right of access to the courts in respect of his common law rights." Wade and Bradley cite similar "principles of interpretation . . . to illustrate how loath the judiciary has hitherto been to construe a statute as changing the basic principles of the common law." *Id.* at 55–56.
8. *See, e.g.,* Califano v. Yamasaki, 442 U.S. 682, 693–97 (1979).
9. *See, e.g.,* Thompson v. Washington, 497 F.2d 626 (D.C. Cir. 1973) (creating a right to public participation in the official forum considering rent increases in low-rent public housing under the National Housing Act).
10. 381 U.S. 497 (1965).
11. *Id.* at 484.

American courts have generally asked whether the process under review is an apt choice amongst all processes that might be legitimate given an appropriate setting. The type of judicial reasoning we are pursuing here thus has both a wider scope and a more contingent application than the analogical development of process proscriptions specifically enunciated in the Constitution. Specific proscriptions and their analogues do have an obvious bearing on these judgments of appropriateness by excluding certain procedures from that set of processes upon which any particular process might appropriately be modelled. But the search for process appropriateness also requires an appreciation of the way any particular procedure fits into the fabric of existing processes dealing with similar questions and connects with the historical development of procedural forms both in that subject matter area and in the legal system as a whole.

APPROPRIATENESS AS A TECHNIQUE AND AS A NORMATIVE IDEAL

The characteristic analytic techniques embedded in the model of appropriateness are evident on the face of the due process jurisprudence and are almost indistinguishable from what might be termed ordinary legal reasoning. A court faced with a claim that one process or another is unconstitutional compares the challenged process with other legal processes to determine whether similar processes have been or are used in analogous legal contexts. The methodology thus might as easily be called "the method of analogy." The judicial search for analogy may investigate a wide range of customs, practices, precedents—even abstract conceptions of process forms or functions—in its quest for relevant contexts and relevant procedural vehicles. Methodologically the model of appropriateness is thus familiar to anyone having a passing acquaintance with legal argumentation.[12]

12. Bruce Ackerman seems to have something very similar in mind when he talks of the lawyer or court as an "ordinary observer" classifying phenomena as they emerge from the facts and circumstances of individual cases. *See* B. ACKERMAN, PRIVATE PROPERTY AND THE CONSTITUTION 88–97 (1977). This conception is played out in various ways in many of the methodological classics on judicial de-

The normative basis for these techniques is more elusive. Indeed, it is characteristic of the methodology to avoid addressing normative questions directly. Everyday legal technique operates at the level of the individual case; it attends much to facts and circumstances and little to general questions of policy or principle. Policy is for the legislature and principle is best understood contextually—as it emerges from or is shaped by an understanding of the facts of the case. Indeed, when broad questions of policy or principle are addressed, it is a signal that the technique is being abandoned for something else. We must therefore construct the fundamental normative grounding for the model of appropriateness in an indirect fashion. The methodology functions *as if* it had a particular normative underpinning—one that must be supplied from outside the system of analysis itself.

The general norm or value that underlies the methodology of appropriateness might be viewed rather grandly as the maintenance of the social order, or at least that portion of it that is affected importantly by legal processes.[13] The precise form of this maintenance function is shaped by the legitimate role of courts, including their ideas about the underlying political ideals that define the constitutional polity. Before we observe the methodology in action, let us look briefly at these abstract normative premises.

Maintenance of the social order would seem to require that the judiciary resolve contests for power by applying principles that the contestants recognize as common social foundations of rights. The particular principles applied define the basic features of the legal order. In a liberal-democratic polity such as our own, those legal principles must support both the ideal of individual self-determination and the maintenance of democratic political institutions.

Every judicial judgment about the appropriateness of proce-

---

cision making. *See, e.g.,* B. Cardoza, The Nature of the Judicial Process (1921); K. Llewelynn, The Common Law Tradition: Deciding Appeals (1960). For a recent incarnation see Bobbitt, *Constitutional Fate*, 58 Tex. L. Rev. 695 (1980).

13. For a somewhat similar view see Scanlon, Due Process, Nomos XVIII, at 93 (J. Pennock & J. Chapman eds. 1977).

dure cannot, of course, be a general inquiry into the maintenance requirements of liberal democracy. Indeed, it would be preposterous to imagine that the claims of individual litigants would provide occasions for illuminating the whole of the legal or constitutional landscape, thereby facilitating fruitful inquiry and sound judgment about the maintenance needs of the social order. Nor need individual lawsuits provide such occasions for general reassessment. For, assuming an acceptable starting point—that is, legal institutions and processes reasonably well-ordered in terms of the society's basic ideals—judicial decisions can be oriented only to the preservation and extension of the existing order by analogizing contemporaneous problems to past instances. These prior legal events are social facts—rules, cases, structures, practices—that embody, presumptively, the survival characteristics of the social order. Their use, analogically, as a measure of the aptness of particular claims of right, promises the continuation of social and political life as it is then understood.

But wait a minute, the reader may say. Have we not just papered over some fundamental problems? What about the basic tension in liberal-democratic theory? How is individual self-realization to be accommodated to collective needs democratically expressed? And how about judicial review? What is to be done about the countermajoritarian difficulty? Moreover, social life is not static. How can an orientation to the past accommodate change? And what precisely is the logic of analogy? How do we tell a good analogy from a bad one? How creative can the analogical method become while still supporting the system-maintenance objective?

These are good and important questions to which we shall often return. It is both the distinctive appeal and the critical failing of the approach we are exploring that these questions should not be addressed directly. Indeed it may be a fundamental political and epistemological premise of the appropriateness model that the problems, collisions, stresses, and inconsistencies of liberal democratic life can be managed—the system maintained—only by not addressing them. For the characteristics that permit the maintenance of this deeply compromised yet apparently good (at least functional) legal order cannot be fully known.

They are imbedded in practice in ways that will not permit analytic dissection, functional analysis, or comprehensive rearrangement by judicial review in a systems engineering mode.[14] To address directly legal questions involving issues of legal technique, political principle, or social welfare, would cut legal reasoning loose from the cultural moorings that give it normative force.

The appeal to tradition through analogy is thus a deeply conservative legal technique, one that might easily be associated with the political ideas of Burke[15] or Von Savigny.[16] Methodologically, it eschews the conceptual for the empirical. It proceeds by degrees, looking not for general principles and unifying themes, but for practice, precedent, and analogy. It judges not for conformity to theory, but for appropriateness, all things considered. Substantively, this approach takes seriously the normative power of the actual. Because governmental forms tend to evolve rather than mutate, most of them will be unobjectionable outgrowths of traditional modes of operation. Appropriateness review should, therefore, produce a generally restrained judicial posture—legislative and administrative judgments will not often be upset. Moreover, attention to the construction and reinforcement of tradition should tend to produce a legal order that is both understandable and predictable. The familiarity of reference points will induce a sense of legal security; the judiciary will be perceived as supporting individual rights without threatening the accomplishment of collective ends. Conflict is mediated without imperiling social order.

A CLOUD OVER CAMELOT

This vision of a stable, evolving social order supported by understandable legal processes is, of course, rather too good to be true. For one thing, social and political life also may have periods of rapid change. Until a reformist movement has been suffi-

---

14. *Cf.* F. Hayek, Law, Legislation and Liberty: A New Statement of the Liberal Principles of Justice and Political Economy (1973).

15. *See, e.g.,* F. O'Gorman, Edmund Burke 45–66 (1973).

16. F. Von Savigny, Of the Vocation of Our Age for Legislation and Jurisprudence (1975).

ciently institutionalized to be explained as the new custom or tradition, judgments founded on old customs and traditions may make courts interventionist. In times of stress the appeal to tradition will appear rigid, perhaps anachronistic. As the familiar confrontation of the Old Court and the New Deal demonstrates, the appeal to appropriateness—interpreted as an appeal to tradition—may provoke a constitutional crisis rather than sustaining a social order.

I do not want to suggest by this extreme example that the model of appropriateness is unable to accommodate change, for that model has always contained more than an appeal to tradition. Assessing the aptness of governmental forms also includes an appeal to contemporaneous practice *and* to the specific social circumstances that have produced a particular decision process. Appropriateness analysis thus is a blend of the customary, the contemporary, the just, and the efficacious. Occasionally a focus on tradition produces obstructionism and crisis, but more often analogical, even metaphorical, extension of existing legal forms yields an acceptance of incremental novelty.

The flexibility of appropriateness analysis, however, solves one problem by creating another. For flexibility suggests judicial choice. Beneath the analogical appeal to functionally opaque, but apparently workable, traditional processes, there appear to be arguments from authority, principle, and policy that inform a judicial judgment that does not adhere precisely to the forms of the past. Flexibility, thus, invites a reinterpretation of how due process review is proceeding. Beneath the modesty of an apparent attention to facts, context, and analogy, the hubris of social engineering may begin to appear in the guise either of the political conservatism of a preservationist judiciary or of a reformist judiciary attempting to anticipate the future.[17]

This book is hardly the first to notice the difficulties that beset a flexible approach to the interpretation of the due process clause. In a seminal article in 1957 entitled "Methodology and Criteria in Due Process Adjudication,"[18] Sanford Kadish suggested that what we are here calling appropriateness analysis ul-

17. This characterization of the judicial task is Alexander Bickel's: A. BICKEL, THE SUPREME COURT AND THE IDEA OF PROGRESS 103–81 (1970).
18. 66 YALE L.J. 319 (1957).

timately is incoherent. Mining the due process jurisprudence for veins of consistent analysis and operation, Kadish was left in the end with two models of due process analysis. One, an appeal to history or custom, he called "tradition." The other could be captured only as "flexible due process"—a hodgepodge of cases in which tradition is abandoned for *something* else that apparently lacks a unifying theme.

Although they agree with Kadish's basic findings, a major purpose of the pages that follow is to suggest that unifying themes can be found. The notion of governmental necessity from which a full-blown functionalism (the model of competence) would later emerge has always been present in the search for appropriateness, along with the dignitary concept of fundamental fairness. These ideas are imbedded in the practices to which a search for tradition makes reference. Yet Kadish was surely correct to note that in 1884, when the Court in *Hurtado v. California*[19] permitted state abandonment of grand jury presentment in a large class of criminal cases and described the due process clause—indeed the whole Constitution—as "made for an undefined and expanding future,"[20] it had cut itself loose from empirical investigation of historic practice in a fashion that demanded a new theory of due process adjudication. It is also true that by the mid-1950s, when Kadish wrote, no coherent explanation of such a new theory had been provided. Indeed, because reaction to *Lochnerian* excesses had made fundamental fairness talk unfashionable, and the possibilities for functional differentiation of the trial model of process were perceived only dimly, the jurisprudence was then in the peculiar disarray that Kadish described.

Nor is the apparent choice between obstructionist traditionalism and incoherent flexibility the only problem for a due process analysis conceived of as a search for apt analogies in custom or practice. There is, in addition, a tendency for this method to degenerate into either formalism or abstraction. Subtle and extensive inquiry into historical and contempory practice is, after all, a costly technique. Courts and lawyers therefore will seek

19. 110 U.S. 516 (1884).
20. *Id.* at 530–31.

continually to short-circuit extended empirical inquiry. Two conventional modes of legal analysis are available.

One apparently efficient device for reducing information costs is precedent. Rather than reinvestigating practices in each case, the information contained in prior cases can be captured and used simply by invoking those cases. To the extent that the new situation is like the prior cases, this technique neither falsifies nor loses information about the tradition. But true or complete redundancy is rare. As precedent accretes, and as it is manipulated without reference to the particular circumstances from which it emerged, judicial activity may become increasingly insular. Rather than pursuing empirical inquiry into the social world, the legal culture may take on a life of its own—one in which cases stand for social facts and manipulation of formal categories replaces factual inquiry as the basis for decision making.[21]

A similar and sometimes related tendency is the lapse into conceptual abstraction. As empirical inquiry may be impounded in case citations, so may cases or actual practices be captured and revealed by a functional or institutional category. The processes of administrative agencies, or those considered in past cases, might be described as judicial, or legislative, or like some other traditional legal process, *e.g.*, contracting or licensing. The new case or situation then need not be compared with precedents or practices. Rather, it can be compared directly with the institution or function that it most resembles. In a sense this seems a step back toward an empirical, rather than a precedent-based, inquiry. But notice that the comparison now is with a concept, not a practice. The image of a court or a legislature or a process of contracting is an abstract representation of activities that may be conceptualized in this way. Comparing adjudicatory activity with the abstract model of a court may thus be a vastly different enterprise than exploring the actual functioning and history of

21. This formalist view of legal reasoning has, of course, not always been viewed as degenerate. Langdell exalted it as scientific. *See* C. LANGDELL, PREFACE TO LAW OF CONTRACTS at vi (1871); and despite the demolition job of the Realists, *see, e.g.,* T. ARNOLD, THE SYMBOLS OF GOVERNMENT (1935) and K. LLEWELYN, *supra* n. 12, the technique continually reemerges. *Cf.* Brilmayer, *How Contacts Count,* 1980 SUP. CT. REV. 77.

similar or related adjudicatory activities. And because, as de Tocqueville reminds us, new things are more easily constructed than new ideas,[22] this ideal-typical analysis may falsify reality as it classifies the process under discussion in terms of an existing set of abstract categories.

I thus call these two movements away from the basic techniques involved in appeals to tradition "degenerate"; they have a tendency to cause the methodology to lose its normative foundation. For as it moves away from its empirical basis, the method of appropriateness also moves away from the social reality it presumptively affirms and preserves. The more formalist and precedent-bound the technique, for example, the less likely it seems that legal forms will be responsive to the underlying needs and values of the social order—that they will in fact serve system maintenance ends. Indeed, formal manipulation of case precedent may undermine normative political acceptability in a more immediate sense. Empirical pursuit of custom and practice is a technique that potentially is open and meaningful to the non-professional. Legal formalism tends to produce a closed system, perhaps transparent only to professionals initiated into its arcane rhetoric.

Abstraction further challenges the conception of a restrained judiciary applying accepted norms embodied in conventional legal forms. The more conceptual the analysis, the less obvious or nonproblematic will be the subsumption of any particular case under any particular category. When plaintiffs and defendants begin to argue about whether a function *is* legislative or judicial rather than about whether it has been carried out in a way roughly comporting with analogous operations in the existing legal order, they increasingly will be seen to be arguing about whether the function *should* be organized in one way or another. For administrative functions do not have essences; they *can* be organized in any number of ways. And because arguments of principle and policy are required to respond to the *ought* question, the capacity of due process adjudication to mediate value conflict by appeal to a conventional social reality will fail just at the point where it is most needed. As we shall see, it then will be child's play to supply the missing premises of legal reasoning in

22. *See* 1 A. DE TOCQUEVILLE, DEMOCRACY IN AMERICA 3–17 (Paris 1835).

the form of the judiciary's approval of or antagonism toward the substantive choices imbedded in particular governmental activities. Conceptualism is easy prey for realist critics disappointed by substantive results.

At least since the 1930s, this historically standard legal technique—the use of custom, precedent, and analogy, unadorned by arguments of policy or principle—has been unfashionable. When the Realists exploded the Langdellian myth of a science of law they replaced it with the idea of law as a purposive activity. The exercise of legal power now must be premised on its instrumental connection to the realization of accepted public values. A legal methodology whose functional underpinnings cannot be analyzed in legal argument seems unlikely to survive in the modern administrative state. Its particularity and obscurantism, indeed its intellectual modesty, are an affront to a legal order increasingly oriented toward generality and rationality—and apparently confident of the power of intellect to know and to shape the social world.

These abstract musings about a particularistic methodology need a firmer empirical foundation. We must immerse ourselves for some time in the cases in order to observe appropriateness analysis in its natural habitat.

APTNESS IN ACTION—EARLY TAX CASES IN THE SUPREME COURT

Given the relatively limited regulatory and redistributional functions of nineteenth-century government, and the ubiquity of taxation in support of public works (general taxes and particularly special assessments for intermittent sewerage, drainage, road, and other projects), the prominence of litigation about tax collection procedures in early due process cases is not surprising. Indeed, tax cases accounted for over 60 percent of all due process cases reaching the U.S. Supreme Court until 1933. The ancient orgins of taxation combined with its proliferation of forms in the various states might well have engendered, as it certainly reinforced, the Court's predisposition to pursue the elaboration of the due process idea as the development of the content of custom.

The earliest attack on administrative procedure on due process grounds, *Murray's Lessee v. Hoboken Land and Improvement Co.*,[23] is both a tax case and a paradigmatic example of empirically based appropriateness analysis. The case involved the validity of a title transferred at a tax sale under what was known as a "distress warrant." Such a warrant operated, under the terms of an 1820 statute, as a lien on the disputed property. The warrant had been issued against the property of a delinquent tax collector after a Treasury audit of his accounts, but without a judicial hearing concerning the accuracy of the audit deficiencies. This lack of judicial process was asserted to violate both the separation of powers principle envisaged in the Article III conferral of judicial power on the courts and the Fifth Amendent's due process clause.

In *Murray's Lessee* Justice Curtis began his opinion for the Court by asserting, somewhat opaquely, that it was "manifest" that the legislature could not "by its mere will" establish just any process. Nor was it enough that the process follow the regular and orderly passage of a statute of general applicability. What would suffice, however, was less clear.

Justice Curtis proposed a two-tier test for determining whether the 1820 act was consistent with "the law of the land," thus assuming the conventional Magna Charta lineage for the due process clause. The first part of this test was a consideration of whether the challenged procedure was in conflict with the Constitution itself. Curtis did not explain what this meant, but is seems probable that he was referring to such specific prohibitions as those against ex post facto laws and bills of attainder. The second part of the test was whether the procedure conformed to "those settled usages and modes of proceeding existing in the common and statute law of England, before the emigration of our ancestors, and which are not shown to have been unsuited to their civil and political condition by having been acted on by them after the settlement of this country." [24] He proposed to settle the question by looking at four factors: the historical practices employed in England, the colonies, and most critically in the various states between the Declaration of Inde-

23. 59 U.S. (18 How.) 272 (1855).
24. *Id.* at 277.

pendence and the ratification of the Constitution; the current practices of the various states; the character or nature of the procedure involved; and the functional necessities of tax administration. Since Curtis thought that all of these factors supported the conclusion that the statute should be upheld, he made no attempt to explain the relative importance of each, or to suggest what the Court would do if they were in conflict.

Curtis found the historical record clear. From at least the reign of Henry VIII (1509-47), English common law had recognized the legitimacy of summary, nonjudicial procedures for the recovery of debts due the sovereign. In particular, the law allowed the use of auditors, inquiry without notice, and summary execution. The Court also found that it was the nearly universal practice of the various states to use some sort of summary distress proceeding. The significance of this finding, both here and in subsequent cases, is ambiguous. As evidence of the fact that once free from royal despotism Americans did not repudiate the practice and thus that it was not inconsistent with the aspirations of a free people, it might have been a kind of historical argument. As a demonstration that summary procedures were ubiquitous, and thus arguably necessary to the orderly collection of taxes, it might have been a kind of functional argument. But it also had an element of a parade of horribles, a raising of the spectre of the confusion that would be created if any administrative procedure so firmly entrenched were declared invalid.

The Court had considerably more difficulty in determining the character of a sale pursuant to a distress warrant. Curtis began by rejecting the contention that it was possible to establish any bright line between judicial acts "in the enlarged sense" and "all those administrative duties the performance of which involves an inquiry into the existence of facts and the application to them of rules of law."[25] He suggested instead that the relevant question was not the the essential nature of the act, but whether the controversy was such that it had to be made the subject of a judicial proceeding. The Court failed, however, to make clear whether this test was only a formal question of where governmental power had been allocated by statute, or was an at-

25. *Id.* at 280.

tempt to define due process in terms of actions that might be said to be exclusively judicial. Subsequent cases treated this part of the opinion as a purely formal statement. In 1877 Justice Miller interpreted the holding of the Court as nothing more than that "the power exercised was executive, not judicial."[26] Justice Field, who by 1884 advocated a much broader reading of the due process clause, was nevertheless equally formal in his approach to the holding in *Murray's Lessee*.[27]

The final factor considered in Justice Curtis's opinion was the interest of the state. Unlike the approach taken by contemporary courts, this functional importance factor was addressed primarily from a historical perspective. The Court made no attempt to balance the interests of collectors, or of taxpayers in general, in a fuller, more judicial proceeding, against the interest of the government in avoiding delaying tactics and securing the immediate payment of taxes. Nor did it consider whether the government might secure the same advantages by less drastic means. It dealt only with the question of whether summary procedures had in general been thought essential to protect the taxing power. While admitting that "due process of law" implied "*actor, reus, judex*" (plaintiff, defendant, judge), taxation was apparently different.

> [T]here are few governments which do or can permit their claims for public taxes, either on the citizen or the officer employed for their collection or disbursement, to become subjects of judicial controversy, according to the course of the law of the land. Imperative necessity has forced a distinction between such claims and all others, which has sometimes been carried out by summary methods of proceeding, and sometimes by systems of fines and penalties, but always in some way observed and yielded to.[28]

Murray's Lessee, thus, touched all the bases of appropriateness analysis: appropriateness viewed historically, appropriateness viewed contemporaneously, appropriateness viewed in terms of governmental necessity. Moreover, the Court recognized a more

26. Davidson v. New Orleans, 96 U.S. 97, 103 (1877).
27. Hagar v. Reclamation Dist. No. 108, 111 U.S. 701, 709–10 (1884).
28. Murray's Lessee v. Hoboken Land and Improvement Co., 59 U.S. (18 How.) 272, 282 (1855).

general ideal of legal appropriateness with respect to contractual property rights—judicial trial. And, while rejecting the Article III argument that only judicial process would do, the Court recognized certain elements of judical trial as the core image of due process of law. That image simply was inapplicable to the peculiar arena of tax collection.

Strangely, given its rather dismal news for taxpayers, the particularistic methodology of the opinion in *Murray's Lessee* seems to have inspired lawyers, after the passage of the Fourteenth Amendment due process clause, to appeal scores of state tax cases to the Supreme Court. By 1877, in *Davidson v. New Orleans*, the Court was feeling oppressed by this nineteenth-century due process revolution. The Court's perception of the role due process was playing, and of the relationship of litigation to its interpretive approach, is worth extensive quotation:

It is not a little remarkable, that while [the due process clause] has been in the constitution of the United States, as a restraint upon the authority of the Federal government, for nearly a century, and while, during all that time, the manner in which the powers of that government have been exercised has been watched with jealousy, and subjected to the most rigid criticism in all its branches, this special limitation upon its powers has rarely been invoked in the judicial forum or the more enlarged theatre of public discussion. But while it has been a part of the Constitution, as a restraint upon the power of the States, only a very few years, the docket of this court is crowded with cases in which we are asked to hold that State courts and State legislatures have deprived their own citizens of life, liberty, or property without due process of law. There is here abundant evidence that there exists some strange misconception of the scope of this provision as found in the fourteenth amendment. In fact, it would seem, from the character of many of the cases before us, and the arguments made in them, that the clause under consideration is looked upon as a means of bringing to the test of the decision of this court the abstract opinions of every unsuccessful litigant in a State court of the justice of the decision against him, and of the merits of the legislation on which such a decision may be founded. If, therefore, it were possible to define what it is for a State to deprive a person of life, liberty, or property without due process of law, in terms which would cover every exercise of power thus forbidden to the State, and exclude those which are not, no more useful construction could be furnished by this or any other court to any part of the fundamental law.

But apart from the imminent risk of failure to give any definition which would be at once perspicuous, comprehensive, and satisfactory, there is wisdom we think, in the ascertaining of the intent and application of such an important phrase in the Federal Constitution, *by the gradual process of judicial inclusion and exclusion, as the cases presented for decision shall require, with the reasoning on which such decision may be founded.* This court is, after an experience of nearly a century, still engaged in defining the obligations of contracts, the regulation of commerce, and other powers conferred on the Federal government, or limitations imposed upon the States.[29] [Emphasis added.]

As much as the Court wanted to get rid of the state tax cases, it resisted altering its methodology. Each question of the appropriateness of administrative (or judicial) procedure would be evaluated in context.

As might be expected, the Court did not in every case provide the exhaustive catalogue of historical and contemporary practices set out in *Murray's Lessee*. It very quickly adopted the citation of precedent as a substitute for redundant empirical investigation and analysis. Yet, repeated recitation of the *Murray's Lessee* and *Davidson* formulations, and continuous judgments for the defendant public authorities, hardly stemmed the tide of tax litigation. In *Springer v. United States*,[30] a vexed Justice Swayne declared, "The idea that every taxpayer is entitled to the delays of litigation is unreason."[31] Three years later[32] Justice Field resorted to an appendix to demonstrate that the tax procedure under attack had close analogues in virtually *every* state in the Union.[33] The turn of the century revealed a Court still trying, without apparent success, to explain that its notion of customary or appropriate legal forms did not entail the invalidity of every process for which there was no identical antecedent.[34]

29. Davidson v. New Orleans, 96 U.S. 97, 103–04 (1877).
30. 102 U.S. 586 (1880).
31. *Id.* at 594.
32. Hagar v. Reclamation Dist. No. 108, 111 U.S. 701 (1884).
33. *Id.* at 713–15.
34. Weyerhauser v. Minnesota, 176 U.S. 550 (1900) (upholding Minnesota

The particularity of the Court's methodology surely contrib-
u.ed to the deluge of tax due process cases. It would be a mistake, however, to imagine that the vision of due process being
propounded in the tax cases had no core ideas, no generalizations to guide application. The opinion in *Murray's Lessee* had
made clear that the most general, customary form for finding
contested facts was trial. The point was that this custom was not
always followed. Particular functions were surrounded by their
own customs which also could be characterized in terms of common elements. In *Davidson v. New Orleans* the Court, "the gradual process of inclusion and exclusion" notwithstanding, had de-
spairingly attempted to capture the essence of due process in the
tax area in this formulation:

> That whenever by the laws of a State, or by State authority, a tax, as-
> sessment, servitude, or other burden is imposed upon property for
> the public use, whether it be for the whole State or some more lim-
> ited portion of the community, and those laws provide for a mode
> of confirming or contesting the charge thus imposed, in the ordi-
> nary courts of justice, with such notice to the person, or such pro-
> ceeding in regard to the property as is appropriate to the nature of
> the case, the judgment in such proceedings cannot be said to de-
> prive the owner of his property without due process of law, how-
> ever, obnoxious it may be to other objections.[35]

To be sure the language permitting such proceedings as
were "appropriate to the nature of the case" suggested flexibility. But in context it seemed to mean only that judicial confirma-
tion did not have to attend every step in the tax collection process—prescription, assessment, valuation, levy, seizure, etc. If
somewhere in the process, perhaps even in an eventual action
against the collector for trespass or conversion,[36] opportunity to
contest were provided, the exigencies of revenue collection demanded that multiple opportunities for judicial review or ap-

provision authorizing the governor to appoint a board to reassess taxable property appearing to have been originally underassessed).

35. 96 U.S. 97, 104–05.

36. *Cf.* McMillan v. Anderson, 95 U.S. 37 (1877) (upholding a Louisiana statute which provided for the summary seizure and sale of property belonging to a
delinquent taxpayer as due process of law on the grounds that an opportunity to
contest the applicability of the license tax in question was available through the
state courts).

proval be excluded. Congress or state legislatures could, therefore, rearrange the myriad details of tax collection in any form
that met the needs of government, as governments had always
done, provided that the core custom of "opportunity to contest"
was *somewhere* maintained.[37]

So viewed, the due process question is not answered, merely
redefined. Opportunity to contest might take many forms. Yet
as the plaintiff in *Murray's Lessee* understood, when he combined
a due process and an Article III claim, those forms draw their
inspiration from the model of judicial trial. The contours and
the occasions for the use of alternative procedure will depend on
the degree to which the "nature of the case" bears close analogy
to cases customarily brought before courts pursuant to civil or
criminal process. Two cases in the second decade of the twentieth century concerning taxation in Denver, Colorado, captured
this idea with a force that has made them leading cases for sev-
enty years.

In the first case, *Londoner v. Denver*,[38] the taxpayer objected
to an assessment against his property based on the benefit alleg-
edly conferred on the property by municipal street paving. Local procedure had permitted a written objection to the assessment but not an oral hearing. The Supreme Court held this
procedure invalid. Due process, the Court declared, demanded
"the right to support . . . allegations by argument, however brief,
and if need be, by proof, however informal."[39] The judicial
model was flexible, but firm at the core.

Yet that model was not always appropriate. Seven years later
in *Bi-Metallic Investment Co. v. State Board of Equalization*,[40] the
Court determined that due process did not require the opportunity to contest a decision increasing, by a substantial percentage,
the tax valuation of all property in Denver. In the Court's view
the action complained of corresponded to another common, but
nonjudicial, governmental process: "General statutes . . . are
passed that affect the person or property of individuals, sometimes to the point of ruin, without giving them a chance to be

37. Hagar v. Reclamation Dist. No. 108, 111 U.S. 701, 710–12 (1884).
38. 210 U.S. 373 (1908).
39. *Id.* at 386.
40. 239 U.S. 441 (1915).

heard. Their rights are protected in the one way that they can be in a complex society, by their power, immediate or remote, over those who make the rule."[41] *Londoner* was distinguished as having involved "a small number of persons, who were exceptionally affected, in each case on individual grounds."

SOME PRELIMINARY REFLECTIONS ON THE TAX DUE PROCESS JURISPRUDENCE

The methodology of appropriateness analysis in the cases we have been considering might be thought of as a dialogue between modal and special conceptions of legal process. The modal process, judicial trial, is so deeply entrenched in the legal culture, not to mention specific provisions of the Constitution, that elaborate discussion of its origins, rationale, and current status would be superfluous. Judicial process is then confronted by processes of administrative decision making that do not conform to the core image of a trial, but that nevertheless claim legitimacy because of their appropriateness to their particular domains of application. That claim is evaluated from several perspectives: (1) Is there historic usage amounting to custom? (2) Is the custom maintained in contemporary legal relations? (3) Does the process chosen have some peculiar functional rationale that connects it with the domain in which it is applied?

This reasoning process obviously leaves much at large. The cautious legislative or administrative draftsman might like the answers to many questions: How important is it that some judicial remedy remain potentially available? How closely should the procedures track the relevant historical analogies? How widespread must be the contemporary usage to make it relevant? How pressing are the functional necessities that will justify continued informality? What if some considerations point in one direction and some in another? These questions call for highly contextualized judgments. General answers will be uninformative or, worse, misleading. We are here in the arena of ordinary legal discourse. Argument is by analogy; reference is to custom and prior holdings; considerations are multiple and un-

41. *Id.* at 445.

weighted. The normative underpinnings of various criteria (the judicial model, usage, governmental necessity) remain amorphous because the "gradual process of inclusion and exclusion" is highly particularistic.

This reasoning process also demonstrates the two degenerate tendencies that we noted earlier—the appeal to precedent and the appeal to abstract institutional concepts. Awash in state tax cases, the Court desperately attempted to signal the redundancy of cases by subsuming them under broader and broader notions of what counted as analogous cases. From *Murray's Lessee* to *Londoner* the dominant predictive fact in the cases was that they were *tax* cases. That alone virtually sealed the taxpayer's fate and often called forth little explanation beyond the citation of prior decisions.[42]

Lying in the background, and occasionally invoked, was the abstract idea of a court-like process for finding contested facts. That image urges forward every plaintiff whose tax administrative process has been unlike at least *some* judicial procedure. And, as *Londoner* demonstrates, someone's facts ultimately will elicit invalidation of an administrative process as insufficiently court-like. Indeed, the Court seemed unable to decide whether the idea of a court trial meant that a truly judicial body had to be used whenever the legislature left any discretion to the tax collectors or whether trial-type procedure before an administrator or commission would suffice.[43] In either case the attributes of a sufficient trial were never specified with any clarity.[44] Appropriateness review thus begins to look like a competition between an empty empiricism (formalistic use of precedent) and the interposition of judicial trial as the constitutional norm.

Such a characterization obviously is too harsh if taken as an accurate description of a complex jurisprudence. Yet it signals a critical issue in the evaluation of this traditional, analogical mode of legal discourse. Whether the analogy is to practice, to precedents, or to abstract models of process, what indeed is the logic

42. *See, e.g.*, Hilton v. Merritt, 110 U.S. 97 (1884).
43. *See* Hagar v. Reclamation Dist. No. 108, 111 U.S. 701 (1884); Spencer v. Merchant, 125 U.S. 345 (1888); Kentucky R.R. Tax Cases, 115 U.S. 321 (1885).
44. *See, e.g.*, Earnshaw v. United States, 146 U.S. 60 (1892); Lent v. Tillson, 140 U.S. 316 (1891); Passavant v. United States; 148 U.S. 214 (1893).

of appropriateness? If the fit of a contested process with the legal order is problematic from any of these perspectives, what—other than the eye of the beholder—informs the answer to the appropriateness issue? It is precisely this metajudgmental issue that the methodology we are discussing cannot address. And, because it cannot, its judgments may take on the character of ipse dixit. Worse, due process review may be seen merely as furthering a substantive judicial program that is itself based largely on the judiciary's agreement or disagreement with the substantive policies embodied in particular types of administrative programs. As due process adjudication moved into the early decades of the twentieth century, these potential methodological problems emerged as political issues.

SUBSTANCE, PROCEDURE, AND THE IMAGE OF A COURT

TAXATION AND SUBSTANTIVE DUE PROCESS

The substantive aspects of due process were recognized explicitly in some of the nineteenth-century tax cases. The *Davidson* majority recognized that many of the cases presented for judgment attacked the "merits of the legislation." And the Court's attempted formulation of a due process test for the validity of tax legislation specified that the tax burden involved be "for the public use, whether it be for the whole state or some more limited portion of the community." Justice Bradley's influential concurrence in that case also focused the Court's attention on the similarity between taxation and "takings," which by virtue of the just compensation provisions of the Fifth Amendment's due process clause could be undertaken only for a public purpose.

To be sure, the Fourteenth Amendment contained no just compensation or public purpose language, but that textual embarrassment was surmounted quite readily in *Loan Association v. Topeka*.[45] The case involved one of that city's schemes for attracting business. Topeka encouraged King Wrought-Iron

45. 87 U.S. (20 Wall.) 655 (1874).

Bridge Manufacturing and Iron Works Company to locate in that city by offering it a "donation" paid for by the sale of one hundred $1,000 interest-bearing bonds, backed by a special municipal tax. The city defaulted on the bonds. When sued by a bondholder, the Cleveland Citizens' Savings and Loan Association, Topeka demurred on the ground that the issuance of the bonds had been illegal. The Supreme Court sustained the demurrer. Quoting *Webster's Dictionary* and Judge Cooley's *Constitutional Limitations*, Justice Miller described a tax as a levy for a public purpose. Topeka's action was not of a public character. The power of taxation could not be used to open the "coffers of the public treasury to the importunities of . . . businessmen."[46]

This noble, if naive, sentiment invited a wide range of challenges to state, federal, and local taxation. Yet the party to which the Court thus called a diverse contingent of revelers was a sombre affair. In subsequent decisions the *Loan Association* case came to stand more for the proposition that taxation for public purposes was a power of almost limitless extent than for the idea, pressed hard by litigants, that taxes had to be general, fair, and beneficial.[47] Only on facts virtually identical to those in the *Loan Association* case was the Court willing to invalidate taxes for failure to serve a public purpose.[48]

The methodology of the substantive public purpose cases is indistinguishable from the tax procedure cases. In both sets of cases the due process issue is consistently viewed as one of the appropriateness of the tax or of the tax collection process when viewed in the context of historic and contemporary governmental functions. Competition for ordinary private industry by "donations" from the public treasury was too novel, or perhaps too blatant, a use of the taxing power to be sustained. But similar actions to obtain a grist mill, an enterprise with a historical aura of publicness, were approved.[49] Ultimately forms, such as simple tax concessions, were adopted that, when combined with the widespread practice of business-seeking by states and localities,

46. *Id.* at 665.
47. *See, e.g.,* Kelly v. Pittsburg, 104 U.S. 78 (1881); Thomas v. Gay, 169 U.S. 264 (1898); Williams v. Eggleston, 170 U.S. 304 (1898).
48. *See* Cole v. LagGange, 113 U.S. 1 (1885).
49. Township of Burlington v. Beasley, 94 U.S. 310 (1876).

legitimated Topeka's perspicuous but premature entry into the tax-subsidy sweepstakes.

THE BATTLE OVER STATE REGULATION

If state taxation was *the* due process issue of the late nineteenth century, state regulation was its successor in the early part of the twentieth. But whereas the tax due process jurisprudence permitted a relatively easy transition from one view of public purposes in economic affairs to another, the Court's traditionalism in state regulatory cases provoked two decades of heated controversy. In the end, in their rather desperate retrenchment to preserve the institution of judicial review, the state regulation cases became the occasion for the Court's attempt to drive a conceptual wedge between procedural and substantive due process. In this there is no little irony, for those cases also demonstrated the inevitable connection between substance and procedure in an analysis based on appropriateness. Indeed, the shift from the broad affirmation of state police powers characteristic of the tax public purpose jurisprudence, and earlier regulatory cases, begins in a procedural due process case, *Chicago Minneapolis & St. Paul Railway Co. v. Minnesota*[50] (hereafter the *Minnesota Railroad Case*), in 1890, a full fifteen years before the famous substantive due process formulations of *Lochner v. New York*.[51]

The *Minnesota Railroad Case* involved an issue dear to the heart of Minnesotans—rates for the transport of milk. The railroad's rates were challenged by shippers as unequal, unreasonable, and therefore, under the applicable law, illegal. Proceedings denominated an "investigation" were held before the Railroad and Warehouse Commission of the State of Minnesota, a body created by statute in 1887. The commission agreed with the complaining parties and ordered the carrier to reduce its rates on several particular routes. When it failed to comply, the commission, following the statutorily prescribed procedure, sought an order of mandamus from the Minnesota Supreme Court. In reply the company demanded that the case be re-

50. 134 U.S. 418 (1890).
51. 198 U.S. 45 (1905).

ferred to a trial docket for the production of evidence on the issues of equality and reasonableness. The Minnesota Supreme Court refused, declaring that the commission's findings were conclusive. Since the company did not deny that it was in violation of the commission's rate order, mandamus was issued.

The railroad appealed to the U.S. Supreme Court urging, among other things, that the regulatory scheme was beyond the legislature's power and, more narrowly, that the absence of trial on the issues of equality and reasonableness had denied it due process of law. The Court made short work of the company's substantive grounds of error. It reaffirmed prior holdings, *Munn v. Illinois*[52] perhaps being the most notable, establishing the general power of state legislatures to regulate rates and to use commissions for that purpose. The opinion also restated the Court's prior position that charters authorizing railroad companies to set tolls and fares in no way barred subsequent legislative action to regulate the rates thus set. But on the procedural point the company obtained a reversal. The language of the opinion is instructive:

> The construction put upon the statute by the Supreme Court of Minnesota must be accepted by this court, for the purposes of the present case, as conclusive and not to be reexamined here as to its propriety or accuracy. The Supreme Court authoritatively declares that it is the expressed intention of the legislature of Minnesota, by the statute, that the rates recommended and published by the commission, if it proceeds in the manner pointed out by the act, are not simply advisory, nor merely prima facie equal and reasonable, but final and conclusive as to what are equal and reasonable charges; that the law neither contemplates nor allows any issue to be made or inquiry to be had as to their equality or reasonableness in fact; that, under the statute, the rates published by the commission are the only ones that are lawful, and, therefore, in contemplation of the law the only ones that are equal and reasonable; and that, in a proceeding for a mandamus under the statute, there is no fact to traverse except the violation of the law in not complying with the recommendations of the commission. In other words, although the railroad company is forbidden to establish rates that are not equal and reasonable, there is no power in the courts to stay the hands of

52. 94 U.S. 113 (1877).

the commission, if it chooses to establish rates that are unequal and unreasonable.

This being the construction of the statute by which we are bound in considering the present case, we are of the opinion that, so construed, it conflicts with the Constitution of the United States in the particular complained of by the railroad company. It deprives the company of its right to a judicial investigation, by due process of law, under the forms and with the machinery provided by the wisdom of successive ages for the investigation judicially of the truth of a matter in controversy, and substitutes therefor, as an absolute finality, the action of a railroad commission which, in view of the powers conceded to it by the state court, cannot be regarded as clothed with judicial functions or possessing the machinery of a court of justice.

Under section 8 of the statute, which the Supreme Court of Minnesota says is the only one which relates to the matter of the fixing by the commission of general schedules of rates, and which section, it says, fully and exclusively provides for that subject, and is complete in itself, all that the commission is required to do is, on the filing with it by a railroad company of copies of its schedules of charges, to "find" that any part thereof is in any respect unequal or unreasonable, and then it is authorized and directed to compel the company to change the same and adopt such charge as the commission shall declare to be equal and reasonable, and, to that end, it is required to inform the company in writing to what respect its charges are unequal and unreasonable. No hearing is provided for, no summons or notice to the company before the commission has found what it is to find and declared what it is to declare, no opportunity provided for the company to introduce witnesses before the commission, in fact, nothing which has the semblance of due process of law; and although, in the present case, it appears that, prior to the decision of the commission, the company appeared before it by its agent, the commission investigated the rates charged by the company for transporting milk, yet it does not appear what the character of the investigation was or how the result was arrived at.[53]

Justice Bradley, joined by Justices Gray and Lamar, dissented.[54] In their view the majority opinion, while apparently

53. Chic., Minn. & St. P. Ry. Co. v. Minnesota, 134 U.S. 418, 456–57 (1890).
54. *Id.* at 461.

reaffirming, virtually overruled *Munn v. Illinois*. Moreover, Justice Bradley believed the Court had misunderstood the function that the Minnesota Commission was performing. Its fact-finding was not judicial, it was legislative. As such, investigation was precisely the usual and appropriate procedure. The dissent proceeds:

> I think it is perfectly clear, and well settled by the decisions of this court, that the legislature might have fixed the rates in question. If it had done so, it would have done it through the aid of committees appointed to investigate the subject, to acquire information, to cite parties, to get all the facts before them, and finally to decide and report. No one could have said that this was not due process of law. And if the legislature itself could do this, acting by its committees, and proceeding according to the usual forms adopted by such bodies, I can see no good reason why it might not delegate the duty to a board of commissioners, charged, as the board in this case was, to regulate and fix the charges, so as to be equal and reasonable. Such a board would have at its command all the means of getting at the truth and ascertaining the reasonableness of fares and freights, which a legislative committee has. It might, or it might not, swear witnesses and examine parties. Its duties being of an administrative character, it would have the widest scope for examination and inquiry. All means of knowledge and information would be at its command—just as they would be at the command of the legislature which created it. Such a body, though not a court, is a proper tribunal for the duties imposed upon it.[55]

Justice Bradley also reminded the Court that it previously had approved of the use of commissions in other contexts, and he implicitly chided it for failing to recognize the applicability of its jurisprudence in the tax area:

> In the case of *Davidson v. City of New Orleans*, 96 U.S. 97, we decided that the appointment of a board of assessors for assessing damages was not only due process of law, but the proper method for making assessments to distribute the burden of a public work amongst those who are benefited by it. No one questions the constitutionality or propriety of boards for assessing property for taxation, or for the improvement of streets, sewers and the like, or of

55. *Id.* at 463–64.

commissions to establish county seats, and for doing many other things appertaining to the administrative management of public affairs. Due process of law does not always require a court. It merely requires such tribunals and proceedings as are proper to the subject at hand.[56]

Which opinion is to be preferred in this dispute about the aptness of analogous governmental forms? Judged by Ernest Freund's monumental comparative survey, *Administrative Powers over Persons and Property*,[57] both the majority and the dissenters clearly were correct. Railroad rate regulation was judicial (commissions were sometimes made courts of record) and it was legislative (often accomplished by special act or charter). How then was the Court to decide? Surely if the method of appropriateness implies only a demand for consistency with historic and contemporary practice, the State of Minnesota should be able to choose among the diverse forms that railroad regulation had taken. It was the rejection of that view which made Justice Bradley fear for the continued stability of *Munn v. Illinois.*

Bradley's anxiety was well-founded. The *Minnesota Railroad Case* signaled the beginning of a more stringent review of state regulation for reasonableness. In some cases that review took the straightforward *Lochner* approach to substantive rationality. Other cases focused, as did the *Minnesota Railroad Case*, on the procedure for furthering rational action. In these latter cases it is hardly surprising that the Court viewed judicial procedure as the epitome of rationality when addressing contested issues of fact. Yet this belief had not occasioned the imposition of judicial forms on state tax collection. Why not?

The answer seems to be that something nontraditional was going on in Minnesota and elsewhere—the emergence of new forms of social and economic regulation that responded to the political demands both of agrarian interests and of the new urban industrial working class. These new forms of regulation subjected property to politics in ways that were unsettling to those whose visions of government were molded by the nineteenth century. They therefore gave rise to claims of right that in their

56. *Id.* at 464.
57. 304–46 (1928).

broadest form were claims to the preservation of the traditional legal order. The *Minnesota Railroad Case* majority may not have been true to the methodology of empirical validation of *procedure,* as practiced in *Murray's Lessee,* but it nevertheless was consistent with a more general and more substantive notion of due process of law—that the traditional was to be preferred to the extraordinary or the innovative. Procedural due process thus became for a time the chief tactical weapon in the legal system's arsenal of defenses against rapid social transformation.

Whereas between 1868 and 1889 seventy-one cases reached the Supreme Court under the Fourteenth Amendment's due process clause, between 1890 and 1901 the number grew to 197.[58] Much of this outpouring was attributable to the *Minnesota Railroad Case,* combined, of course, with the temper of the times. As Charles M. Haugh put it in his elegant Frank Irvine Foundation Lecture at Cornell in 1918: "War memories were fading fast, greater societies needed more government than farm townships, increasing wealth tempted taxation, ambitious local improvements demanded it, and heavily indebted transportation lines controlled by distant security holders continued to irritate an increasing population that owed its existence to that which excited its anger."[59] Haugh's angry populations sought regulation of the great (and some of the small) businesses. The businesses fought back in the courts. The *Minnesota Railroad Case* was the first of few judicial victories, but reward enough to energize the fight.

This history is sufficiently familiar that it need not long detain us. The twin possibilities of the *Minnesota Railroad* opinion—that due process required (1) a *trial-type* procedure or (2) a *judicial* determination of basic questions of fact—were played out in numerous cases over the next forty-odd years. In the process, review of state economic regulation gave rise to doctrines that still haunt administrative law,[60] and spilled over into other

58. Corwin, *The Doctrine of Due Process of Law before the Civil War* (pt. 1) 24 HARV. L. REV. 366 (1911).

59. Haugh, *Due Process of Law—Today,* 32 HARV. L. REV. 218, 227 (1918).

60. *See generally* L. JAFFEE, JUDICIAL CONTROL OF ADMINISTRATIVE ACTION 636–53 (1965).

areas of federal administrative action to provide protection
against the actions of immigration officials[61] and even against
an occasional tax collector, as *Londoner v. Denver* attests.

But, by the passage of time and laws, social and economic
regulation became customary, and judicial deference reasserted
itself. Moreover, as substance became familiar and accepted,
Justice Bradley's procedural paradigm regained ascendancy.
Not only is today's Court prepared to view rate making as quasi-
legislative and therefore subject only to the *Bi-Metallic* constitutional process of representative government;[62] it is prepared to
allow regulatory agencies to shift from an adjudicative to a legislative mode, virtually at will,[63] and to free them from virtually
all demands for trial-type proceedings not mandated by a specific statute.[64]

A 1978 decision, *New Motor Vehicle Board v. Orrin W. Fox,
Co.*,[65] brings us almost precisely full circle from the *Minnesota
Railroad Case*. The respondent attacked a California statute that
required the New Motor Vehicle Board's approval of the location or relocation of an automobile dealership whenever there
was objection from a dealer in the same line of cars who was located within a ten-mile radius of the proposed new
distributorship. Pending that approval, after a full hearing, the
proposed location or relocation could not be effected. Orrin W.
Fox, Co. claimed that this procedure, in particular a board order
to desist pending a hearing, was tantamount to the issuance of a
court injunction on the basis of a simple "I object" from a competitor. Because injunctions are extraordinary remedies and are
available in preliminary form only after demonstration of a
prima facie case, a high probability of success, and irreparable
interim injury—none of which was satisfied by a competitor's
mere objection—the procedure was claimed to violate basic and
traditional notions of adjudicatory fairness.

61. *See, e.g.*, Ng Fung Ho v. White, 259 U.S. 276 (1922).
62. *See, e.g.*, United States v. Florida East Coast Ry. Co., 410 U.S. 224 (1973).
63. *See, e.g.*, F.P.C. v. Texaco Inc., 377 U.S. 33 (1964).
64. *See* Vermont Yankee Nuclear Power Corp. v. Natural Resources Defense
Council Inc., 435 U.S. 519 (1978).
65. 439 U.S. 96 (1978).

Fox's case was an attractive one, and for reasons detailed elsewhere,[66] I believe it should have called forth a response in terms of the almost moribund public purpose strain of the due process jurisprudence. For present purposes, however, the interesting feature of the *Fox* opinion is that only Justice Stevens thought that adjudication was even involved. A majority of the Court returned to the idea, first developed in the nineteenth-century tax jurisprudence, that when the administrator has no discretion his action is legislative. Because a competitor's objection triggered an automatic stay under the California scheme, the stay was a product of the legislation. And in the post-*Lochner* world, legislative action in areas of social and economic policy is immune to due process review. As the activist state has moved in our political consciousness from the novel to the traditional, the characterizations and the results in economic regulation cases have simply been reversed.

The elusiveness and manipulability of appropriateness analysis in this form is not, it should be noted, confined to the legislative/judicial debate that swirls around the jurisprudence of economic substantive due process. Whether modern forms of administrative social regulation *are* legislative or judicial in character or, alternatively, whether the function is some hybrid form that should be given a distinct shape by active judicial review seemed to be *the* administrative law issue of the 1970s.[67] But neither the analyses of litigants, courts, and commentators, nor the Supreme Court's ultimate insistence that the rulemaking function is legislative and subject to legislative procedural specification, has done much to allay the anxiety about the pervasive effects of administrative rules and the administrative exercise of political power that they represent. In fact, at least two members of the Court now seem convinced that because the power to make general substantive rules is legislative, it is, when put in the hands of administrators, an improper delegation of the legislature's lawmaking powers and, therefore, unconstitutional.[68]

---

66. Mashaw, *Constitutional Deregulation: Notes Toward a Public, Public Law*, 54 TUL. L. REV. 849 (1980).

67. *See, e.g.,* Diver, *Policymaking Paradigms in Administrative Law*, 95 HARV. L. REV. 393 (1981) and authorities there cited.

68. Indus. Union Dep't v. Am. Petroleum Inst., 448 U.S. 607, 672–88 (1980)

These shifts in the form of the judicial/legislative debate signal not only the continuation of concern about the soundness, if not the legitimacy, of economic and social regulation, but also the unpersuasiveness of a methodology based on abstract categories. Contemporary administrative rulemaking is neither judicial nor legislative; it is something of both. In the absence of a conventional paradigm that effectively captures the behavior of regulatory agencies, at least in the legal imagination, a jurisprudence seeking appropriateness by reference to these abstractions oscillates between the image of a court and the image of legislative action. As Justice Bradley recognized a long time ago, because the "What is it?" question, as a normative standard, merely camouflages a "What should it be?" issue, formal categorization ultimately will reveal a substantive agenda.

The Proliferation of Formal Models

To this point the question of appropriate legal form has been presented as a simple, and apparently sometimes simpleminded, choice between legislative and adjudicative modalities. We might hope, therefore, to avoid the sterility and disingenuous character of that choice by constructing a broader set of models, each capturing the essence of some traditional aspect of the legal culture and available for analogical comparison to apparently novel and potentially objectionable governmental forms. Unfortunately, however, models seem to have a modest resolving power. The addition of new candidates from the legal lexicon of appropriate forms may add complexity without aiding the clarity or persuasiveness of the analysis.

Consider, for example, a group of due process cases that were generated by one of the great political issues of the 1950s, a group that I shall term loosely the "Communist stigma" cases. For our purposes they begin with *Joint Anti-Fascist Refugee Committee v. McGrath*.[69] The petitioning committee in *McGrath* complained of its inclusion on the attorney general's list of fascist, communist, totalitarian, or subversive organizations. Although

---

(Rehnquist, J., concurring); Am. Textile Mfrs. Inst. Inc. v. Donovan, 452 U.S. 490, 543–48 (1981) (Rehnquist, J. and Burger, C.J., dissenting).

   69. 341 U.S. 123 (1951).

listing had no direct legal effect on the organizations, the list was required by executive order to be disseminated to all executive departments and to the Loyalty Review Board. Membership in a listed organization could raise the issue of a federal employee's loyalty and might result in removal or a refusal of employment. Departments might also make other uses of the list, and inclusion was a ground for public disapprobation. These effects made it virtually impossible, so it was alleged, for the committee to carry on its principal purpose—collecting and providing aid to anti-Franco refugees of the Spanish Civil War. The committee claimed that inclusion on the list without notice and opportunity to contest was unconstitutional, as well as unauthorized by the governing statutes and executive orders.

In approaching the case, Justice Frankfurter, in his famous concurrence, gave ringing reaffirmation to the appropriateness model. "[D]ue process," proceed the often-quoted lines, "unlike some legal rules is not a technical conception with a fixed content . . . [It is] compounded of history, reason, the course of past decisions. . . ."[70] In Frankfurter's view, the Court interpreting the due process clause had been "entrusted with [its] unfolding" in an ever-changing social and governmental context. But Frankfurter did more than reaffirm the basic model; he wrote an opinion that illustrated its many facets and demonstrated a subtle understanding of its nuances and ambiguities.

Frankfurter begins with the core notion of judicial trial, the provision of notice and hearing before judgment where an individual may suffer a serious loss. He reinforces the centrality of this conception by exploring judicial precedent to demonstrate that deviations from the judicial or quasi-judicial norm are exceptional. Trial as the heart of accepted legal procedure is further documented by noting that federal statutes and administrative practices are to the same effect. (Happily for Frankfurter, or for his law clerk, the work on statutory and administrative history had been done recently by the attorney general's Committee on Administrative Procedure.) To be sure the general picture that Frankfurter paints must, as his opinion recognizes, be qualified by exceptions for action of a legislative nature and for

70. *Id.* at 162–63.

exigent circumstances. But this pattern of rule and exception suggested to Frankfurter that there was a burden on those who would characterize the case as exceptional.

Turning to a search for exceptional circumstances in the case before him, Justice Frankfurter saw nothing in the charge to the attorney general to make the list, or in the statutes supporting the overall loyalty-security program, which required summary process for listing. Some exceptional protections might have to be afforded confidential informants and so on, but these details could await the event. Frankfurter recognized that the function involved in *McGrath* was rather novel. Listing was neither obviously legislative nor obviously judicial in character. Yet, looking at listing in terms of its operational content, it clearly was an individualized judgment about status or attributes that was likely to have drastic and particular real world effects. This suggested the presumptive applicability of the core notice and hearing ideal, which, in the absence of a persuasive demonstration of the necessity for avoiding it, was the command of due process.

No other justice signed the Frankfurter concurrence, although it is by far the most often cited opinion in *McGrath*. The case splintered the Court. The decision was five to three, but all five of the justices in the majority wrote separate opinions. An opinion by Justice Burton, joined only by Justice Douglas (who also concurred specially), became the plurality opinion. It ruled on the narrowest possible ground.[71] The case had been disposed of below on a motion to dismiss. Thus Burton asserted that the committee's pleadings had to be taken as true. So viewed this was a case in which the attorney general had branded the committee "communist" when the only facts of record, those in the committee's initial pleading, claimed that it was not. A ruling so plainly counter to the accepted facts was arbitrary. Because the executive order by which the attorney general had acted expressed concern to preserve both national security *and* the rights of federal employees, Justice Burton could not believe that it authorized arbitrary findings that might form the basis for later actions against government personnel. The attorney general's action without notice and hearing therefore was illegal because it

71. *Id.* at 124.

violated the executive order. The constitutional due process issue need not be reached.

Justice Black, concurring, agreed that the attorney general had no authority to list the committee; his agreement was, by contrast, based on the broadest of constitutional premises.[72] In his view neither the president nor the Congress *could* authorize the listing because listing effectively punished persons for their beliefs and associations in violation of the First Amendment. Moreover, although prepared by an executive office, the list was, in Black's view, tantamount to a bill of attainder. In support of his proposition that the officer or body actually drawing the bill was not critical to its status as prohibited attainder, Black appended to his opinion[73] MacCauley's account of the great Act of Attainder passed by the first Irish parliament called by James II after his removal to Ireland. In making up the list of proscribed persons, and getting parliamentary assent to each name, it seems to have been enough to say, "I have heard the King say some hard things of that Lord." The king clearly had the controlling influence on the bill, and it was precisely such abuses of power that the attainder clause in the U.S. Constitution had been designed to prevent. That design should not be thwarted, Black believed, just because the list involved in *McGrath* was only a pseudoattainder,[74] prepared by the attorney general pursuant to a joint legislative-executive program to ensure the loyalty of federal employees.

Thus far then, we have our customary two characterizations, judicial and legislative. The only novelty is that both point toward the same result. But the plot thickens. While Justice Black thought it nonproblematic that the listing imposed punishment, the dissenting justices thought it had no legal effect whatever. It was, therefore, not susceptible to any more due process objection than a governmental *press release*.[75] For it was obvious to them that there were no legal effects on the organization as a result of listing. To be sure, there was disadvantage, but to constitute a deprivation of liberty or property the dissenters believed that there would have to be a direct invasion of organizational or

72. *Id.* at 142.
73. *Id.* at 146.
74. *Id.* at 144.
75. *Id.* at 183.

individual rights. Justice Reed's minority opinion could not find, for neither the organization's nor its members' legal positions were changed by the listing. Reed further noted that although the organization might have a tort suit for defamation against a party not privileged, the United States and the attorney general were immune from such interference in the ordinary, internal business of government. Moreover, public employees had no right to any particular standards for qualification or procedures for removal beyond those specified in the civil service regulations. Organizational listing and the use of membership in a listed organization as evidence in a loyalty-security hearing in no way impaired those rights.

The dissenting opinion thus expresses views similar to those of the circuit court in *Bailey v. Richardson*,[76] affirmed per curiam[77] by an equally divided Court on the same day that *McGrath* was handed down. In *Bailey* the suit concerned the procedures for removal of a probationary employee on grounds of probable disloyalty. The challenged regulations provided for notice and hearing but did not permit confrontation or cross-examination of opposing confidential witnesses. In the circuit court the decision for the government proceeded from two traditional bases: (1) Government employment itself was simply a contractual relationship carrying with it such conditions, including summary dismissal for suspected disloyalty, as were customary or were stipulated by statute or regulation. (2) Government action, for example, comments in legislative debates or hearings, often might stigmatize; but to the extent that such action was in pursuit of public purposes, it was not actionable defamation because the government was immune. In short, customary legal rights sounding in either contract or tort were not implicated and the due process clause, therefore, was not applicable.

Bailey and *McGrath* obviously reflected a deep division on the Supreme Court. Equally obviously, abstract characterizations of the process involved simply evoked different images of the relevant tradition within which to gauge the appropriateness of the contested procedures. Part of the Court seems to imagine the substitution of a legislative act or a summary executive determi-

76. 182 F.2d 46 (1950).
77. 341 U.S. 918 (1951).

nation for a judicial finding of guilt. Other members are operating with a vision of government action within the tradition of government contracts and government torts. From this perspective the government's exercise of a reserved power to terminate a contract without holding a hearing is perfectly conventional. Moreover, even if the termination is carried on in a way that involves incidental injury, that hardly can justify a demand for a hearing. The same considerations of governmental necessity that underlie tort immunity support the denial of a preaction hearing.

Throughout the fifties the Supreme Court seems to recognize and embrace the *McGrath–Bailey* doctrinal confusion, while reinforcing the view that the government could attach stigmatizing labels to persons or groups only after procedures approximating a judicial trial. This conceptually awkward posture was maintained via the *McGrath* plurality's device of nonconstitutional interpretation. When confronted with procedural claims relating to loyalty-security actions the Court could invoke both *McGrath* and *Bailey* to demonstrate that a difficult constitutional issue was raised. It then would avoid that issue by construing the statutes or regulations in question as not clearly authorizing the procedures complained of. This practice steadily reinforced the view that the Court's rulings were in fact constitutionally based because the assertion of lack of authority in most cases was rather transparently false.[78]

In *Cafeteria Workers v. McElroy*[79] in 1961, the Court finally abandoned the authority dodge and confronted a case on the constitutional merits. Rachel Brawner's security badge was revoked without notice, hearing, or explanation by the commander of a naval base. Without it she was ineligible to work in the base canteen and could not be employed there by the private firm which operated the base food concessions. The appropriate union, on behalf of Ms. Brawner, sued for notice and hearing.

The Supreme Court held that the procedures used were adequate under the Constitution in an opinion that affirms *both* the independent constitutional relevance of stigma claims and Cir-

---

78. *See* Greene v. McElroy, 360 U.S. 474 (1959); Vitarelli v. Seaton, 359 U.S. 535 (1959); Service v. Dallas, 354 U.S. 363 (1957); Peters v. Hobby, 349 U.S. 331 (1955); Cole v. Young, 351 U.S. 536 (1956).
79. 367 U.S. 886 (1961).

cuit Judge Prettyman's proprietary function analysis in *Bailey v. Richardson*. The Court begins with the usual genuflection to *McGrath*'s flexible approach—or rather to the language of Justice Frankfurter's concurrence. It rejects the notion that access to the naval base, because a mere privilege, could be accorded or withheld free of due process controls. The opinion then makes it determinative of the required due process procedures that the exclusion was in connection with the *proprietary* functions of the government, management of a naval base, over which the government traditionally had exercised unfettered control. Governmental regulatory functions were distinguished.

In the loyalty-security cases a determination of subversiveness or probable disloyalty is, indeed, a many splendored thing. Sometimes it is like a criminal trial or a grand jury investigation; sometimes like a legislative classification or a bill of attainder; sometimes like defamation; sometimes like a mere press release; and sometimes like contract termination. It may even resemble ejection of trespassers from real property. The function itself —the basic process of gathering and manipulating information to come to a decision about individual or group loyalty—is unchanging. It is alternatively characterized in terms of the perceived purposes and the effects of the decision. Depending on the characterization chosen, the stigma suffered by the complaining party will be punishment, injury, or unfortunate side effect. Moreover, not only may differing characterizations yield the same legal conclusions (witness Frankfurter and Black in *McGrath*), the same characterization may yield conflicting legal implications. As *Bailey* and *McGrath* illustrate, the tort analogy may cause one court or justice to see an injury, leading to a due process demand for decisional care, where another will see an immunity that negates the plaintiff's claim of an analogous common law right and renders due process talk superfluous.

THE IMPLICATIONS OF METHODOLOGICAL DRIFT

THE DANGERS OF ABSTRACTION

One way to think about the empirically oriented appropriateness paradigm with which we began is as a means for embedding procedural due process analysis in the substantive reality of administration. The search is for how a particular governmental function has been or is being carried out. The discovery that an appropriateness analysis, operating in an abstract analogical mode ("Is it like a court or a legislature?"), seems to be manipulable by reference to the underlying substantive issues is then, in one sense, only the perception of methodological drift from a concrete and transparent concern with substance-procedure linkages to an abstract and veiled concern with the same issues. Yet it is surely more than that. For it is a shift from a concern with the lessons that custom and practice have to teach about the fit between procedure and substance to a concern with the way procedural devices support or retard the development or implementation of substantive rights. As such, the methodology becomes suspect.

It is suspect first because it may misdirect the Court's substantive analysis. Reconsider *McGrath* and *Bailey* from a substantive perspective. From this viewpoint *McGrath* is concerned, not with due process ideas, but with the First Amendment's guarantees of freedom of speech and association. Associational labeling or stigmatizing thus impels the Court toward procedural intervention to protect these substantive constitutional interests. On the other hand, *Bailey v. Richardson,* to the extent that it involves substantive constitutional questions, provokes separation of powers concerns. As Judge Prettyman points out, the *Meyers*[80] case makes clear that the executive branch need not retain, even if so directed by Congress, officers and employees in whom it has no confidence. Moreover, if viewed as an attempt to control government processes in order to deter incidental injuries, *Bailey* implicates the government's quasi-constitutional immunity from suit. In substantive terms, then, *McGrath* is a First Amendment case, while *Bailey* is a public employment or public civil liability case. Government is on a short leash in the first arena, but has wide latitude when dealing with the latter categories.

This explanation fails to explain why *McGrath* is not also a civil liability case. More important, the very need for such an explanation of supposedly procedural due process cases in First Amendment, or government employment, or some other sub-

80. Meyers v. United States, 272 U.S. 52 (1926).

stantive terms, raises fundamental issues concerning the Court's post–New Deal attempt to sharply differentiate substantive and procedural due process. If the attorney general's listing inhibits free speech or association, should the Court not, as Justice Black did, address that issue? What is the relationship of improved listing procedures to First Amendment protections? Surely it cannot be to insure that only the *correct* groups have their First Amendment rights impaired. And if these rights are *not* impaired by listings, how could they be impaired by erroneous or unfair listings? Making sense out of administrative due process cases by attention to the substantive rights that are implicated may indicate that the Court is making hash out of both procedural due process analysis and the substantive constitutional jurisprudence. Is the Court, to put the question uncharitably, operating in some netherworld of otherwise nonenforceable quasi-rights that are being judicially implemented by apparently unrelated procedural remedies?

Conversely, why should the existence of substantial governmental power to discharge an employee influence the process by which a further action, deprivation of reputation, is accomplished? The government did not discharge Mrs. Bailey for no apparent reason—an action it clearly had the power to take— it said that she was a security risk. In short, if other areas of constitutional law explain these cases, this type of analysis may be detrimental in four dimensions. By confusing the focus of constitutional claims it risks under- and over-protection of both substantive and procedural rights.

A substantive orientation also tends to delegitimate judicial review by inviting straightforward explanation of results in terms of political preferences or other poorly hidden agendas. Tracing the stigma cases beyond the concern of the 1950s with internal subversion is instructive. Consider the following two cases.

The United States Commission on Civil Rights has since 1957 been charged with collecting information about "legal developments constituting a denial of equal protection of the laws" and reporting to the president and the Congress on its findings and recommendations. Although at its hearings the commission may inquire into the specific activities of named individuals, thereby exposing them to possible public opprobrium and retaliation, the Supreme Court held in *Hannah v. Larche*[81] that the commission must not identify the persons who have filed charges of racial discrimination with it nor need it allow cross-examination of adverse witnesses. In passing on the due process question the Court, speaking through Chief Justice Warren, said:

> Whether the Constitution requires that a particular right obtain in a specific proceeding depends upon a complexity of factors. The nature of the alleged right involved, the nature of the proceeding, and the possible burden on that proceeding, are all considerations which must be taken into account. An analysis of these factors demonstrates why it is that the particular rights claimed by the respondents need not be conferred upon those appearing before purely investigative agencies, of which the Commission on Civil Rights is one.
>
> It is probably sufficient merely to indicate that the rights claimed by respondents are normally associated only with adjudicatory proceedings, and that since the Commission does not adjudicate, it need not be bound by adjudicatory procedures. Yet, the respondents contend, and the court below implied, that such procedures are required since the Commission's proceedings might irreparably harm those being investigated by subjecting them to public opprobrium and scorn, and the distinct likelihood of losing their jobs, and the possibility of criminal prosecutions. That any of these consequences will result is purely conjectural. There is nothing on the record to indicate that such will be the case or that past Commission hearings have had any harmful effects upon witnesses appearing before the Commission. However, even if such collateral consequences were to flow from the Commission's investigations, they would not be the result of any affirmative determinations made by the Commission, and they would not affect the legitimacy of the Commission's investigative function.
>
> On the other hand, the investigative process could be completely disrupted if investigative hearings were transformed into trial-like proceedings, and if persons who might be indirectly affected by an investigation were given an absolute right to cross-examine every witness called to testify. Fact-finding agencies without any power to adjudicate would be diverted from their legitimate duties and would be plagued by the injection of collateral issues that would

81. 363 U.S. 420 (1960).

make the investigation interminable. Even a person not called as a witness could demand the right to appear at the hearing, cross-examine any witness whose testimony or sworn affidavit defamed or incriminated him. and call an unlimited number of witnesses of his own selection. This type of proceeding would make a shambles of the investigation and stifle the agency in its gathering of facts.[82]

A decade later, in *Jenkins v. McKeithen*,[83] the Court was called upon to review the processes of a state commission whose charter was drafted with a careful eye on *Hannah v. Larche*. The commission was the Labor–Management Commission of In-quiry, set up by the Louisiana legislature to hold hearings on alleged labor racketeering in the construction industry. Commission action after such hearings was limited to public findings of whether there was reasonable cause to believe that violations of existing state or federal criminal laws had been committed. The Supreme Court summarized the commission's hearing procedures:

> [T]he Commission has the power to compel the attendance of wit-nesses. A witness is given notice of the general subject matter of the investigation before being asked to appear and testify. A witness has the right to the presence and advice of counsel, "subject to such rea-sonable limitations as the commission may impose in order to pre-vent obstruction of or interference with the orderly conduct of the hearing." Counsel may question his client as to any relevant matters, but the right of a witness or his counsel to examine other witnesses is limited:
>
>> In no event shall counsel for any witness have any right to exam-ine or cross-examine any other witness but he may submit to the commission proposed questions to be asked of any other witness appearing before the commission, and the commission shall ask the witness such of the questions as it deems to be appropriate to its inquiry.
>
> With one limited exception to be discussed below, neither a witness or any other private party has the right to call anyone to testify be-fore the Commission.
>
> Although the Commission must base its findings and reports only on evidence and testimony given at public hearings, the Act

82. *Id.* at 442–44.
83. 395 U.S. 411 (1969).

does provide for executive session when it appears that the testimony to be given "may tend to degrade, defame or incriminate any person." In executive session the Commission must allow the person who might be degraded, defamed, or incriminated an opportunity to appear and be heard, and to call a reasonable number of witnesses on his behalf. However, the Commission may decide that the evidence or testimony shall be heard in a public hearing, regardless of its effect on any particular person. In that case, the person affected has the right to appear as a "voluntary witness" and may submit "pertinent" statements of others. He may submit a list of additional witnesses, but subpoenas will be issued only in the discretion of the Commission.[81]

Jenkins claimed that these procedures were constitutionally defective because of their limitations on the rights to confront and cross-examine adverse witnesses and to present evidence by live testimony. The state defended the procedures as sufficient under *Hannah v. Larche* for a commission whose job was merely to find facts. The Supreme Court agreed with the plaintiff, stating in part:

> We reaffirm the decision to *Hannah*. In our view, however, the Commission in the present case differs in a substantial respect from the Civil Rights Commission and the other examples cited by the court in *Hannah*. It is true, as the Supreme Court of Louisiana has held . . . that the Commission does not adjudicate in the sense that a court does, nor does the Commission conduct, strictly speaking, a criminal proceeding. Nevertheless, the Act, when analyzed in light of the allegations of the complaint, makes it clear that the Commission exercises a function very much akin to making an official adjudication of criminal culpability. . . .
>
> The Commission is limited to criminal law violations; the Act explicitly provides that the Commission shall have no jurisdiction over civil matters in the labor-management relations field. Indeed, the Commission is even limited to certain types of criminal activities. As noted above, nothing in the Act indicates that the Commission's findings are to be used for legislative purposes. Rather, everything in the Act points to the fact that it is concerned only with exposing violations of criminal laws by specific individuals. In short, the Commission very clearly exercises an accusatory function; it is empowered to be used and allegedly is used to find named individuals

84. *Id.* at 417–18.

guilty of violating the criminal laws of Louisiana and the United States and to brand them as criminals in public.[85]

These disparate results are explicable superficially in analogical appropriateness terms. *Hannah* involved legislative investigation; *Jenkins* a process that was similar to a criminal trial, but without its safeguards. Yet this distinction hardly is satisfactory. Both bodies made findings of fact that stigmatized. In both cases these findings, if made by a civil or criminal court, would have involved serious legal consequences. Almost inexorably one is led to the conclusion that the Court's decisions make sense only as part of a substantive judicial program to promote civil rights and to protect labor organizations from harassment. Indeed, the legal literature is replete with excellent articles describing the real substantive agenda that is being played out in one or another arena of due process adjudication.[86]

THE INDETERMINACIES OF FORMALISM

One would expect appropriateness analysis to segment procedural due process cases in terms of their subject matter. Given natural lawyerly tendencies to cite cases having similar facts, the search for appropriateness rapidly becomes a search for case precedent closely related to the case at hand. Wide-ranging review of historical practices, contemporary statutes, and functional requirements thus gives way to the citation of cases. Tax cases cite tax cases;[87] immigration cases cite immigration cases;[88] rate cases cite rate cases;[89] nuisance regulation cases cite nuisance regulation cases;[90] and so on. Cross-fertilization of the jurisprudence occurs primarily when some new governmental function emerges for review (witness Justice Frankfurter's

85. *Id.* at 427–28.
86. *See, e.g.,* Burt, *The Constitution of the Family,* 1979 SUP. CT. REV. 329; Wilkinson, *Goss v. Lopez: The Supreme Court as School Superintendent,* 1975 SUP. CT. REV. 25.
87. *See, e.g.,* Bi-Metallic Inv. Co. v. State Bd. of Equalization, 239 U.S. 441 (1915).
88. *See, e.g.,* United States v. Ju Toy, 198 U.S. 253 (1905).
89. *See, e.g.,* The New England Divs. Case, 261 U.S. 184 (1923).
90. *See, e.g.,* Lawton v. Steele, 152 U.S. 133 (1894); N. Am. Storage Co. v. Chicago, 211 U.S. 306 (1908).

opinion in *McGrath*), or in dissenting opinions objecting to the majority's too facile characterization of the case (witness the *Minnesota Railroad Case*). Indeed, in heavily litigated areas, like taxation, one finds subcompartmentalization into customs cases[91] or special assessment cases[92] that cite no authority outside their particular domains. Moreover, the appropriateness model's segmentation of the jurisprudence by substantive field remains highly influential. Several modern casebooks on administrative law, for example, present due process cases as a series of discrete arenas of procedural conflict, oriented to contemporary concern with substantive issues such as welfare rights, public employment, public education, or prison administration.[93]

Notwithstanding the important efficiency properties of impounding practice into precedent, which then can be applied without reexamination of run-of-the-mine cases, the subject matter compartmentalization and predictable application that precedent entails should not be overvalued. In all the jurisprudentially important cases the technique unravels in much the same way that we witnessed with respect to abstract functional characterization. The subject matter of a case is not self-defining. To ask what a case is like in terms of the prior jurisprudence may evoke a variety of responses leading to different lines of authority and different outcomes. Subject matter compartmentalization is necessarily fragile in a legal culture that strives for generality and coherence.

For example, notice how easily we fell into talk about the stigma cases. But from the perspective of subject matter orientation those cases are not necessarily stigma cases. They can be characterized as dealing with widely disparate governmental functions: *McGrath* involves an executive department information function; *Bailey v. Richardson* is a public employment case; *Cafeteria Workers* involves governmental proprietary action; *Hannah* implicates civil rights investigations; and *Jenkins* is a labor case. How could we have thought that they were related? Well,

---

91. *See, e.g.*, Sampson v. Peaslee, 61 (20 How.) 571 (1857); Passavant v. United States, 148 U.S. 214 (1893).
92. *See, e.g.*, Paulsen v. Portland, 149 U.S. 30 (1893); Hancock v. City of Muskogee, 250 U.S. 454 (1919).
93. *See, e.g.*, S. BREYER & R. STEWART, ADMINISTRATIVE LAW AND REGULATORY POLICY (1979); G. ROBINSON, E. GELLHORN, & H. BRUFF, THE ADMINISTRATIVE PROCESS (2d ed. 1980).

because they did involve governmentally imposed reputational harms. Moreover, the later cases cited the earlier cases as *if* they were related. Two later decisions illustrate how right and how wrong we were.

The first is *Wisconsin v. Constantineau*.[94] There the complainant had been determined by state beverage control officials to be a habitual drunkard. Pursuant to state law her name was posted in all state liquor stores and while posted she was denied the right to purchase alcoholic beverages. In the course of deciding that the posted person was entitled to notice and hearing prior to posting, the Supreme Court said, "The only issue present here is whether the label or characterization given a person by posting . . . is . . . such a stigma or badge of disgrace that procedural due process requires notice and an opportunity to be heard." In deciding that this state scheme did impose such a stigma, the Court cited many of the cases we have previously discussed as stigma cases. So far, so good.

But then came *Paul v. Davis*.[95] There the complaining party had been included in a list of active shoplifters circulated to local businesses by the Louisville, Kentucky, police department. In fact, the plaintiff had been arrested for shoplifting only once, and that charge had been dropped. He sued for damages claiming that this obviously harmful action was taken without any notice, hearing, or other process to ascertain the accuracy of the information upon which the action was based. On the authority of *Constantineau, inter alia*, the lower courts granted relief. But the Supreme Court reversed. In the majority's view all of the prior stigma cases had been predicated not on a notion of a constitutional right to avoid stigma without due process, but, instead, on a right to be free from incidental stigma associated with the invasion of some other liberty or property interest without due process. *Constantineau* thus became a case involving invasion of liberty of contract (freedom to purchase liquor). Similarly, intervening school suspension[96] and public college employment[97] cases employing stigma language were interpreted as

94. 400 U.S. 433 (1971).
95. 424 U.S. 693 (1976).
96. Goss v. Lopez, 419 U.S. 565 (1975).
97. Bd. of Regents v. Roth, 408 U.S. 564 (1972).

cases involving rights to public schooling or to maintenance of academic tenure.

The *Paul v. Davis* analysis of the precedents hardly makes compelling sense of *McGrath* or *Jenkins*, as the dissenters pointed out at length.[98] But these cases may have turned on yet other axes; it is as yet unclear what sort of case *Paul v. Davis* was. Perhaps it will turn out to be a public safety case.[99] Perhaps its import lies primarily in the protection from federal constitutionalization that *Paul v. Davis* affords state private law.[100] Closely allied to this federalism dimension is an interpretation that would connect *Paul* to other recent cases that seek to restrict the growth of amorphous and remedially awkward federal rights.[101]

These speculations suggest that, as usual, a case is not precedent until it is used. And in that use a court does not so much recreate the past as mold the present and suggest the future. In this gradual unfolding due process cases may have many lives. They certainly cannot be expected to remain locked in intellectual categories bounded by the subject matter of the underlying administrative function or of the type of harm involved. When the search for appropriateness is a search for precedent, it is a search along multiple dimensions of the potentially applicable jurisprudence. Administrative function, the nature of the personal interest implicated, structural constitutional features relating to federal jurisdiction and to federal creation of a remedial common law, separation of powers concerns, may all play a part as analysis responds to the many lines of force in the precedents that might pull the decision into their orbit. Here appropriate-

98. 424 U.S. at 724–32.

99. *See, e.g.*, Fed. Trade Comm'n v. Cinderella Career & Finishing Schools, Inc., 404 F.2d 1308 (D.C. Cir. 1968).

100. *See, e.g.*, Bishop v. Wood, 426 U.S. 341 (1976); Cort v. Ash, 422 U.S. 66 (1975).

101. *Cf.* Pennhurst State School & Hospital v. Halderman, 451 U.S. 1 (1981) (holding that the Developmentally Disabled Assistance and Bill of Rights Act did not create a federal substantive right to "appropriate treatment" in the "least restrictive" environment for the mentally retarded); Carey v. Piphus, 435 U.S. 247 (1978) (holding that public school students bringing actions under 42 U.S.L.C. § 1983 against school officials, for the students' suspension without procedural due process, were entitled to recover only nominal damages—absent proof of actual injury).

ness analysis takes on its most general form. It asks no less than how a decision for or against certain process rights fits within the whole fabric of our constitutional jurisprudence.

So put, the appropriateness issue is difficult, interesting, perhaps inevitable, but it is far from our original impression of the function of precedent. This is no simple impounding of custom into doctrine, thereby facilitating retrieval and application. Indeed, far from the good signaling qualities that our naive view of precedent implied, precedents now impinge on cases from every direction. Each suggests some important dimension of the constitutional tradition that makes a claim to be preserved in the pool of ideas and values from which further doctrine will be selected. Interpretive use of precedent thus demands that subtle form of judicial decision making Alex Bickel called "anticipating the future"[102]—a multidimensional constitutional future at that. Peering into a jurisprudential crystal ball seems very far removed from the primarily backward-looking search for tradition with which we began.

APPROPRIATENESS—A PRELIMINARY APPRAISAL

Poking holes in the logic of a due process jurisprudence that judges the appropriateness of governmental forms "all things considered" is indeed child's play. Criteria seem to be given different weights in different contexts, and the formal lines of precedent through which the analysis is given structure are continuously giving off ambiguous, if not frankly contradictory, signals. Yet we should not get carried away with this portrait of intellectual chaos. For logic is not the promise of the method of appropriateness. The promise instead is the maintenance of a moderately workable system whose internal linkages may be too complex and subtle for complete understanding, much less description. After all, we have survived a due process jurisprudence that for most of its history is best described by Justice Frankfurter's *McGrath* concurrence as "compounded of reason, history, the course of past decisions," or perhaps simply as, in

102. A. BICKEL, *supra* n. 17.

Davidson v. New Orleans, "the gradual process of inclusion and exclusion."

SOME STRENGTHS

The valuable survival characteristics of the appropriateness methodology are apparent in several ways. Although "all things considered" suggests an immodest intellectual task for the judiciary, the decisions themselves rarely upset the techniques or structures established by the legislative and executive branches or by state governments. Immodest reach combined with modest grasp seems built into the methodology. If the search is for concrete analogy in order to analyze contested structures or processes, one would have to imagine legislative or administrative creativity on a grand scale to believe that historical or contemporary analogues will not be available for most of the situations that confront the Court.

To be sure the Court may become fixated on a particular aspect of legal tradition. In the familiar *Lochner* fashion, for example, it may for a time exalt contract over legislation as the appropriate form for ordering a particular set of legal relations. Yet we also must recognize that the idea of constitutional protections is to restrain government. The period of activist judicial intervention in state economic regulation was a period in which the scale of legislative experimentation ultimately transformed the dominant vision of how social relations were structured by law. Judicial resistance to this transformation supported precisely the values of regularity, security, and incremental change that the appropriateness methodology purports to respect.

I have suggested that compartmentalization of precedent is fragile, and it is. Yet separate lines of authority are discernible. Within the due process jurisprudence it is certainly meaningful to talk about tax cases, immigration cases, loyalty-security cases, and so on. One steeped in a particular jurisprudential subject matter will have little doubt about the core of due process requirements in that area. Moreover, the generally modest demands of the case law produce wide margins for contextual variation. Processes for licensing attorneys do not have to be the same in every state, nor need the licensing of liquor dealers conform to the model employed by lawyers. Balkanization of precedent and resort to highly contextualized practice thus can promote both certainty of expectations and opportunities for change.

The search for appropriateness also permits an easy association of substantive and procedural concerns. Whether something is appropriate necessitates attention to the question, "To or for what?" What is appropriate to tax collection may not be appropriate to occupational licensing. The form of governmental power thus is not separated from its extent. The mediation of the conflict between collective power and individual right can go on in somewhat different ways in different subject matter arenas.

A SUBSTANTIAL DOUBT

We need not repeat our previous misgivings about the tendencies of the appropriateness methodology to degenerate into a battle of abstract forms or of competing lines of precedent. Those concerns remain, for they are the flip side of flexibility. Yet there is every reason to believe that the appropriateness methodology has reasonably good regulative properties. The run-of-the-mill case should be fairly predictable.

The fundamental problem with the appropriateness methodology—at least as I have portrayed it—is that it fails us when the going gets tough. When it is clear that choices must be made among competing precedents and models, the appropriateness methodology provides no means for structuring the constitutional conversation. Thus, to take *Goldberg v. Kelly* as an example, the majority apparently views the government as seeking to terminate a property interest and concludes that due process consistently has demanded prior hearings for such actions, except in special circumstances. Transposed to the welfare context, this implies that payments must continue on a disputed claim until a hearing can be provided.

Justice Black, dissenting, views the situation as analogous to nonperformance of an executory contract. In such disputes he says: "I know of no situation in our legal system in which the person alleged to owe money to another is required by law to

continue making payments to a judgment-proof claimant without the benefit of any security or bond to insure that these payments can be recovered if he wins his legal argument."[103]

Both opinions clearly identify a way that the situation might
be characterized. Which is correct? Appropriateness analysis
cannot tell us. In order not to remain mute the justices must
abandon it for something else. Thus, in *Goldberg* the majority's
basic argument is simply that it is unfair to put the risk of administrative error on recipients who may not know where they will
get their next meal. Justice Black, in a prescient description of
the dynamics of post-*Goldberg* welfare administration, argues
that however humane the majority's procedural innovations, society will view the costs as excessive and will find a way to tax the
recipient class for them. What the *Goldberg* opinions fail to tell us
is why *that* unfairness is unconstitutional or why public perceptions of costs are relevant to constitutional adjudication.

The explanatory failures of the appropriateness methodology are not limited to cases where legal characterizations of a situation conflict. Recall the discussion of *O'Bannon v. Town Court
Nursing Home* in chapter 1. The underprotectionist critic is unlikely to deny that the residents are claiming something analogous to intervention of right in a civil proceeding. Indeed, the
critic probably would prefer that characterization to one that described the residents as attacking the rationality of the legislative-regulatory scheme or as seeking a quasi-legislative forum in
which to change the state's certification policy. Instead of attacking the characterization, the underprotectionist—dissatisfied with the results that follow it—wants to know why the aptness of the analogy determines the outcome. The most that the
Court could respond from within the appropriateness methodology is something like: "Reasoning by analogy seems to have
good survival characteristics." Or: "That's legal method." Or,
more trenchantly: "Next case."

Whatever one thinks of the underprotectionist thesis, from a
contemporary perspective this silence is suspicious. The idea of
legality in modern, bureaucratic society is precisely that law em-

103. 397 U.S. at 277–78 (Black, J., dissenting).

bodies general, rational, and transparent rules.[104] Law in this conception derives legitimacy from its instrumental rationality. It seeks the realization of certain values and, if rational and legitimate, will therefore take on a consistent, coherent, and explicable form. Ours is a legal world in which particularism and tradition seem to have lost their legitimating force. They instead have become puzzles to be solved, masks for subterranean purposes, or anachronistic pockets of traditional authority that must be stripped away to construct a fully legitimate legal order. To bring conviction to the modern mind, Burkean obscurantism—which makes the mere existence of a practice or institution an argument for its legitimacy—must be replaced by some neo-Weberian explanation of the way particular decisional structures realize basic political ideals. For the particularistic, almost anthropological,[105] investigation of practice, there must be substituted a more general and transparently rational inquiry into means and ends.

This is precisely the sort of inquiry into basic values and their pursuit that the appropriateness methodology cannot undertake. The answers to that method's "What is it?" or "What is it like?" questions may be thought to proceed from some invisible intuition that answers the question "What should it be?" But that latter question cannot be addressed directly. There are no sources within the methodology from which it *could* be answered. Therefore, it is not surprising that under pressure to come to terms with the administrative state and its instrumental rationality paradigm, the Supreme Court in *Goldberg* switched to a more modern conception of due process analysis. As the next chapter details, modernity is no bargain.

---

104. *See generally* M. WEBER, THE THEORY OF SOCIAL AND ECONOMIC ORGANIZATION 324–37 (A. Henderson & T. Parsons trans. 1947).
105. *See generally* C. GEERTZ, THE INTERPRETATION OF CULTURES 3–30 (1973).

3 / *The Model of Competence*

The obscurity, particularity, and complexity of the appropriateness model apparently was supplanted in the 1970s by a new form of due process analysis—one that promised transparency, generality, and simplicity. This new approach seemed functionally oriented and quasi-scientific in its methodology; it made the guarantee of due process a guarantee of accurate and cost-effective decision making. As the leading case, *Mathews v. Eldridge*, put the constitutional test:

> [T]he identification of the specific dictates of due process generally requires consideration of three distinct factors: First, the private interest that will be affected by the official action; second, the risk of erroneous deprivation of such interest through the procedures used, and the probable value, if any, of additional or substitute procedural safeguards; and finally, the Government's interest, including the function involved and the fiscal and administrative burdens that the additional or substitute procedural requirement would entail.[1]

Here at last, it would seem, is a formulation of administrative due process criteria suitable for the modern administrative state. Instrumental rationality is recognized as the goal of administrative decision making. Procedure is to be evaluated in terms of its competence, in particular, its propensity to prevent error. The necessary trade-offs between individual protection from

1. 424 U.S. 319, 334–35 (1976).

102

erroneous deprivations and the accomplishment of collective ends through governmental action are to be considered explicitly. Due process adjudication henceforth should proceed not as a battle of obscure and competing precedents, analogies, and abstract legal characterizations, but by attention to the costs and benefits of organizing administrative decision making in one form or another.

A BRIEF HISTORY OF THE MODEL OF COMPETENCE

DOCTRINAL PRECURSORS

Various aspects of the model of competence are present in the appropriateness jurisprudence that chapter 2 depicts. The idea of procedural costs or governmental necessities was set out as early as *Murray's Lessee*,[2] and we have found the Court often hotly disputing the nature of the plaintiff's interest.[3] Yet the line of cases culminating in the *Eldridge* formulation seems to begin about 1960 with the statement in *Hannah v. Larche* that "the nature of the alleged right involved, the nature of the proceeding, and the possible burden of that proceeding, are all considerations that must be taken into account."[4] Although this three-factor test, involving an explicit balancing of private and governmental interests, played only a modest supporting role in the *Hannah* opinion, the notion of balancing private and public interests was given greater prominence one year later in *Cafeteria and Restaurant Workers' Union v. McElroy*.[5]

Functional redefinition of the "nature-of-the-proceeding" consideration, in terms of the contribution of the procedures requested, to *accuracy* did not appear, however, until *Goldberg v. Kelly*.[6] The quest for accuracy emerged as an element of the specification of the government's interest in procedural expedition and, in *Goldberg*, served to subordinate that interest where welfare pretermination hearings were concerned.

2. See discussion *supra*, chapter 2 at 64.
3. See discussion *supra*, chapter 2 at 81–95.
4. 363 U.S. 420, 442 (1960).
5. 367 U.S. 886, 895 (1961).
6. 397 U.S. 254 (1970).

Public assistance . . . is not mere charity, but a means to "promote the general Welfare, and secure the Blessings of liberty to ourselves and our Posterity." The same governmental interests that counsel the provision of welfare, counsel as well its uninterrupted provision to those eligible to receive it; pre-termination evidentiary hearings are indispensable to that end.[7]

This demand for accuracy played a similar role in several due process cases decided between *Goldberg* and *Eldridge*; that is, accurate decision making was equated with the state's interest (and hearings with accuracy), tipping the balance forcefully in favor of the private party's procedural demands.[8] It was not, however, until *Eldridge*, in 1976, that accuracy was given a fully independent status in constitutional doctrine. For in *Eldridge* it became clear that the public interest was not an interest in getting every decision right, but rather an interest in a generally reliable process of decision. The *Eldridge* opinion thus indicated both a revised due process criterion and, considering accuracy's pro-plaintiff history, a retrenchment on the apparent procedural promises of *Goldberg*. Yet this short doctrinal pedigree belies the much longer intellectual history of the model of competence.

On Embracing Bentham

The critical literature on the recent work of the Supreme Court attacks the Court's use of what we are calling "the model of competence" many fronts. The Court's instrumentalism is criticized by those who suggest that processes may have inherent values.[9] Its use of positive law to determine the nature of a plaintiff's interest is decried because that approach ignores nonpositivist associational values that legal processes might further.[10] The Court's apparent utilitarianism is criticized as substituting interest balancing for a constitutional theory of individ-

7. 397 U.S. at 265.

8. *See, e.g.*, Stanley v. Illinois, 405 U.S. 645 (1972); Morrisey v. Brewer, 408 U.S. 471 (1972).

9. *See, e.g.*, Saphire, *Specifying Due Process Values: Toward a More Responsive Approach to Procedural Protection*, 127 U. Pa. L. Rev. 111 (1978).

10. *E.g.*, Michelman, *Formal and Associational Aims in Procedural Due Process*, in Due Process, Nomos XVIII, at 126 (J. Pennock & J. Chapman eds. 1977).

ual rights.[11] At this point I do not want to discuss the merits of these criticisms. I only want to note that the critics—whatever their disagreements about whether the real culprit is instrumentalism, positivism, or utilitarianism—have not unfairly characterized the jurisprudence. Moreover, they have properly (although not purposefully) described the procedural views of Jeremy Bentham. The model currently under consideration is instrumentalist, positivist, and utilitarian; and, as Gerald Postema has reminded us,[12] it was set out some years before *Murray's Lessee v. Hoboken Land and Development Co.*, as well as *Hannah v. Larche, Goldberg v. Kelly,* and *Mathews v. Eldridge.*

Indeed, Bentham put the instrumentalist point of the model with a rhetorical force that has shaped our general legal language. He called procedure "adjective law" because, just as adjectives have no meaning without a noun to modify, procedure has no value apart from substantive law. Well-chosen adjectives carry accurate information about nouns; well-chosen procedures effectively implement the policies of substantive law. When the Supreme Court asks what the contribution of a procedure is to accurate application of a statute, it implicitly agrees with this particular version of procedural instrumentalism.

I say "this particular version" advisedly. After all, one could conceive of process as instrumental to the development (rather than the implementation) of substantive law, or to the creation of a sense of community, or to individual self-respect, or to any number of other goals. The choice of the end served—accurate implementation of the substantive law—therefore gives the instrumentalist procedural theory we are considering its positivist cast. As an adjective with no reference to a noun can be greeted only with puzzlement, so a claim to legal procedure divorced from a recognized claim of substantive entitlement must be treated as legally (or for Bentham, philosophically) meaningless.

To be sure, Bentham's conception of law was positivist in a rather extreme form; he had a decided preference for statutes

11. Note, *Specifying the Procedure Required by Due Process: Towards Limits on the Use of Interest Balancing*, 88 HARV. L. REV. 1510 (1975).

12. Postema, *The Principle of Utility and the Law of Procedure: Bentham's Theory of Adjudication*, 11 GA. L. REV. 1393 (1977).

and rules as compared with court precedents and general principles. But the Supreme Court's contemporary practice is not markedly dissimilar.[13] Although common law rights are not ignored, the Court looks for substantive claims primarily in statutory form. It demands to know how due process claimants' interests conform to preexisting characterizations of legal entitlement; it is loathe to create new substantive interests by judicial fiat in cases that are, ostensibly, procedurally oriented. The Court is sometimes uneasy about this stance, but its concerns may be with the ambiguities of positivism, not with the basic theory.[14]

This instrumentalist-positivist perspective, however, provides only a frame of reference for due process analysis, a way of knowing what procedure talk is about and when it is constitutionally relevant for the Court to assess the adequacy of processes. A normative model requires more: a theory of the good is also necessary. For Bentham that theory was obvious. Procedures are valuable to the extent that they increase social welfare. Thus one can easily imagine processes that are excellent vehicles for accurately applying positive law, but that are counterproductive from the perspective of social welfare because they require that we give up other things having higher social value. We surely are not prepared to devote the whole of the national budget to the assurance of the accuracy of all social welfare decisions. The appropriate implementation of positive law is important, but it does not exhaust our demand for a good life.

The Supreme Court's utilitarianism is less obvious, but arguable. The Court talks about balancing the interest of the party claiming a process right to an accurate determination of a substantive claim against the public interest in low-cost or expeditious procedures. Putting the matter this way seems to distinguish qualitatively between public and private interests, rather than to weigh them on the same social welfare scale. This may reflect only some loose language in the *Eldridge* formulation. As the doctrinal roots of the *Eldridge* formula attest, the private party's interest in accuracy is not viewed as being held by him alone.

13. *See generally* Monagham, *Of "Liberty" and "Property,"* 62 Cornell L. Rev. 405 (1977).
14. See discussion *infra* at pp. 145–51.

The public also has an interest in accurate implementation and assigns a *social* value to it. The question is how much society is prepared to spend for the accurate decision of any particular sort of claim.[15]

The *Mathews v. Eldridge* statement of the relevant factors is evidence that a Benthamite procedural model is imbedded in the Supreme Court's contemporary model of competence. The post-*Eldridge* doctrine is structured largely in terms of questions such as: What is at stake? How does the procedure requested further the implementation of the substantive norm that underlies the claimed entitlement? What are the relative magnitudes of the social costs and benefits that flow from granting or denying access to the claimed procedure? Yet a survey of post-*Eldrige* cases hardly suggests a compulsive commitment to the methodology of the model of competence. *Eldridge* almost always is cited, and in a few cases the three-factor test is applied in a straightforward (albeit problematic) fashion.[16] Some cases, nevertheless, simply ignore *Eldridge* and its purportedly controlling test.[17] One even finds the Court, when deciding two licensing due process cases on the same day, applying the competence

15. It is worth noting that the cost-minimization approach just presented is not an approach based upon notions of economic efficiency and does not implicitly assert that the maximization of aggregate economic wealth is a constitutional value—or a value at all. *See* Dworkin, *Is Wealth a Value?*, 9 J. Legal Stud. 191 (1980). *See generally Symposium on Efficiency As a Legal Concern*, 8 Hofstra L. Rev. 485 (1980). An economic efficiency analysis cannot, in fact, be made applicable to a procedural analysis such as the *Goldberg-Eldridge* approach, which views process accuracy as instrumental to programmatic goals that are distributive rather than efficiency oriented. Or, to put the point differently, an efficiency analysis would have to abandon any close association with markets as sources of information about values and seek to assign monetary values to distributional purposes. One might then question whether the economic analysis was distinguishable from the utilitarian analysis in either its basic moral assertions or its analytic technique.

Nevertheless, analysis of procedure in economic efficiency terms may be superior to a social welfare approach with respect to that arguably large class of substantive legal norms that rather clearly serve efficiency ends. And it is undeniably the case that much of the technical apparatus for talking about social welfare calculations is borrowed from economic analysis. *See generally* Posner, *An Economic Approach to Legal Procedure and Judicial Administration*, 2 J. Legal Stud. 399 (1973).

16. *See, e.g.*, Dixon v. Love, 431 U.S. 105 (1977); Macky v. Montrym, 443 U.S. 1 (1979).

17. *See, e.g.*, Board v. Horowitz, 435 U.S. 78 (1978).

model in one,[18] while resolving the other wholly in terms of analogy to three pre-*Eldridge* decisions.[19]

The Court's methodological commitment to the model is not just erratic, it also is limited. Often the Court looks at only one of the three factors.[20] Moreover, it is intensely concerned in some cases with whether a substantive entitlement exists to which the demand for procedural protection can be attached,[21] but in other cases that presumably threshold requirement seems to be ignored.[22] Stranger still, the Court has in two cases suggested that the *Eldridge* test somehow is to be combined with Justice Frankfurter's *McGrath*[23] appropriateness formulation,[24] and with prior precedents enunciated in terms of fundamental fairness.[25] Yet it decides other cases, to which these particular precedents are arguably as relevant, by torturing the *Eldridge* analysis until it yields a result that could have been rationalized much more easily and convincingly on grounds of appropriateness[26] or some notion of fundamental fairness.[27] Bentham has been embraced, but apparently with some reluctance.

POST-*ELDRIDGE* DOCTRINAL INCOHERENCE

The Court's ambivalence about utilizing the model of competence is combined with, and perhaps explains, its incoherent application of the *Eldridge* criteria. We shall examine here only some of the more obvious examples. Consider first the question of whether the complaining party has a life, liberty, or property interest sufficient to trigger concerns about the accuracy of the legal processes by which that interest is protected. This is the qualitative aspect of the first *Eldridge* factor. As noted in chapter

18. Macky v. Montrym, 443 U.S. 1 (1979).

19. Barry v. Banchi, 443 U.S. 55 (1979).

20. *See, e.g.*, United States v. Raddatz, 447 U.S. 667 (1980); Greenholtz v. Inmates, 442 U.S. 1 (1979).

21. *E.g.*, Memphis Light, Gas, and Water Div. v. Craft, 436 U.S. 1 (1978).

22. *E.g.*, Vitek v. Jones, 445 U.S. 480 (1980).

23. See discussion in chapter 2 *supra*, at 82–83.

24. *E.g.*, Ingraham v. Wright, 430 U.S. 651, 653 (1977).

25. Lassiter v. Dep't of Social Services, 452 U.S. 18, 26–27 (1981).

26. *Cf.* Califano v. Yamasaki, 442 U.S. 682 (1979).

27. *Cf.* Santosky v. Kramer, 450 U.S. 993 (1982).

1, there is substantial confusion in the jurisprudence about how rights or entitlements emerge and take shape apart from the legal processes through which they are implemented. But for now we shall be concerned only with one corner of this issue—how the recognition or nonrecognition of rights at common law affects the existence of a legal interest for purposes of administrative due process review.

Two cases, *Paul v. Davis*[28] and *Bishop v. Wood*,[29] decided in the same term as *Eldridge*—indeed, that with *Eldridge* gave shape to the competence model—provided early suggestions of the doctrinal incoherence that was to follow. *Paul* was the stigma case involving mistaken inclusion of the plaintiff on a police list of active shoplifters.[30] There the Court concluded that no separate legal interest in preventing stigmatizing governmental action existed that alone would require any particular processes of decision be employed to prevent error. This was supported by the finding that the plaintiff might have an action for defamation against the responsible officials. In short, *Paul* seems to establish the proposition: If the common law recognizes the plaintiff's substantive right, then the common law processes for that right's protection are exclusive. Yet in *Bishop v. Wood*,[31] the police officer dismissal case, the fact that state common law made employment "at will" defeated the plaintiff's claimed entitlement, pursuant to a state statute, to dismissal only for cause. With the nonrecognition of the substantive entitlement, of course, there is nonrecognition of due process procedural protections in this model. Thus, *Bishop* seems to stand for the proposition: No common law right, no due process entitlement.

It may be suggested that these two holdings are not contradictory. They demonstrate only that the common law treatment of an interest has no effect on the due process characterization of an entitlement. The true rule is "Heads the state wins, tails the private party loses." Talk about the common law is simply makeweight.

If such talk is makeweight, it does not always rest on the same

28. 424 U.S. 693 (1976).
29. 426 U.S. 341 (1976).
30. See discussion *supra*, chapter 2 at 95–96.
31. See also discussion *supra*, chapter 2 at 85–86.

side of the scale. Two years after *Paul* and *Bishop*, the Court heard *Memphis Light, Gas, and Water Division v. Craft*,[32] a case involving the adequacy of a municipal utility's dispute resolution procedure. Craft complained that the utility had failed to notify him of the availability of the company's pretermination review procedure when threatening him with termination of service for nonpayment. The company admitted its failure to notify, but argued that the available common law remedies—pretermination injunction, posttermination damages, and a postpayment action for refund—defined the extent of the plaintiff's rights against the publicly owned company. Not so, said the Court. "The availability of such local-law remedies is evidence of the State's recognition of a protected interest."[33]

As *Craft* illustrates, the common law seems to be a wild card, whether the discussion is about the existence of a legal interest or about the accuracy-enhancing power of a procedural protection. The Memphis company paraded the available common law remedies not only as evidence of Craft's exclusive interest, but also as evidence that a pretermination conference would add little to his existing rights. It was surprised to learn that this argument, relating to the second factor in the *Eldridge* test, also was wrong. Those common law remedies were not, said the Court, "an adequate substitute for a pre-termination review of the disputed bill with a designated employee."[34]

Yet the utility surely must be forgiven its mistake. Only one term earlier the Court had held there was no need for "prepaddling" hearings in a school system employing corporal punishment precisely because "the available civil and criminal sanctions for abuse . . . afford significant protection against unjustified corporal punishment."[35] Indeed, the Memphis defendant probably thought it had an a fortiori case. The school discipline holding that gave the company comfort emerged from a context in which (a) the common law remedy was only for abuse, not error; (b) no prepunishment common law remedy was thought to exist; and (c) no court in the affected state ever

32. 436 U.S. 1 (1978).
33. 436 U.S. at 11.
34. 436 U.S. at 20.
35. Ingraham v. Wright, 430 U.S. 651, 678 (1977).

had recognized a remedy against a teacher for corporal punishment.

The significance accorded the existence or nonexistence of common law remedies is but one of the inconsistencies in the Court's analysis of the second factor in the competence analysis. A brace of cases concerning psychiatric assessment, and a similar pair relating to decisions based on character, intelligence, and good faith, continue the tale of a wildly erratic jurisprudence. Consider first *Parham v. J.R.*[36] and *Vitek v. Jones*[37] decided the same Term and published in the same volume of the United States Reports.

In *Parham* the issue was whether a minor need be given a hearing prior to commitment to an institution for treatment of mental illness. The Court thought not, apparently in substantial part, because a hearing would provide little additional protection from error: "Common human experience and scholarly opinions suggest that the proposed protections of an adversary hearing to determine the appropriateness of medical decisions for the commitment and treatment of mental and emotional illness may well be more illusory than real."[38] Yet, somehow, when in *Vitek* the question was whether a prisoner should have a hearing prior to being transferred to a mental hospital, the suggestion that psychiatric judgment was involved elicited the following judicial response: "The medical nature of the inquiry . . . does not justify dispensing with due process requirements. *It is precisely [t]he subtleties and nuances of psychiatric diagnoses that justify the requirement of adversary hearings.*"[39]

Greenholtz v. Inmates[40] and *Califano v. Yamasaki*[41]—again, same Term, same volume—are hardly less baffling. *Greenholtz* holds that a face-to-face, oral hearing is not required to make parole decisions based on an assessment of the offender's personality, readiness to undertake responsibilities, intelligence, training, "mental and physical makeup," attitude toward law

36. 445 U.S. 584 (1979).
37. 445 U.S. 480 (1980).
38. 445 U.S. at 609.
39. 445 U.S. at 495 (quoting *Addington v. Tex.*, 441 U.S. 418, 430 (1979) (emphasis supplied).
40. 442 U.S. 1 (1979).
41. 442 U.S. 682 (1979).

and authority, and any other factors the parole board deems relevant. Accuracy, the Court ruled, could be achieved by a review of the prisoner's files. Yet *Yamasaki* requires an oral hearing (at least a conversation) whenever the secretary of Health and Human Services decides whether to waive recoupment of improperly paid disability benefits because the waiver standard, lack of fault, rests "on an evaluation of all 'pertinent circumstances' including the recipient's intelligence . . . and physical and mental condition as well as his good faith."[42]

That doctrine is contradictory does not imply necessarily that any of the cases were wrongly decided. The point is more limited: the post-*Eldridge* cases are not consistently or convincingly explained by the Court in terms of the *Eldridge* criteria. Indeed, these cases reveal judicial reason giving that sometimes seems to border on the lunatic. If the Court cannot explain its decisions in a coherent and convincing fashion, then sooner or later the legitimacy of its decisions will be called into question. One is tempted to suggest that attachment to Jeremy Bentham may be doing for the Burger Court what a fondness for Herbert Spencer did for the Court during the *Lochner* era.

I do not, however, want to be too strident in the claim that the Court is committed to the Benthamite theory of procedural due process that I have called the model of competence. At least some of the Court's gyrations might be explained by suggesting that it is only quasi-positivist, is interested in process characteristics unrelated to accuracy, and has some notion of balancing that is not utilitarian. The Court appears to be searching, at least some of the time, for a model that goes beyond the ideal of competence. That search raises two significant questions. First, what motivates the search? Second, for what is the Court searching? An answer to the first question will make up the bulk of the remainder of this chapter. The case, in brief, is that the model of competence, although it surely identifies issues of interest and importance, has three major flaws: (1) It is intellectually overambitious. The criteria it enunciates cannot be put into practice in constitutional adjudication. (2) The formula, notwithstanding its generality and overambitiousness, is also underinclusive. It pro-

42. 442 U.S. at 696–97 (quoting 10 C.F.R. § 404.507 (1978)).

vides no technique for addressing major due process concerns that have no relationship to accurate decision making and that are not allayed by competent implementation of positive law. (3) The approach involves the judiciary in general welfare calculations that appear, simultaneously, unsuitable for judicial judgment and underprotective of individual rights. As we shall see, the first problem can be somewhat ameliorated by various techniques for economizing on the information demanded for adjudicatory judgment. Problems two and three are more resistant to reform from within the model of competence itself. Exploring them will establish the direction of our search for a model that will provide an adequate constitutional approach to administrative due process. Let us examine the competence model's major flaws in turn.

THE INTELLECTUAL HUBRIS OF SOCIAL COST ACCOUNTING

The discussion that follows explores the use of the model of competence in the context of determining entitlements to social welfare payments. *Goldberg v. Kelly*[43] and *Mathews v. Eldridge*[44] provide the focus. Because these decisions are, doctrinally, the two most significant administrative due process cases since the 1930s and, for purposes of examining the content of the model of competence, are indistinguishable analytically from cases in other areas of administrative activity, no loss of generality results from this choice. Throughout the discussion we will concentrate on the analytic content of the opinions in these cases and will ignore explanations of the Court's behavior that rely on shifting personnel, personal philosophies, general political context, or alternative analytic models. The issue to be addressed is what it means to confront due process questions in accordance with the criteria that comprise the model of competence.

In *Goldberg*, the Court decided that benefits under the program Aid to Families with Dependent Children (AFDC) could not, as a matter of due process of law, be terminated before the recipient was provided with a trial-type hearing (including spe-

43. 397 U.S. 254 (1970).
44. 424 U.S. 319 (1976).

cific notice of issues, opportunity to present evidence orally and to confront and cross-examine adverse witnesses, a neutral decider, a decision based wholly on the hearing record, and an opportunity to be represented by counsel). The prior administrative decision structure for AFDC payments—which included a notice indicating the intention to terminate benefits and the grounds for termination, as well as an opportunity to submit written objections prior to termination—was determined to be constitutionally inadequate.

Six years later in *Eldridge*, the Court faced the same issue—a claim of constitutional entitlement to a pretermination oral hearing—with respect to Social Security Disability Insurance (DI) benefits. It held that a pretermination oral hearing was not required.[45] This meant the Social Security Administration (SSA) could terminate benefits, constitutionally, on the basis of (1) documentary evidence submitted by treating and consulting physicians that had never been made available to the claimant and (2) information submitted by the claimant pursuant to a general request for information concerning his or her condition. In neither case would the claimant be given specific notice of the information relied upon to initiate a termination notice.

The difference in the *Goldberg* and *Eldridge* results does not indicate a doctrinal shift. Although the *Eldridge* statement of the due process criteria is a dramatic crystallation of the Court's approach, in both *Goldberg* and *Eldridge* the Court considered the familiar three factors: (1) the interests of the claimants in the receipt of benefits; (2) the contribution of the requested procedures to avoiding erroneous terminations; and (3) the fiscal, administrative, and other burdens of the requested procedures. Yet, as the majority opinion in *Eldridge* reflects, the Court perceived critical differences in the magnitude of the relevant costs and benefits at stake in the two cases.[46] The Court described the situation of terminated AFDC recipients as "immediately desperate," whereas it believed DI recipients to be in less-straitened circumstances. The claimant's interest in avoiding erroneous deprivation was therefore more significant in the AFDC than in

45. 424 U.S. at 349.
46. *Id*. at 339–43.

the DI program. Moreover, the Court believed that adding formal procedures would substantially improve accuracy in AFDC determinations, but not in DI cases. Having made these two distinctions, and having no reason to believe that adding procedural safeguards was cheaper in DI than it had been in AFDC, the Court decided not to impose the *Goldberg* hearing requirements on DI determinations.

As I have argued elsewhere, the Court's conclusions are deeply problematic on empirical grounds. It is likely that terminated DI recipients are very nearly as "desperate" as terminated AFDC recipients, that oral hearings are peculiarly important to the determination of many DI claims, and that the administrative costs of pretermination hearings in AFDC cases are higher than they would be in the DI program.[47] More important for this discussion, the problematic character of the Court's *Eldridge* conclusions seems predictable in nearly every due process case. The model of competence has an enormous appetite for data that is disputable, unknown, and, sometimes, unknowable. To understand why this is the case requires a discussion of what it might mean to take the model seriously in the *Goldberg-Eldridge* context.

INTERESTS, BURDENS, AND SOCIAL WELFARE: AN APPROACH
TO SOCIAL COST ACCOUNTING

As a preliminary matter we first must give the model of competence as it appears in these cases a somewhat more precise formulation. In doing so, we will offer some evidence to indicate that the Court has been approaching the cases in roughly the same terms. It seems clear, for example, that the claimant's interest criterion cannot be viewed as a question of how the claimant subjectively would value the continuous receipt of payments. Nor does the Court search for evidence of actual claimant valuation, even in qualitative terms like "desperation." Indeed, such an approach would be surprising. The Court has often made clear that the subjective expectation of a claimant is not the con-

47. *See* Mashaw, *The Supreme Court's Due Process Calculus for Administrative Adjudication in* Mathews v. Eldridge: *Three Factors in Search of a Theory of Value*, 44 U. CHI. L. REV. 28 (1976).

stitutionally relevant measure of the importance of a substantive claim of right.[48] Similarly, dollar values of benefits cannot be the issue. A dollar is a dollar, and DI beneficiaries receive more of them per claim than AFDC beneficiaries. Using this measure, the Court would have come to opposite conclusions when comparing the interests at stake in the two cases.[49] What, then, is the Court seeking to count?

Within the model of competence the Court should be viewed as searching for the relative social value or utility of transferring dollars from taxpayers to AFDC and DI claimants. As in most constitutional adjudication, the Court must specify some consensus, or at least widely held values, as a starting point for analysis. Here, claimants may make successful claims to societal resources in the form of additional procedural protections only to the extent that those procedures convincingly support the general welfare. That conviction will follow, at least in part, from a perception that accurate decision making, with respect to the claimants' underlying substantive interests, is of substantial social importance. Potential desperation is thus a proxy for general social concern with the claimant's plight. The Court, believing that greater desperation occurs among terminated AFDC recipients than among terminated DI recipients, therefore found it socially more valuable to avoid erroneous AFDC terminations than to avoid erroneous DI terminations.

Assuming that the Court is, indeed, interested in the social value of protecting the claimant's interest, is it similarly interested in the social costs of respecting that interest via procedural safeguards? In a special sense of "social costs," the Court is concerned. It mentioned administrative and societal costs—costs that are social at least in the sense of "paid out of public monies."[50] But what of other social costs, for example, the dissatisfaction of taxpayers compelled to support ineligible persons pending a hearing on their proposed termination? Are these considerations also to be included on the cost side of the equation?

It seems reasonable to presume they should be. There is evi-

48. *See, e.g.*, Bishop v. Wood, 426 U.S. 341, 343–47 (1976).
49. Mashaw, *supra* note 47, at 39–45.
50. 424 U.S. at 347.

dence from other cases that suggests the Court is concerned with the effects of procedural formality on the accomplishment of public purposes. That concern is not solely with the budgetary costs of procedure, but with a procedure's potential to inhibit the achievement of important social objectives.[51] Moreover, the cases from *Goldberg* forward that developed the notion of accuracy as the goal of governmental decision making viewed at least the benefits of accuracy as a social or public value.[52] A coherent social welfare calculation would require that the costs of error be counted in the same way.

From the foregoing one can see that there are two types of social costs of AFDC and DI claims adjudications. First, there are the social benefits foregone when eligible persons are denied, and social costs incurred when grants are made to ineligibles. These are the error costs of the system. Second, there are the direct costs of running the adjudicatory system (personnel and so on) and the indirect costs of various types of adjudicatory processes (administrative inefficiency, delay, and the like). These are the administrative costs of the system. Minimizing the sum of these costs seems desirable.

This type of cost minimization appears to be what the Court had in mind when it said it must consider, along with the cost of any procedural safeguard, the contribution it (in this case, pretermination hearings) will make in preventing erroneous decisions. Any procedural device that yields a savings in error costs in excess of its administrative costs is desirable. As a standard for constitutional adjudication, the point seems to be that at some level of failure to capture these potential benefits, administrative procedures will be considered irrational, arbitrary, and, therefore, a violation of the due process clause.

One might object to this calculus as incomplete. It neglects the costs and benefits of processes—not as instrumental devices for achieving substantive social goals—but as devices for self-realization, participatory governance, and the like, or for their opposites, alienation and anomie.[53] Or, it may be asserted at the outset that general social welfare calculations do not provide an

51. *See, e.g.*, Hannah v. Larche, 363 U.S. 420, 443–44 (1960).
52. See discussion *infra* at 103–04.
53. *See* Saphire, *supra* note 9.

appropriate methodology for judicial decision making.[54] In one sense, such arguments relate to the comparative goodness of other approaches to due process review. They assert that there are better ways of deciding. Such claims would require for their evaluation a full explication of those alternative perspectives.

In a second sense, however, these objections may be asserting that a social welfare approach is ineffectual or inappropriate in more absolute terms. It may be argued, for example, that social welfare talk implies combining individual preferences, and that we have no adequate technique for aggregating interpersonal utilities.[55] Or it might be suggested that any judicial attempt to assess general welfare consequences either subordinates judicial review to a prior social welfare calculation at the legislative level or impermissibly invades the legislative function of making policy based on general welfare calculations.

The discussion that follows will cast some light on these sorts of issues. For the efficacy question turns on the degree to which a social welfare approach can say plausible, coherent, and useful things about social welfare functions, given the inaccessibility of much important data concerning individual or aggregated preferences. And, in turn, the appropriateness of a judicial, social welfare calculation depends upon the types of value assertions and the level of the information demands that a conscientious court might make when attempting to do its sums correctly.

A BETTER SPECIFIED MODEL OF THE SOCIAL COSTS OF ERROR

At this point I will introduce a graphic representation of the social gains and losses from accurate and erroneous decision making in the AFDC and DI programs. The graph establishes an analytic framework for the remainder of the discussion, and permits the isolation of a number of critical issues that the Supreme Court in *Goldberg* and *Eldridge* dealt with on only an intuitive level, if at all.

Figure 1 assumes several—I believe reasonable—things about legislative decisions to make income transfers. First, the

54. *See* Note, *supra* note 11.
55. *See* Arrow, *Values and Collective Decision Making*, in PHILOSOPHY, POLITICS AND SOCIETY 215, 225–32 (3d series P. Laslett & W. Runciman eds. 1967).

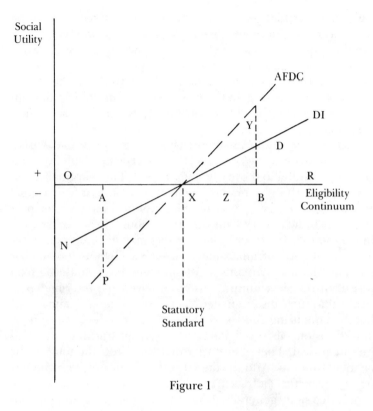

Figure 1

graph assumes that claimants are more or less deserving rather than absolutely eligible or ineligible, as the decisions concerning individual entitlements would imply. Common sense suggests that we will care more about the support of some eligibles than others and be more outraged by some erroneous transfers than others. Moreover, from the perspective of a social welfare calculus, it seems plausible to describe the legislative adoption of various income-transfer programs as a series of attempts to define as eligible for a transfer anyone to whom the transfer can be made at a net social benefit. The legislature may have stopped short of this goal, thus failing to capture all available social benefits, or may have overshot the mark, thus making transfers to some persons at a net social cost. But, in the ideal realm of positivist, instrumentalist, utilitarian, judicial review, the legislature must be viewed as having defined eligibility in a way that attempts to capture the available social benefits from a particular type of transfer program. Claimants and recipients range on both sides of this eligibility criterion, or legislative standard, from the clearly inappropriate (small gain/large cost), to the marginally ineligible, to the marginally eligible, to the clearly appropriate (large gain/small cost).[56]

Second, the graph assumes that the legislature makes flat-rate payments to those who meet or exceed the eligibility standard and nothing to those who fall below it. The marginally ineligible get nothing, whereas the marginal and inframarginal eligibles get the same payment. Although income-transfer programs, including AFDC, do vary the amounts paid to eligibles, they do so in gross terms. One sensibly may imagine significant numbers of both inframarginal transferees to whom too much is paid and denied claimants to whom something would be paid were transfers less lumpy. Moreover, even if prescribed payment amounts discriminated perfectly among claimants — thereby equalizing the social value of all transfers at the margin — decisions about eligibility in nearly all transfer programs are categorical. They therefore often will affect the total of the payment amount. And in contexts other than programs involving cash transfers (job security, civil commitment, licensure, and so on), decisions generally involve allocating very lumpy goods and bads.

The social welfare functions described on the graph by *XAFDC* and *XDI* constitute one plausible representation of the Supreme Court's view of the net social utility to be derived from making payments to claimants who lie at various places along the

56. Note that both the horizontal and vertical axes employ a cardinal, but undisclosed, ordering. One way to imagine the construction of the horizontal axis is a perfect plebiscite in which voters assign deservedness numbers on a scale of 1 to 100 to well-defined clusters of relevant personal characteristics. The task of administration is then to assign individual claimants to the correct characteristics cluster, and to determine whether the cluster falls below or above the score that has been determined necessary for eligibility. The vertical scale is constructed in the same way, this time asking voters to indicate the intensity of their joy or happiness at the prospect of a public transfer of a specified size being made to persons occupying various places on the horizontal scale.

eligibility continuum OR.[57] Thus, a payment at point B would produce net utility BD in the DI program, and a greater net utility, BY, in the AFDC program. The payoff from eliminating negative errors is obviously much greater in AFDC than in DI. And, because the Court assumes that the same procedures would eliminate more negative errors for point B AFDC claimants than for point B DI claimants, the case for increased procedural safeguards becomes even stronger. The *Goldberg* opinion might be described as holding that, under these circumstances, it is irrational not to attempt to capture the social welfare gains from more accurate decision making.

SOME OBVIOUS PROBLEMS WITH *Goldberg-Eldridge*-STYLE CALCULATIONS

Describing the Comparative Heights of Social Welfare Functions. The comparison of current with past cases is a standard technique of legal analysis. The *Eldridge* Court compared that case with *Goldberg* and found larger social costs associated with AFDC errors than with DI errors. But how does the Court know how to describe the social welfare functions of the two programs even in comparative terms? The number of imponderable issues raised by an attempt at such a description is indeed awesome.

If we assume that the legislature is concerned with maximizing social welfare, it would seem to follow that it would define AFDC and DI eligibility in a fashion that made identical the marginal social returns of payments under the two programs. But this only tells us that the marginal payments—those immediately above and immediately below the statutory standard—have similar social benefits and costs. It says nothing about infra-

57. Another possibility, of course, is that the Court viewed the social welfare functions as dichotomous and unequal—for example, as in figure 2, which appears later in this chapter. This description fits the Court's analysis, but it seems implausible as a description of the relevant social values. It is simply hard to believe that society views the support of all DI recipients (those with lower back pain and those in iron lungs) and all AFDC recipients (unwed teenage mothers and widowed middle-aged housewives) as equally valuable. We apparently do not want to bear the costs associated with a legislative or administrative system that attempts to make these sorts of worthiness discriminations, but that is a quite different matter from asserting that the same social consensus underlies every transfer.

marginal transfers and, therefore, nothing much about the shape or heights of the social welfare curves. The one interesting property of this observation is the suggestion that it would be wrong to assume that the DI and AFDC social welfare functions have different shapes throughout their respective ranges. At least at the margin, the benefits and costs are the same.

Of course, the *Eldridge* Court did not assert that the social value of AFDC and DI payments is the same at every point on the curves. Rather, a careful reading of the cases suggests an assertion that the average social value of AFDC payments exceeds that of DI payments. But, given the pervasive uncertainty concerning the shape of the two welfare functions, is there any reason to credit this assertion? I think not. The Court makes its assertion on the basis of the greater need of AFDC recipients. As an empirical matter, the Court *may* have correctly assessed the average relative need of recipients under the two programs. But as a conceptual matter, it has not explained why relative need defines relative social value.

If the social value of transfers is something that the Court seeks to establish by considering evidence of legislative intent, then the criterion of need clearly is wrong. To ask whether the DI recipient is as needy or desperate as the AFDC recipient is to treat the social costs of negative error in the two programs as if both programs were premised on the need of recipients. But the DI program has no need standard. Its payments are based on a combination of prior FICA contributions and medical impairment. In that program the social costs associated with negative error may result as much from a large component of demoralization costs—that is, a denial of what was thought to be a secure entitlement—as from the desperation of claimants. The Court can assert that the social welfare schedule for AFDC payments is higher than that for DI payments only if it ignores the different legislative bases for the two types of payments.

The Court may be prepared to say that need is the only constitutionally relevant criterion for assessing the social costs of error. But such an assertion would be both inconsistent with the general pattern of its jurisprudence[58] and impolitic in the ex-

---

58. *See, e.g.*, San Antonio Ind. School Dist. v. Rodriquez, 411 U.S. 1, 23–24 (1973) (equal protection claim not established where lack of personal resources

treme. That one's security of expectations with respect to governmental action should be inversely related to wealth is not a novel constitutional theory,[39] but it is not a theory the Court previously has rushed to embrace.

The Failure to Address the Problems of Positive Errors. The question of the comparative heights of the social welfare functions in the *OX* segment of the graph is never addressed by the Court. In its discussion of fiscal and administrative costs, the Court does not identify the costs resulting from the positive errors induced by pretermination hearings. Possibly the Court believed that procedures that decreased negative errors would have no impact on positive errors (defining a point *A* claimant as eligible)—in which case the shape of the curves between *O* and *X* is clearly irrelevant. If so, it also clearly was wrong. Because the requested procedures in *Goldberg* and *Eldridge* (pretermination hearings) *must* induce some positive errors (not all appellants win, but they are paid pending a hearing decision), the heights of the social welfare functions and the distribution of positive errors in the two programs are important.

The Court might believe that positive-error costs are nearly identical for the two programs. This could be true under any of a number of conditions, including: (1) the social welfare functions have the same shape between *O* and *X* (either *PX* or *NX*), and errors are identically distributed (by both position and number) along *OX* for both programs; (2) the social welfare functions in the *OX* range are the reverse of those represented, and the distribution of errors is similar for the two programs; (3) the social welfare functions are as represented, and errors are similarly distributed, but fewer positive errors would be induced in the AFDC program; and (4) positive errors in AFDC are systematically skewed toward the marginally ineligible (near *X* on *OX*), whereas DI positive errors are not. The opinions in

does not occasion absolute deprivation of educational benefits); Griffin v. Ill., 351 U.S. 12, 20 (1956) (state need not purchase stenographic transcript for defendant where other means affording adequate and effective appellate review available to indigent defendants).

59. *See* Michelman, *Foreword, On Protecting the Poor through the Fourteenth Amendment*, 83 HARV. L. REV. 7 (1969). *See also*, Lubman, *Mao and Mediation: Politics and Dispute Resolution in Communist China*, 55 CAL. L. REV. 1284 (1967).

Goldberg and *Eldridge*, however, provide no guidance on these questions.

The Failure to Consider the Distribution of Errors. Although the relative heights of the functions *XAFDC* and *XDI* apparently were treated as critical, the Court largely ignored the question of the distribution of errors in the *XR* segment of the eligibility continuum. If AFDC negative errors related predominantly to type *Z* claimants, whereas DI errors related predominantly to type *B* claimants (and errors were of roughly equal numbers), the social costs of negative errors would be equivalent in the two programs. Alternatively, were the DI program more error-prone at the initial stages than the AFDC program, DI errors in the aggregate might be more costly than AFDC errors, even if each individual DI error were less costly than its AFDC counterpart.

SOMEWHAT LESS OBVIOUS ANALYTIC DIFFICULTIES

Error, Error, Who's Got the Error. The preceding discussion treats errors as if they were nonproblematic facts, the incidence of which the Court might have—and, given its own decision rule, should have—considered. The reality is, of course, different. Decisions on AFDC and DI claims are judgments based on a partial knowledge of facts—facts that often nudge the decision maker in different directions. Even perfect information concerning the relevant objective facts would not prevent disputes about the ultimate facts from which legal consequences flow. One disability examiner's "broken-down manual laborer" is another's "malingerer"; one AFDC eligibility technician's "good cause" for refusing employment is another's "lame excuse." What does an error mean in a system of judgmental administration?

The question is difficult, perhaps ultimately unanswerable. Even so, it seems clear that, with respect to the AFDC and DI programs, "error" should not mean what the Court's discussion in both cases takes it to mean: reversal on appeal. Appeals are de novo in both programs; not only may new evidence be taken, but a new judgment is rendered, which is wholly independent of the prior determination. There is no reason a priori to consider the second judgment superior to the first. In addition, a reversal-rate approach to the incidence of error provides no information on *unappealed* cases. The Court had no information on false positives. Moreover, it might easily have been induced to believe that the error rate for appealed cases was equally representative of the false negatives in unappealed cases—a relationship that has also never been established. In short, when the Court in *Goldberg* and *Eldridge* spoke of the error-proneness of AFDC and DI initial decisions, it actually was talking about the incidence of conflicting de novo judgments in a small subset of initially rejected claims—a quite different matter.

Procedural Power. From what has been said about the relationship of reversal rates to errors, the Supreme Court's refusal in *Goldberg* and *Eldridge* to gauge the error-preventing power of hearings by the reversal-rate statistics should be applauded. And its functional approach to the role of various aspects of hearings (for example, cross-examination) deserves similar praise. Yet the discussion one finds in the two cases still falls remarkably short of the demands of a probing social welfare calculation.

The Court dealt in stereotypes concerning the bases for termination decisions (witness testimony in AFDC cases, disinterested and routine medical records in DI cases), and then it evaluated the need for hearings to buttress that evidence from the perspective of the function of hearings in civil litigation. There was no attempt to evaluate the degree to which, or how often, the stereotypic evidence dominates the decision matrix in AFDC or DI termination cases. Nor was there an attempt to investigate how a technique like cross-examination, or a view of the witness-claimant, functions in the special context of benefits determinations. A serious inquiry into these issues might reveal, for example, that testimonial evidence is not a common basis for AFDC terminations, and that an opportunity to view and question the claimant is considered the most important evidence in DI hearings.

This stereotypic analysis may reintroduce the confusion between reversals and errors. Much of the design of trial procedure is premised on preserving either unrelated substantive values or equality between legal combatants, not on truth-seeking. The reputed capacity of the heat of civil trial to separate precious metal from slag is more an engaging metaphor than an empirical finding.[60] The conventional wisdom of the civil trial stereotype is lawyer's wisdom, predicated on experience concerning the power of a procedure to turn decisions around. This experience has dubious value when assessing the issue of accuracy made relevant by the Supreme Court's due process calculus.

Dynamic Effects. Finally, we have said little about the dynamic or systemic effects of changes in procedural rules. Justice Black, however, noted this problem in his *Goldberg* dissent. If the Court skews the system in favor of positive errors, by procedurally constraining negative decisions at one decision point, what is to prevent administrative self-correction? As Justice Black suggested, if terminations are judicially constrained, then decisions concerning initial acceptances into the program might be reduced administratively in order to maintain an acceptable level of disbursements.[61] Moreover, because the Court cannot know how the balance will be reestablished, it cannot know whether the combination of error and administrative costs in the new equilibrium will be the same, greater, or less than those costs under the prereview system. As noted in chapter 1, commentators have produced social cost accountings for the Court's due process rulings that falls into all of these categories.

The position of the Court when pursuing a model of competence analysis is indeed unenviable. It needs information on the causes and incidence of errors, the social valuation of both positive and negative errors, the error-correcting power of various procedural devices, and the dynamic adjustments that may result from any changes that are ordered. It has no information on most of these questions other than potentially false proxies and conventional wisdom. Nor, as we shall see, is it likely to get any.

---

60. *See* Frankel, *The Search for Truth: An Umpireal View*, 123 U. Pa. L. Rev. 1031, 1036 (1975).
61. 397 U.S. at 297 (Black, J., dissenting).

STRATEGIES FOR MANAGING THE INFORMATION DEMANDS
OF A SOCIAL WELFARE CALCULUS

From what has been said, it seems clear that the Supreme Court's approach to *Goldberg* and *Eldridge* left unanswered —indeed, unasked—a number of questions that are critical to a serious calculation of social utility. The accounting task that a thorough analysis of social costs and benefits would impose on the Court is simply too formidable. The slope of the social welfare functions for various transfer programs cannot be determined with precision. The number and positions on those curves of positive and negative errors, even the existence of errors, cannot conclusively be established. The procedural power of various adjudicative techniques is unknown. The dynamic effects of procedural change are unpredictable.

But, regardless of the imponderables, the Court must decide. The question, then, is whether it should face up to the information demands of its due process calculus, and if it does, what that candor implies. One possible implication is that where decisions require highly indeterminate social welfare judgments, the Court is a poor institution for resolving competitive claims. In the absence of appropriate information, a judgment about process seems to be merely an instinct about whose interests are to be preferred, rather than a judgment about aggregate social welfare. Surely that sort of choice is for the legislature, or for the good faith judgments of the legislature's administrative delegate, as the final paragraphs of the *Eldridge* opinion suggest.[62]

Yet, we hardly can accept the notion that due process means merely whatever process the legislature and administrators devise. Whether we applaud due process review, or only view it as an established part of the constitutional landscape, a full-fledged judicial withdrawal from due process review seems improbable. If we do not shift to due process review on some radically different basis, then the question is whether there are any strategies for managing the indeterminacies of the cost-minimization model without, as the Court seems to do in *Goldberg* and *Eldridge*,

62. 424 U.S. at 347–49.

making wholly intuitive, and therefore unconvincing, assertions about social valuations, procedural power, and the like. Let us return to the various problems with the Court's analysis, and see what headway can be made.

Describing and Comparing Social Welfare Functions. I can make very little progress in describing the social welfare functions for AFDC and DI in a convincing way. It seems reasonable to believe that their shapes are more like the curves in figure 1 than those in figure 2. But when called upon to justify the continuous structure of the figure 1 curves, I would have to fall back on a negative assertion: I have no good reason to introduce kinks into the curves except possibly to recognize peculiarly high demoralization costs for obvious errors affecting claims at the tails of the eligibility continuum. Of course, this says nothing about heights.

Perhaps the best that can be done is to combine traditional legal technique, judicial modesty, and game theory. The Court does not usually reason in a vacuum. As in *Eldridge*, it compares cases. The question, then, is whether the social value of accuracy in a current case is greater or less than in prior similar cases. I already have argued that there is no valid basis for either assertion. That being the situation, a reasonable strategy might be to treat the pervasive uncertainty of relative social values as a ground for assuming their equivalence. This is, after all, a standard technique in estimating the probability of outcomes when no information exists concerning the likelihood of any particular outcome. But if uncertainty is indeed the norm, this implies a decision rule having a rather peculiar form. Instead of merely treating *like* cases alike, the operational reality will be to treat *all* cases alike. Judicial modesty in these circumstances certainly would counsel affirming legislative-administrative choice. In short we are back to de facto abandonment of due process review.

The Distribution of Errors. Assuming that the social welfare functions are roughly the same in the AFDC and DI programs (and, for that matter, in other transfer programs), the Court also must establish the number and position of positive and negative errors on the social welfare curve. How can this be done? First,

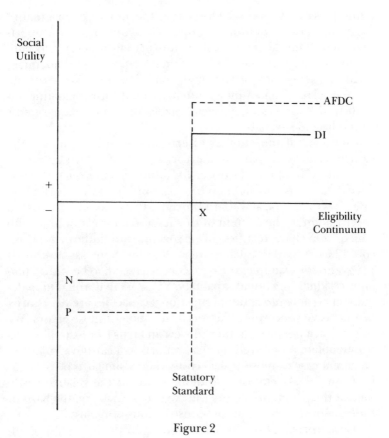

Figure 2

some progress can be made in establishing the definition of an error and determining how often errors occur. Although reversal rates are not good proxies for error rates, other more useful data, generated by administrative quality assurance activities, often are available.[63] I have argued elsewhere that the nonexistence of reasonably reliable error-rate data might itself constitute

63. Chassman & Rolston, *Social Security Disability Hearings: A Case Study in Quality Assurance and Due Process*, 65 CORNELL L. REV. 801, 810–14 (1980); Mashaw, *The Management Side of Due Process: Some Theoretical and Litigation Notes on the Assurance of Accuracy, Fairness and Timeliness in the Adjudication of Social Welfare Claims*, 59 CORNELL L. REV. 772, 791–804 (1974).

a due process violation.[64] The critical function of error identification in a cost-minimization approach to due process supports that view. The failure to collect information necessary to both administrative and judicial evaluation of procedural adequacy seems arbitrary, absent very high collection costs. Were the absence of error data an independent ground for invalidating administrative processes, it seems likely that such data rapidly would become available.

But, even if the number of errors is quantified, how is the Court to locate any particular error or group of errors on the social welfare function? In order for administrative quality assurance data to cast any light on the relationship of the distribution of errors to the social welfare function, there would have to be a specification of the content of the deservedness continuum with which the characteristics of erroneously adjudicated claims could be compared. Such a prospect seems hopeless. In the DI program, for example, the core concerns seem to be with claimants' residual functional capability. Yet, data that would map decisional errors onto residual functional capacities are necessarily inconclusive concerning the social valuation of those errors. We simply have no idea whether to view an error (for example, failure to obtain a required medical report) in a cardiovascular impairment case as more or less costly than a similar type of error in a musculoskeletal case. Judgments about the relative costliness of the programs' errors will have to be made on the basis of hunches or, at best, plausible constructions of reality.

Certain aspects of the DI program do provide some guidance. For example, termination decisions should rarely introduce errors at the tails of the social welfare function. Objective bases qualify the very severely disabled at the initial stages of the determination process, and practically none of these cases subsequently is terminated on a nonobjective basis. Conversely, decisions continuing support payments to persons who previously have been determined totally incapable of working at any job in the national economy are unlikely to introduce positive errors that would affect a robust segment of the population.

It seems reasonable to believe, therefore, that errors in the

64. Mashaw, *supra* note 63, at 775–76, 807.

DI program are likely to occur in marginal cases—cases in which the social costs of error are modest. This assumes, of course, that the social welfare function is not very steep with respect to claims that are just to one side of the statutory standard. That assumption also seems plausible to me. Large social welfare costs are likely to result primarily from widespread perceptions of either injustice (negative errors) or rip-offs (positive errors). But these perceptions should not be expected to attend cases where the decision is arguable either way.[65]

If this is correct, the Court might justify a refusal to upset the DI legislative scheme on constitutional grounds with the rough judgment that at most there are modest social welfare gains to be had from eliminating negative errors in the DI program. Given the somewhat tenuous connection between procedure and accuracy anyway, only a refusal to attempt to eliminate substantial error costs by providing procedural protection will be considered so irrational as to be a failure to provide due, or on this model, competent, process.

When one attempts to model the distribution of errors in AFDC, the situation is more complex. Need is a major criterion of eligibility from the legislative perspective and is a significant factor in eligibility disputes; but it does not dominate the decisional matrix the way functional capacity seems to dominate the disability decision. Factors like family composition, residency, cooperation in locating relatives, and willingness to seek employment also are critically important. What this suggests is that we cannot confidently assert that the circumstances constraining errors with respect to one aspect of eligibility would tend to confine errors to the marginal cases. Because the eligibility continuum presents a complex of factors affecting a recipient's deservedness, and because each factor must be independently satisfied, errors concerning any issue—however effective the decision process is generally concerning that issue—might affect recipients whose composite claim strengths are very high.[66] Er-

65. I must confess, however, that I am far from certain. *See* Mashaw, *How Much of What Quality: A Comment on Conscientious Procedure Design*, 65 CORNELL L. REV. 823, 828–31 (1980).

66. Imagine, for example, ten separate criteria for eligibility; a 1 to 10 scale of satisfaction for each criterion (which might represent either degrees of satis-

roneous termination might affect recipients at any position on the deservedness continuum, including the tail. Thus there is less reason to believe that the distribution of errors in AFDC is constrained to marginal and, therefore, low-cost cases. In the face of this level of uncertainty concerning the social costs of any particular termination, the Court might conclude that failing to provide extensive procedural safeguards is recklessly imprudent.

SOME PROBLEMS WITH OUR STRATEGIES

Where is the Social Welfare Gain from Trading Negative Errors for Positive Ones? A revised social welfare model, one that reflects a unitary social welfare function for AFDC and DI payments and a guess at the distribution of errors in the two programs, appears as figure 3. A glance at it suggests a problem. The assumptions in figures 1 and 3, that the social welfare function is linear and, in figure 3, that the distribution of claim strength is symmetrical around the statutory criteria, imply that by preventing the termination of ineligibles, pretermination hearings would add social costs from false positives equal to the savings from the avoidance of false negatives. If the effect of the pretermination hearings for AFDC involves a simple trade-off of equivalent costs attached to different forms of error, where is the social gain?

One answer might be that the distribution of AFDC errors is, in fact, skewed in such a way that the Court reasonably might anticipate that high-cost negative errors would be traded for low-cost positive ones. The complex of eligibility criteria—with a requirement that each condition be satisfied independently—supports an expectation that negative errors may affect any portion of the eligible sector of the eligibility continuum. Positive errors, however, are in principle more constrained. If we as-

---

faction of the criterion or degrees of certainty with respect to binary judgments); and a requirement that claimants score at least 5 on *each* of the ten scales to be eligible. The minimum eligibility score is thus 50, and one might imagine that a marginal case would be in the range of 40 to 60. But a claimant rating an overall 96 could be disqualified by a 2-point mistake in classification with respect to one factor.

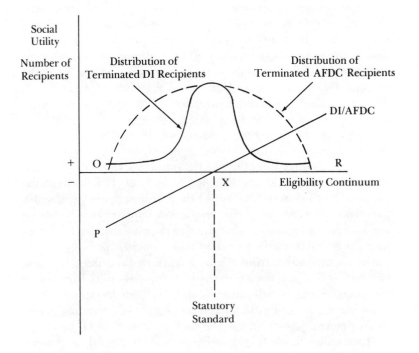

Figure 3

sume that the incorrectly decided grant contains an error with respect to only one aspect of eligibility, then presumably the recipient is at least marginally eligible with respect to all other criteria. Unless the controls on positive error with respect to separate characteristics of recipients are very poor, large numbers of high-cost mistakes should not occur. In any event, the agency remains free to institute controls to protect against high-cost positive errors. Thus, it remains free to insure that, by and large, the cases that remain eligible pending a hearing are marginal cases.

Another possibility may be that the social welfare gain results from the shorter time period within which the social costs of negative errors will be borne. Where only the direct administrative costs of providing hearings show up in administrative budgets, governmental agencies may be willing to tolerate the social costs of negative error for substantial periods. Where the administrator faces the costs not only of the hearing apparatus, but also of the positive errors induced by a pretermination hearing requirement, he or she has incentives to trade these costs at the margin. Given the usual magnitudes of the two costs, hearing delays are likely to become dramatically shorter under such a system. With rapid claims processing, the costs of induced false positives will be negligible, and *presumably* the hearings themselves will limit the costs of false negatives.

How does this distinguish AFDC terminations from DI terminations? Why should the SSA not be induced to behave in the fashion just suggested for state AFDC administrators faced with a pretermination hearing requirement? An answer that builds on the foregoing analysis is that the direct costs of prior hearings, including the continued payment to ineligible persons, would outweigh any gains from the avoidance of false negatives that currently are not reflected in the institutional utility function of the Social Security Administration. This assertion implies relatively strong belief in the limited social value of avoiding errors in DI determinations and in the substantial cost of DI hearings. As I have shown, the former belief must be premised on assumptions about the distribution of claim strength that may be reasonable, but hardly are conclusive. Nevertheless, an administrator or a legislature that held this belief certainly could not be called arbitrary, and a procedural system explicable in terms of a nonarbitrary assumption about social costs probably meets the constitutional standard the Court has articulated.

Yet, even here, where our attempts at rationalization seem to have made some progress, notice that the due process decision really turns on a presumption of regularity built into a modest judicial posture. An attempt to address the cost-benefit question in a relatively rigorous fashion has demonstrated our (and any reviewing court's) inability to obtain the necessary data to refute that presumption convincingly. Analysis according to the competence model must proceed on the basis of rough judgments, assumptions, and case comparisons. And, if the post-*Eldridge* Supreme Court cases are any guide, those approaches have produced dramatic variance in judicial judgments and a nearly incomprehensible jurisprudence. The Court in *Eldridge*, ignorant of the facts, affirms the legislative-administrative judgment. Its only alternative seems to be the *Goldberg* approach—an approach that, similarly uninformed, merely affirms a different, more interventionist, vision of the judicial function.

The Problem of Assessing Errors. The difficulties of error assessment are perhaps even more daunting than our prior discussion has suggested. In programs like AFDC and DI there are quality assurance data that provide some basis for assessing error rates, and independent studies that use other techniques might sometimes be available. Yet these devices have the ironic feature of mocking the quest for accuracy, while simultaneously providing new information on its success. Consider, for example, a quality assurance (QA) system.[67] Such a system has two basic techniques at its disposal when reviewing a sample of claims decisions for correctness: it may focus on the outputs or on the inputs. If it chooses the former, it necessarily is second-guessing the initial decider. Moreover, it will be doing so on the basis of a cold record and outside the local context, which may lend weight to, or subtract it from, various information sources. How is the quality assurance reviewer to know that he or she is not introducing new errors rather than finding old ones?

The solution to this problem, adopted by almost every quality assurance system, is to limit the quality review concerning output errors to clear errors—situations in which there is no evidence to support the critical findings of fact. A quality reviewer who merely disagrees with the initial decision may be authorized to note a judgmental deficiency, but not an error. The structure of a QA review thus recognizes that there often is no objective and recognizable external referent for the decision being made. That a worker will be unable for the next twelve months to engage in substantial gainful activity is a prediction. A finding of "disabled" merely disguises this prediction as a fact.

Because of these inherent limitations on measuring output

---

67. For a general description of such a system see authorities cited at note 63 *supra*.

quality, quality assurance systems are oriented primarily to issues of development and documentation—to whether the examiner has compiled a record that provides an adequate basis for judgment. In short, a good quality assurance system is more concerned with inputs—the process of decision—than with second-guessing outputs; it recognizes the ultimately ineffable quality of accuracy. Error rates for QA are thus much more likely to produce information on how well low-level adjudicators follow procedural and evidentiary instructions than on how accurate their decisions are. Quality assurance data will only tell the Court how well the agency follows its own approved decisional routines.

This in no way suggests that a well-designed quality assurance system is not an extraordinarily useful management tool for discovering apparent trouble spots, for providing continuous feedback to decision makers, and for promoting consistency across deciders. It says instead that systematic efforts to improve quality, based on continuous collection and analysis of information about decisions, generally recognize that the relationship between the system's judgments about the quality of decisions and true states of the world is deeply problematic. A court attempting to use the findings of such a system to gauge the accuracy of a given decision process thus would have to know a great deal about the quality assurance system's design and about the dynamics of its operation in order to interpret the error-rate data that it produced.[68]

Determining Procedural Power. Like error assessment, the question of procedural power may be soluble, in part, if sufficient investment is made in its pursuit. In principle, for the administration of programs like AFDC or DI, the question can be answered. The design of a scientific investigation of the effects on accuracy of particular forms of hearing processes is certainly within the competence of social scientists, *provided*, of course, that they are prepared to use some proxies (the findings of a quality assurance review, the judgment of experts, the mean findings of multiple or repeated decisions, or something else)

68. *See generally* J. Mashaw, Bureaucratic Justice (1983).

for correctness. But it is unlikely that a more refined analysis of the effects on accuracy of some particular procedure—specific notice, oral versus written presentation, or the like—will be available when due process litigation arises. Experiments would have to be designed and run at substantial expense.

A serious demand for this sort of information thus begins to raise traditional legal issues of information costs—issues usually resolved by legal rules concerning the location of the burden of proof. Should we say that plaintiffs who fail to produce good data on procedural power lose? If so, we seem to be saying that all plaintiffs, at least of the *Goldberg-Eldridge* sort, lose. Or should we place the burden of production on the agency, provided that the plaintiffs make some plausible showing concerning the procedural power of their requested protection? And, if the latter, what could we mean by "plausible showing" other than arguments from the previously decried conventional wisdom?

A court could demand that litigants direct their attention to effects on accuracy rather than effects on reversals. Next, it could demand that arguments take account of the peculiar features of the program under review. For instance, who are the deciders? What is their training? Within what sort of incentive structure do they function? What are the discrete mental operations necessary for a decision? What information is necessary to these operations? Where is that information located, and who has the responsibility for producing it? What are the customary informational gaps? What are the decision rules for judgments under uncertainty? In this way, a functional context might be constructed within which to analyze or predict the effects on accuracy of changing one or several of the system's procedural characteristics.

This sort of approach is possible, and it may in part avoid the conventional wisdom. Nevertheless, it is time-consuming, costly, and problematic. A nonstereotyped, functional analysis of agency decision processes often will raise as many questions as it answers.[69] It perhaps also will suggest that modifications of the decision process, in ways that exceed the lawyer's usual proce-

---

69. *See generally* M. FEELEY, THE PROCESS IS THE PUNISHMENT (1979); J. MASHAW, C. GOETZ, F. GOODMAN, W. SCHWARTZ, P. VERKUIL, & M. CARROW, SOCIAL SECURITY HEARINGS AND APPEALS (1978).

dural claims, are necessary to assure accuracy. Such an inquiry thus broadens every judicial review proceeding into a general, albeit unscientific, study of the agency's structure, management, and processes. It invites all manner of novel claims concerning the decision process most appropriate to the activity under review. Once again the information demands of the competence methodology seem to trap us in a dilemma—a choice between ignorant abstention and a series of global inquiries that are themselves radically interventionist.

Controlling for Dynamic Effects. A highly specific inquiry into the functioning and relationship of various aspects of the decision process also will lead almost ineluctably to the question of how any change would affect patterns of behavior over time. The Supreme Court, obviously, needs some basis for believing that its reform of any particular area of procedure or practice will in fact have the salutary social welfare enhancing effects asserted to attend it. Indeed, a prediction about dynamic effects was used earlier as a strategic justification for shifting symmetrically distributed error costs from negative to positive ones in AFDC, but not in DI. This or any prediction about dynamic effects, however, clearly will be a risky business.

Not only do we lack the facts about future states of the world within which the procedural system will operate, but we also lack a good theory of the behavior of the agents who manipulate a procedural system in a well-defined universe. The prior assertion, that DI administrators might overreact to budgetary costs that exceeded social costs, presumed that the administrators would be concerned to constrain their budgets. Yet some explanations of administrative behavior argue that administrators instead are concerned with maximizing or stabilizing all or some part of their budgets.[70] These theories assert that budget constraint is externally imposed. Hence, our previous assumptions could be supported only by a specification of the external controls applicable to particular administrators, the preference orderings of these controlling institutions, and the expected equi-

70. *See generally* D. ARNOLD, CONGRESS AND THE BUREAUCRACY 20–26 (1979).

librium in the bargaining process between administrators and their external controllers.

Putting the question this way suggests that it is unanswerable. There are competing theories concerning the goals that motivate administrative, legislative, and pressure-group behavior. Even if there were agreement on the bargaining positions of the parties, that agreement would describe only a set of possible bargains. If a unique solution is required, it will not be forthcoming without some heroic assumptions. But we should not get carried away by this catalog of uncertainties. In the ordinary affairs of life, we do not expect to be able to control and predict all dynamic effects. Moreover, it seems clear that decisions not to act —to retain the status quo—also have unpredictable dynamic effects. We really have no choice but to choose. The question is: What can one say about sensible judicial management of the dynamic effects of judicial review of procedural adequacy?

The foregoing discussion suggests at least one caveat and one technique. The caveat is that the Court should not implicitly adopt a theory of bureaucratic behavior as a basis for predicting dynamic consequences without carefully examining it. It seems that reviewing courts often do just that; they seem to assume that a change will be made in legal procedures and that that change will have its desired instrumental effects. Because, over time, *ceteris* never is *paribus*, this would occur only if subsequent dynamic changes were managed in a way that protected the goal of social-cost minimization. But this assumes the relevant administrators have internalized that goal, are capable of acting on it, and accurately perceive the social context—in which case the arbitrariness of those administrators' prior procedures becomes inexplicable. Or, alternatively, it assumes the judicial decision subsequently will dominate all other forces in shaping the administrators' actions. In essence, this is what is sometimes called the "lawyer-domination" theory of bureaucratic behavior. That theory may be correct, but no one yet has demonstrated that it is. Nor can the Court content itself with the implicit adoption of this view simply because it supports the ideal of administrative regularity or the rule of law. The cost-minimization approach demands functional analysis of the efficacy of ideals.

The remedial technique suggested by a need to control dynamic effects is the so-called structural injunction. It probably is necessary to put the whole system at issue in every due process case in the way that a willingness to issue broad structural injunctions does. This would provide an incentive for the parties to address the procedural system as a whole, and to develop expert opinion or consensus on questions like procedural power or the dynamic effects of proposed changes. In many cases it may be necessary to initiate simultaneously a series of related structural changes in order to achieve the basic goals of social-cost reduction. Yet, saying this not only reinforces the idea that the model of competence makes immodest demands for information, it also raises in a stark form the much-rehearsed question of the appropriate role of courts in constitutional adjudication.

THE MODEL OF COMPETENCE AND THE CONSTITUTIONAL POSITION OF DUE PROCESS ADJUDICATION

The information demands of a social welfare calculation seem to make a restrained judicial posture very difficult to maintain. It is simply not possible to take competence seriously and, simultaneously, to make modest demands for information about the operation, context, and consequences of procedural systems. This holistic approach to procedural revision, including the ever-present possibility of structural injunction, indeed suggests a court sitting as supermanager of bureaucratic decision processes. An information-demanding posture is not necessarily an objectionable form of judicial activism. In the context of reviewing the substantive agency judgments for rationality, the Supreme Court has said that the inquiry may be searching, but the ultimate judgment deferential.[71] Administrators perhaps are less sanguine about the prospects for judgmental modesty after prodigious inquiry. More important, the inquiry/judgment distinction may miss the point. The prospect of searching inquiry may itself skew administrative responses to proceduralist de-

71. *See, e.g.*, Citizens to Preserve Overton Park Inc. v. Volpe, 401 U.S. 402, 416 (1971) ("Although this inquiry into the facts is to be searching and careful, the ultimate standard of review is a narrow one.").

mands in socially nonbeneficial directions. The judiciary may intrude as a threatening presence as well as by decree.

In reality, the Court has been restrained both in its inquiry and in its judgments. Administrative procedures have been rejected as inadequate in only about one in four of the post-*Eldridge* administrative due process cases decided by full opinion. Moreover, the Court's demands for factual information about procedural systems have been extremely modest. For inappropriate intervention describes only one horn of the judicial dilemma. The model of competence provides even richer possibilities for complete escape from judicial review of administrative process. Indeed, under one interpretation of the model's positivist orientation, abdication of constitutional review seems logically necessary. To observe the techniques by which restraint has been achieved without complete abdication of procedural due process review is thus to observe a Court in the process of rejecting the model that it is applying.

THE TECHNIQUES OF RESTRAINT

Given the breadth of civil rights actions pursuant to 42 U.S.C. §1983,[72] the availability of actions directly on the Constitution,[73] and the ease with which claims of inadequate process escape preliminary hurdles such as exhaustion of administrative remedies,[74] judicial restraint in administrative due process cases generally entails a judgment on the merits that approves legislative or administrative procedural choices. Techniques for implementing the passive virtues are often unavailable. The Court seems, nevertheless, to have at least three means for making merits judgments, while avoiding the exhaustive investigation into the facts and analysis of potential costs and benefits that the *Eldridge* criteria make relevant. The first is to emphasize the Court's limited scope of review and the primary responsibility of legislators and administrators for procedural design. The second is to deny that the claim relates to an interest that merits due process protection. The third is to take a commonsense ap-

72. *See, e.g.*, Carey v. Piphus, 435 U.S. 247 (1978).
73. *See, e.g.*, Butz v. Economou, 438 U.S. 478 (1978).
74. *See, e.g.*, Mathews v. Eldridge, 424 U.S. 319 (1976).

proach that makes all three factors point in the same (acceptable) direction.

THE CLOAK OF ADMINISTRATIVE DISCRETION

The "they're-the-experts" technique looked promising in *Eldridge* but has received very modest play since. Why this should be so is not obvious from the cases, nor indeed from the basic logic of the model of competence. If a wide-ranging exploration of the social costs of error, the influence of various procedural devices on accuracy, and the administrative context and political dynamics of decision making is required in order to make sensible judgments about procedural design; then surely time, resources, and experience all are on the side of nonjudicial institutions. Having explored the intricacies of the calculus in a few contexts, the Court might have done well to follow Justice Powell's lead in *Eldridge* and, by constantly asserting deference, to unify the jurisprudence of substantive procedural due process with that of substantive economic due process, around the rational-basis test.[75]

We can only speculate why this has not occurred, but the speculation does not operate in a vacuum: the Court has been unable to shed sufficient constitutional history to apply its modern criteria in a logical fashion. One of the great constitutional myths of the post-*Lochner* era is that—whatever its deference to the administrative state on matters concerning the *substance* of economic and social policy—legal *procedure*, judicially formulated and enforced, stands between the citizen and the government. This idea is given a definite form, as we saw in the discussion of the model of appropriateness, by the notion that *procedure* means preeminently judicial trial. It is reinforced by the companion convention that the experts with respect to trial technique, the courts, need not be intensely concerned when addressing process questions about their own competence vis-á-vis the judgments of coordinate or political branches of government. Procedural protection thus lies firmly within the Court's constitutional mandate.

75. The Court might be thought occasionally to have done so. *Cf*. New Motor Vehicle Bd. v. Orrin W. Fox Co., 439 U.S. 96 (1978).

These process myths represent the conventional wisdom of contemporary lawyers and courts. I do not want to attack them here beyond the reminder that much that I have said thus far argues against the possibility of untangling procedural and substantive questions. The more important point for present purposes is that, by subscribing to this conventional wisdom, the Court almost necessarily rejects the model of competence. For if the courts do have a special role to play in procedural matters, and if the model of judicial trial has (as Justice Frankfurter asserted in *McGrath*) an independent constitutional status, then it cannot also be the case that procedure is merely an instrumental device for the accomplishment of substantive or programmatic objectives devised by the legislature—unless one also makes the heroic assumption that trial-type processes are usually the best means for implementing legislative objectives.

I do not claim that this form of judicial heroism can never be discerned from the cases. It is amply displayed in the opinion in *Califano v. Yamasaki*.[76] But *Yamasaki* seems to me a demonstration more of the Court's rejection of the competence model and return to appropriateness analysis than an application of the *Eldridge* formula. *Yamasaki*, remember, involved a demand for an oral hearing as a prerequisite to SSA recoupment of overpayments from Social Security disability beneficiaries. The Social Security Act authorized recoupment of overpayments by deduction from future monthly benefits. Section 204(b) of the Act prohibits recoupment, however, if adjustment or recovery would tend either to "defeat the purposes" of the Act or to "be against equity and good conscience."[77] By rule, the Department of Health and Human Services had defined "equity and good conscience" to mean detrimental reliance on receipt of the incorrect amount when the beneficiary was in "good faith" and without "fault."[78] Under the challenged scheme, when a beneficiary applied for a waiver of the recoupment, both the determination that overpayment had occurred and the decision on the waiver application were made without providing the beneficiary with any personal access to the decision maker. Beneficiaries could,

76. 442 U.S. 682 (1979).
77. 42 U.S.C. § 404b (1976).
78. 20 C.F.R. § 404, 509 (1980).

however, obtain a subsequent oral hearing before an administrative law judge.

Employing the *Eldridge* error-costs approach, the *Yamasaki* Court approved SSA's procedure for determining the existence of overpayments without a hearing: "[T]he rare instance in which a credibility dispute is relevant to a[n overpayments] claim is [not] sufficient to require the Secretary to sift through all requests for reconsideration and grant a hearing to the few that involve credibility."[79] In short, the increased accuracy was not worth the cost.

The Court viewed the waiver question differently, however. It read the statute, which was entirely silent on the question, as requiring an oral hearing on waiver petitions prior to recoupment.[80] And, it came to this conclusion apparently by employing the *Eldridge* formula as a guide to statutory interpretation. First, the Court gave the waiver provision a strained reading by stressing the statute's imperative voice when it states that "there shall be no [recoupment]" from any person who qualifies for waiver.[81] Initially the argument seems to be that the legislature, rather than the due process clause, has demanded accuracy. The only wrinkle is that the statute demands perfection. No errors are tolerable. Yet if pressed, the Court surely would have to admit that eligibility conditions in a statutory benefits program could hardly be precatory; the imperative voice is standard legislative drafting. Moreover, given that certainty is infinitely elusive and, therefore, infinitely expensive, it hardly seems sensible to read the Congress as having demanded *that* level of accuracy for rejecting waivers although remaining satisfied, à la *Eldridge*, with a much less searching inquiry when rejecting claims. The opposite would make more sense.

Therefore, eschewing demands for the impossible, the distinction between the approved overpayments determination and the disapproved waiver determination should turn, in the standard *Eldridge* fashion, either on differences in the likelihood of error when making the determinations or on the power of hearings to produce accurate fact-finding. The Court, having no

79. 442 U.S. at 696.
80. *Id*. at 695.
81. *Id*. at 693–94.

data on either of these issues, chose the latter, relying on law-yers' conventional wisdom: "As the Secretary's regulations made clear, 'fault' depends on an evaluation of 'all pertinent circum-stances.' . . . Evaluating fault, like judging detrimental reliance, usually requires an assessment of the recipient's credibility, and written submissions are a particularly inappropriate way to dis-tinguish a genuine hard luck story from a fabricated tall tale."[82]

Perhaps this is so, but it certainly is unclear how the Court knows it. Experienced judges have testified vigorously that the traditional oral confrontational process enhances accuracy very modestly, if at all.[83] Furthermore, the Court does not know that any increased accuracy will be worth the cost. Is cost irrelevant because of the statute's imperative instruction to get it right? More fundamental, what does it mean to establish accurately someone's good or bad faith, fault or faultlessness? Are these characteristics facts? Or are they instead moral conclusions? And, if there are all these doubts about the worth of orality, how does the Court know that a silent Congress wanted it?

The answer, of course, is that the Court does not know it. *Yamasaki*, although apparently employing the *Eldridge* criteria, falls back on the intuitive bedrock of the appropriateness model —individual decisions should be made by oral, confrontational, trial-like processes. The model of competence provides abso-lutely no basis for making such an assumption. In adopting it the Court not only makes heroic assumptions, it also obviously lacks the courage of the model of competence's instrumentalist convictions. For those convictions demand either a more search-ing inquiry or, as *Eldridge* suggests, deference to informed ad-ministrative discretion.

Positivist Traps for the Unwary Proceduralist

The Court's ambivalence about the positivism of the compe-tence model is even clearer from the jurisprudence. A majority has refused to subscribe to Justice Rehnquist's bittersweet theory of protected entitlements. Indeed, the Court only intermittently

82. *Id.* at 697.
83. *See* Frankel *supra* note 60.

explores the question of entitlement with any seriousness. The occasions on which it has focused on the entitlements question and has refused to review contested procedures are sufficient to drive process-oriented constitutional law scholars quite wild.[84] Yet the logic of the positivist position, like the logic of legislative and administrative expertise, would imply a complete abdication of procedural due process review. Consider the following imaginary colloquy:[85]

COURT: What is your claim?

CITIZEN (former public school teacher): I was fired from my teaching job without a hearing. I am here to claim my due process rights.

COURT: What is your interest in this claim?

CITIZEN (puzzled): Well, isn't that obvious? I want a chance to defend myself, and I want my job back.

COURT: Wait, you misunderstood me. I want to know what interest you have that qualifies under the due process clause as an interest in "life, liberty, or property."

CITIZEN: Well, it's my life, isn't it? And, if I can't teach where I want to, I have lost my liberty. It is even possible, I guess, to say that I have lost property—my income—but that way of talking seems a little funny to me.

COURT: Where does it say that you have a "liberty" to teach in your former school?

CITIZEN: Eh?

COURT: Well, surely there is no general liberty to teach in your school. People can't walk in off the street and take up teaching anytime they want. What gives you that "liberty"?

CITIZEN: Oh, I get it. The school board hired me to teach there.

COURT: OK. So your "liberty" interest—or maybe we had better call it a "property" interest—is based on a contract with the school board. What does the contract say?

84. *See, e.g.*, Tushnet, *The Newer Property: A Suggestion for the Revival of Substantive Due Process*, 1975 SUP. CT. REV. 261.

85. The dialogue is suggested by the facts of Bd. of Regents v. Roth, 408 U.S. 564 (1972).

CITIZEN: Well, it doesn't really say anything much. I have a letter that says that I was appointed at such and such a salary. But that's about it.

COURT: Did the notice of appointment say anything about removal?

CITIZEN: No. But I assumed, if it came to that, there would be some fair way of going about it—not just dismissal with no hearing.

COURT: But surely you didn't think you can force a hearing on the board just because you assumed there would be one? You wouldn't think that the board could require you to clean the school's restrooms just because they had assumed when you were hired that you wouldn't mind adding that to your duties?

CITIZEN: Well, no, but . . .

COURT: Now, I don't mean to say that you don't have a property interest here in retaining your job until dismissed after a fair hearing. It may be that such an interest is "implied" in the contract of employment.

CITIZEN (warily): You say "implied" like it has some special meaning. How do we find out whether hearings are "implied" by my contract?

COURT: Well, there are several places to look. The school board may have rules or regulations that say something about dismissal. There may be general statutes or common law principles in your state that provide an interest in hearings before dismissal from public employment. Indeed, if you could establish that hearings were the practice of the school board in such cases, or that it led teachers generally to believe that there would be hearings associated with dismissals, I might find that you had a sufficiently reasonable expectation of a hearing that it was an implicit part of your property interest in your teaching contract.

CITIZEN: OK. I will see what I can find.

(Later, dejectedly) Well, I am afraid I couldn't find much. The rules just say that "teachers' appointments are for a stated term or during adequate performance." I am not even sure what that means. The only mention of a process relating to dismissal is a voting rule for the board that requires a majority vote for personnel actions made on the recommendation of a school principal and a two-thirds majority for all such actions in other cases. So far as I can tell, there have never been any hearings—at least there aren't any records. The general statutes are silent and the courts have never really decided the question. In all candor, though, I have to tell you that there is a lot of stuff in some judicial opinions about the "presumption" that employment contracts are terminable "at will."

COURT: Well, I am not too surprised. State law is often like that. But, as you seem to suspect, this report eliminates your due process claim. You don't have a "legal interest" to assert.

CITIZEN: I rather thought you might say that. I'll go away now, but before I go, could I ask a question?

COURT: Sure.

CITIZEN: Why is it that, although I came in here to assert a federal constitutional right, all we have talked about are contracts, state statutes, school board regulations, and state common law?

COURT: Because that's where we find the interests that the due process clause talks about, in the existing positive law of some jurisdiction. You don't expect us to just make these interests up, do you?

CITIZEN: No, I guess not. But I didn't expect the school board to get to make them up either. In fact, if they had agreed by contract or regulation to give me a hearing, I don't see why I would need a constitutional protection in the first place.

COURT: Next case.

The positivist trap need not, of course, have sprung shut on our citizen school teacher at the threshold of the claim. Back with a report on the state of the positive law in the jurisdiction, a more sympathetic response was possible:

COURT: I see. Well, the school board's rules certainly suggest something more than tenure at will. They seem to contemplate either a fixed term or tenure during good behavior. And the latter standard must presume some good faith method of determining the adequacy of the teacher's performance. Otherwise "adequate performance" would be the functional equivalent of "at will." I think you have demonstrated a sufficient property interest to justify a claim that due process demands some reasonable procedure for ascertaining the facts concerning the grounds for dismissal. Let's go forward with an inquiry into what process was, indeed, due here.

But the steel spring of positivist logic remains cocked. The satisfaction of positivism's threshold test does not preclude the application of positivism to the case later on, when it comes time to elaborate the specific requirements of due process. Let us return to the courtroom.

CITIZEN: Great. When do I get my hearing? Who issues the subpoenas for my witnesses? Will the board get a stenographer, or should I bring my tape recorder? What . . .

COURT: Not so fast. We haven't decided what kind of hearing is necessary here. Besides, the City Attorney is waving something at me.

CITY ATTORNEY: That's right, your honor. I have an affidavit here that states that the dismissal in question was by majority vote of the board on the basis of a recommendation of the teacher's principal. This case should be dismissed.

COURT: Well, I am glad to hear that the board followed its own rules. But what does that have to do with the plaintiff's due process claim?

CITY ATTORNEY: That's perfectly straightforward, your honor. The plaintiff's interest is one based on the implied promise of the board's rules. But, surely he can't read some but not all of the rules. And, the rules provide a procedure—recommendation of the principal plus a majority vote of the board. If the plaintiff expected more, that expectation had no basis in the rules or the general law of this state. It was a simple, subjective expectation (indeed, I might call it a hope or a wish), and we already know that that cannot provide the basis for imposing additional procedures on the board. The plaintiff has had the process that was due.

COURT: There is a certain logic to your position. But how does this fit into the *Mathews v. Eldridge* balancing test?

CITY ATTORNEY: Perfectly. The first question in that test is the importance of the claimant's interest. Now, as we know, that can't mean the importance the claimant attaches to it. Otherwise we are back to subjective measures—every person would be able to define his or her own process. The question is what importance or value can be reasonably assigned to the interest asserted.

Now it's obvious that the value of an interest includes not

only its substantive definition, but also the prospect that any particular person can claim or defend it. In short, the value of an interest is precisely its substantive value to the holder discounted by the probability of its retention. And, of course, the probability of retention is determined by the security of expectations provided by the process for allocating the substantive interest.

In this case, if you allow the plaintiff more process than the rules specify, you are creating that process for the protection of an interest that is *nowhere specified in the positive law*. The process set out in the rules both determines the real value of the plaintiff's interest in his employment contract and protects it to the full extent that procedural protection is due.

COURT: I am still troubled. What role is there for the due process clause in all this?

CITY ATTORNEY: In a case like this, only to stand behind the rules and ensure uniform application—no cooking up of special procedures for particular cases. If there were no procedure specified at all, then you might have to supply some via due process.

CITIZEN: But this is an outrage. Surely the court doesn't sit here to enforce the school board's crummy rules?

CITY ATTORNEY: I understand that you are angry. But the law doesn't operate on your sense of outrage. The question is what was a reasonable expectation concerning security of tenure under the positive law in existence. The answer to that question defines your interest. And, it hardly seems outrageous to treat your interest precisely as the rules say it will be treated. Maybe you, and other teachers, should have greater security in your jobs. But surely that is a substantive policy issue for legislative judgment.

Besides, the rules give you greater interests, both substantively and procedurally, than the general law of this jurisdiction concerning employment contracts. Your definition of your interest of necessity relies exclusively on the board's rules. As Justice Rehnquist says, you have to take the bitter with the sweet.

COURT (to Citizen): I am afraid he's right. I can't go around making up new values or interests and then new procedures to protect them. That's not my role.

Good luck in your job search.

CITIZEN: I think you've done it again—read the due process clause right out of the Constitution.

COURT: Next case.

There really is no escape from this position except to reject positivism. The Court must have done so,[86] otherwise its approach to due process cases would be limited to a (perhaps *Yamasaki*-style) determination of whether the procedure intended by the legislature or its delegate was in fact being used.

NINE UNHAPPY UTILITARIANS

As the Court's practice with respect to the first two techniques of judicial restraint suggests an inability to maintain its commitment to a model of due process adjudication that is positivist and instrumentalist, so too its practice in making social welfare assessments undermines belief in its commitment to utilitarianism. The Court seems determined not to engage in trade-offs, but instead to analyze each of the *Eldridge* factors in a

---

86. I use a logical deduction from behavior here rather than a survey of doctrine because, once again, confusion reigns. It is not really possible to determine what a majority of the Justices believe at this point. The remarkable twists and turns of individual Justices in procedural due process cases are worthy of a study in themselves. Perhaps the following will suffice to set the tone: In *Bishop v. Wood*, 426 U.S. 341 (1976), Justice White begins a dissent for himself and Justices Brennan, Marshall, and Blackmun by saying, "I dissent because the decision of the majority rests upon a proposition [the positivist trap] which was squarely addressed and in my view correctly rejected by six Members of this Court in *Arnett v. Kennedy*" *Id.* at 355 (White, J., dissenting). That statement implicitly criticizes Justice Powell, who—although he was caught with the majority in *Bishop*—rejected the lure of the trap in *Arnett v. Kennedy*, 416 U.S. 134, 166–67 (1974) (Powell, J., concurring in part and concurring in the result in part).

Justice White and his *Bishop* companions should not, however, wax too self-righteous. A look at *New Motor Vehicle Bd. v. Orrin W. Fox Co.*, 439 U.S. 96 (1978), reveals Justice White to have joined in a majority opinion written by Justice Brennan that is so wedded to the positivist view that it cannot distinguish a procedural from a substantive issue. *See* 439 U.S. at 106–08. And Justice Blackmun concurs in the classic *Bishop v. Wood* majority's style: "The abstract expectations of a new franchise does not qualify as a property interest." 439 U.S. at 113 (Blackmun, J., concurring). Meanwhile, Justice Stevens, who wrote the majority opinion in *Bishop*, was the sole dissenter in *Fox*, on grounds that necessarily give independent normative force to the words of the due process clause. *See* 439 U.S. at 114 (Stevens, J., dissenting).

fashion that permits each to serve as an independent ground for decision. It is this sort of rationalization that produced most of the outright contradictions recounted earlier. Some of the Court's other statements when it operates in this advocacy mode are equally wonderful. It has claimed, for example, that students do not really have an interest in hearings before being paddled because the delay engendered by hearings will intensify their anxiety and make the punishment more severe.[87] That remark caused one of *my* students to wonder whether the Court's sympathy someday would extend to summary capital punishment—at least for students.

The complexity of the analysis required by the model of competence cannot fully explain these contortions. The Court could eschew detailed investigation without insisting that every factor pointed in the same direction. The aversion here is not just to extensive investigation. It is to balancing interests in the course of a demonstration that general social welfare demands the suppression of individual claims to procedural protection.

The reason for this aversion is not difficult to fathom. A claim to due process, like a claim to any other Bill of Rights protection, is precisely a claim to the protection of minority interests in the face of majority desires. If the greatest good for the greatest number is the test for constitutionality under the due process clause, then it is hard to escape the notion that the best evidence of social welfare will always be the judgment of the legislature or its delegate. It is the Congress (and state legislatures), not the Court, that has the constitutional mandate to "promote the general welfare." The Court's accepted role is to say when individual constitutional rights trump legislative welfare judgments. To engage in real balancing is to rip the due process clause loose from its constitutional moorings and to reveal the Court engaged in a truly legislative function. General welfare simply will not do as a judicial measure of constitutional right. The Court, therefore, must deny that any serious trading of individual for collective interests is going on.

87. Ingraham v. Wright, 430 U.S. 651 (1977).

CONTINUING CONFUSION
AND THE PATH TO REFORM

Due process doctrine is at present at least as confused as when Professor Kadish reviewed it in the 1950s. The model of competence is a fiasco at the level of judicial review. Although promising transparency and generality, it has produced instead an opaque and Balkanized jurisprudence that can only hope to be understood within the particular context of specific programs or substantive fields of activity (education, public employment, or the like).[88] Indeed, one case seems to say that the due process question is a question of fact to be assessed differently by different trial and appellate courts hearing cases raising identical issues about identical administrative functions.[89] By comparison, the model of appropriateness is not only modest and wise, it is clear. Moreover, to the extent that there is a substantive thread in the jurisprudence, some find that it is not support for the rational impersonality of bureaucratic legality—the rule of law in the administrative state—but rather a shoring up of the traditional personal authority of parents, teachers, doctors, and public employers.[90]

The model of competence asks an important functional question, but it is a question that cannot be answered within the context of constitutional adjudication. The question is one of policy highly dependent upon unavailable social facts. In this functional failure, the methodology reveals its symbolic inappropriateness. For there is no principle here that can be defended against majoritarian desire. The general welfare, the greatest good for the greatest number, in this model *is* the principle purportedly to be defended. Where the Court gets better information about general welfare than the legislature, however, remains mysterious. And why it should continue to try to do so is explained neither by the success of its doctrinal explanations nor

88. *See, e.g.*, Wilkinson, *Goss v. Lopez: The Supreme Court as School Superintendent*, 1975 Sup. Ct. Rev. 25.
89. Lassiter v. Dep't of Social Servs., 452 U.S. 18, 31 (1981).
90. *See* Burt, *The Constitution of the Family*, 1979 Sup. Ct. Rev. 329.

by the structure of the Constitution. As a means for structuring the constitutional conversation about governmental forms the model of competence surely deserves to be abandoned at the earliest opportunity.

It may be possible to modify any or all of the competence model's attributes to provide a more satisfactory account of the post-*Goldberg* jurisprudence. But the definition of a coherent and acceptable approach to administrative due process questions is not advanced very far by recharacterizing the jurisprudence as *sometimes* positivist; *usually*, but not always, instrumentalist in an accuracy-seeking mode; and interest balancing, but *not necessarily* utilitarian. If positive law does not provide the identification and relative value of interests, what does? If process promotes something other than accuracy, what is it? And, if the Court is to balance interests without becoming utilitarian, or perhaps to eschew interest balancing in favor of rights enforcing, exactly how is it to go about these things in a coherent and acceptable fashion?

There are no answers to these questions in the contemporary jurisprudence. Nevertheless, to address them preliminarily will give us some idea of the sort of theory that we must pursue in the pages that follow. They point out the starting point of the path to reform.

Nonutilitarian Interest Balancing

Suppose we abandon social welfare talk. What then are the possibilities for a theory of due process? Such a theory might be of two general types. One would eschew interest balancing in favor of rights enforcing. But this hardly seems promising. It would require first that due process be given a determinate content and that that well-defined decision process be applied in all relevant contexts of administrative decision making. The Court has always—well, usually—resisted this particular temptation. And whereas one might point out any number of defects in such an approach in the specific context of the due process clause, we might rest content with one general objection: we cannot sustain a vision of the world in which rights ring out true and clear, unencumbered by the consideration of the conflicting claims of others to scarce social resources. It is the fundamentally compromised nature of social life that interest balancing recognizes and confronts. Any attempt at absolute rights can result only in the subsumption of problem solving in formal categories and in the misdirection and hypocrisy that the degenerate tendencies of the appropriateness model demonstrated so well.

Rights theorists, nevertheless, clearly are concerned with a critical issue. The requirement that rights be asserted provides both a legitimate occasion for judicial intervention and a means for restricting the domain of judicial action. The demand for a claim of right can prevent the Court from becoming a simple council of revision. Moreover, whether we call these claims to due process rights or interests, and whether we balance or not, we have to have some idea of what the Court is protecting with the due process clause. The rights theorist is surely correct that there can be no neutral constitutional decision making. We must know what counts as constitutional value, and if we balance, how to go about balancing the things that count against each other when they inevitably conflict. It is this question, above all, that an adequate theory of due process adjudication should address.

Quasi Positivism

The positivist, of course, has an answer to the "what's-being-protected" question. The interest that gives rise to the due process claim is the interest to be balanced against other competing interests. Yet this position is hardly satisfactory. For one thing, it results in some of the perverse conclusions that we have previously encountered—for example, that nursing home residents have no recognizable interest whatever in the decertification of their nursing home, whereas a prisoner's traditional common law property interest in a lost $23.50 hobby kit demands full-dress appraisal of whether his due process rights have been infringed. And, second, the positivist position provides no basis for second-guessing the balance of interests that the legislature has provided through whatever procedural vehicles exist for the protection of the interests recognized by the positive law.

We can of course imagine, indeed describe, the Court as not committed to the extreme positivist position, which would recognize only clear common law or statutory interests as worthy of protection and which would abandon further constitutional due process review. But to what is it or should it be committed? If positive law does not define exhaustively the relevant interests to be protected, what does? The Court? How? What are the criteria of recognition? And when protecting entitlements that are positively defined, how can the Court escape the second positivist trap, without asserting that procedure just happens to be the Court's business rather than the legislature's? That is a decidedly odd assertion in a constitutional system that presumes that the source of the Court's jurisdiction to make its *own* procedural rules is delegated legislative power. To become quasi positivist is thus only to raise, not to answer, the basic questions of the source and nature of the interests that due process adjudication protects.

Accuracy as a Function of X

Another way of conceiving of the right that is at stake in due process adjudication is as a right to an accurate determination. I have already suggested that this conception is underinclusive. We may be concerned, as the Court is in *Yamasaki* and in the irrebuttable presumption cases, with the use of general and impersonal rules to decide highly individualized and context-specific questions such as good faith or parental fitness. But accuracy or potential inaccuracy hardly captures our concern. Moreover, to the extent that official processes *create*, or simultaneously create and apply, legal norms, accurate implementation is irrelevant. We are understandably uncomfortable with the notion that wherever accuracy is not a principle goal of decision making, due process is inapplicable. Indeed, once total positivism is eschewed, there seems no reason to imagine that accurate implementation captures all, or even the core, of what is meant to be protected by due process of law.

Moreover, it is not possible to think of accuracy as a due process right without a further elaboration of the values that accuracy might support. Eschewing the impossible dream of perfect accuracy, surely the constitutional command could be only a requirement of reasonable accuracy. But reasonable in relation to what? In order to answer that question, we have to know what values accuracy supports and how administrative decision processes affect those values. Having abandoned positivism, we seem to be left only with a placeholder, $f(X)$. Giving content to this unknown term in the due process equation is the task of the next three chapters.

4 / *Toward a Model of Dignitary Values*

THE NATURAL RIGHTS TRADITION IN
DUE PROCESS ADJUDICATION

The Supreme Court's approach to the due process clause always has been something more than a search for appropriateness and competence. History and precedent may be *evidence* of the constitutional limits on legitimate governmental activity that are appropriate to maintaining the conception of individual liberty that we affirm; reasonably accurate processes of decision making may be instrumentally essential to individual security; but these traditional legal forms and intermediate values seem in the end only means for approaching and supporting some more fundamental conception of due process. They do not define the core ideal. It thus is not surprising that the Court has sought sometimes to consult directly the basic values that are instinct in American constitutionalism in order to discern from them the limitations that due process imposes on the forms of collective governance. Indeed, this direct, generally intuitive, approach to the development of the natural rights of individuals, and derivatively the fundamental features of procedural fairness, has a strong historical claim to our attention. For in *Hurtado v. California*,[1] only thirty years after *Murray's Lessee*, the Court seemed to

1. 110 U.S. 516 (1884).

158

abandon the sanctions of custom and precedent for a test that asked only whether a procedure was "essential to the idea of due process of law."[2]

At issue in *Hurtado* was whether the Fourteenth Amendment's due process clause required that California employ grand jury indictment, rather than prosecutorial information, for capital offenses. Although grand jury indictment was the practice in England, at the federal level in the United States and in all states save California, the Court held that grand jury indictment was not required by due process of law. Indeed, *Hurtado* declared, "to hold that such a characteristic is essential to due process of law, would be to deny every quality of the law but its age, and to render it incapable of progress or improvement."[3] Due process did not demand particular historic forms of procedure, but rather protection of "the very substance of individual rights to life, liberty and property."[4] Equally interesting, the *Hurtado* Court made explicit the potential link between legislative action and the individual's rights to due process of law. For the Court continues, the "greatest security" for those rights "resides in the right of the people to make their own laws and alter them at their pleasure."[5]

Hurtado is in no sense a "sport." Although, historically, appropriateness has been the dominant methodological strain in the jurisprudence, *Hurtado's* conception of natural rights, or fundamental principles of liberty and justice, is both a close competitor and a methodological partner to the model of appropriateness. Indeed, many might view the historic competition between these two models as a draw, or perhaps give the edge to the natural rights contender. There is repeated evidence of natural rights thinking, for example, in pre-*Hurtado* constructions of the Fourteenth Amendment.[6] The economic substantive due

2. 110 U.S. at 529.
3. *Id.*
4. 110 U.S. at 532.
5. 110 U.S. at 534–35.
6. *See, e.g.*, The Slaughterhouse Cases, 83 U.S. (16 Wall.) 36, 116 (1873) (dissenting opinion of Justice Field), Butcher's Union, Co. v. Crescent City, Co., 111 U.S. 746, 762 (1883) (concurring opinion of Justice Bradley); Loan Ass'n v. Topeka, 87 U.S. 655, 662 (1874).

process cases of the late nineteenth and early twentieth centuries clearly were saturated with natural rights ideas.[7] And when the Court abandoned economic liberty or liberty of contract as a constitutional ideal, it did not abandon the notion of natural rights. For it is the idea of fundamental individual liberties that underlies the selective incorporation of Bill of Rights protections in Fourteenth Amendment due process[8] and the development of additional nonenumerated protections for familial integrity[9] and individual physical autonomy.[10] Moreover, fundamental fairness has, since *Hurtado*, been the cornerstone of due process adjudication relating to criminal (and quasi-criminal) procedural and evidentiary standards.

The partnership of the fundamental fairness and appropriateness approaches is equally pervasive, but often subtle and ambiguous. What we called the core of the appropriateness model —the model of judicial trial—for example, might be characterized as the method that best captures the sense of fairness in a common law culture. Conversely, the search for ideas of fairness that are fundamental may, as *Hurtado* demonstrates, include a wide-ranging investigation of custom and the history of legal institutions. Supreme Court majorities may include justices whose opinions emphasize tradition and custom along with those emphasizing fundamental fairness ideas. The same cases thus often serve as examples of both methodologies.[11]

CONTEMPORARY INTEREST IN THE NATURAL RIGHTS APPROACH

Natural rights ideas increasingly have populated the contemporary debate concerning administrative due process. For however confusing the Court's words in the post-*Eldridge* due pro-

---

7. *See, e.g.*, Mugler v. Kan., 123 U.S. 623 (1887); Allgeyer v. La., 165 578 (1897); Lochner v. N.Y., 198 U.S. 45 (1905).

8. *E.g.*, Powell v. Ala., 287 U.S. 45 (1932); Betts v. Brady, 316 U.S. 455 (1941); Palko v. Conn., 302 U.S. 319 (1937); Adamson v. Cal., 332 U.S. 45 (1946).

9. *E.g.*, Griswold v. Conn., 381 U.S. 479 (1965).

10. *E.g.*, Roe v. Wade, 410 U.S. 113 (1973).

11. *See, e.g.*, Chicago, B. & Q. R.R. v. Chicago, 166 U.S. 226 (1897); Twining v. N.J., 211 U.S. 78 (1908); Powell v. Ala., 287 U.S. 45 (1932).

cess jurisprudence, its actions reveal a significant retrenchment from its procedurally interventionist posture in the early 1970s. And as the due process promises of *Goldberg v. Kelly* were revealed to contain conditions that rendered those promises non-negotiable in a variety of contexts,[12] legal scholars attempted to change the shape and direction of the analysis used in defining administrative due process. Commentators demanded a more "responsive approach to procedural protection,"[13] discussed "the limits of interest balancing,"[14] attempted to patch up the "cracks in the new property,"[15] and described "associational aims"[16] in processes of public decision making. Indeed, quite apart from constitutional analysis of the due process clause, Richard Stewart described the modern contours of administrative law—as defined both by statute and by judicial decree—as shaped by an "interest representation model" of administration that seeks to involve in the process of decision making all of the persons or groups affected by any administrative action.[17] More general still, Robert Summers made a "plea for process values"[18] with respect to all public decisional processes. The unifying thread in this literature[19] is the belief that the ways in which legal processes define participants and regulate participa-

12. Paul v. Davis, 424 U.S. 693 (1976) (hearing or other procedures *not* required before state withdraws or alters status not initially recognized by state law); Mathews v. Eldridge, 424 U.S. 319 (1976) (hearing *not* required before termination of Social Security disability payments); Bd. of Regents v. Roth, 408 U.S. 564 (1972) (hearing *not* required before nonrenewal of nontenured state teacher's employment contract).

13. Saphire, *Specifying Due Process Values: Toward a More Responsive Approach to Procedural Protection*, 127 U. Pa. L. Rev. 111 (1978).

14. Note, *Specifying the Procedures Required by Due Process: Towards Limits on the Use of Interest Balancing*, 88 Harv. L. Rev. 1510 (1975).

15. Van Alstyne, *Cracks in "The New Property": Adjudicative Due Process in the Administrative State*, 62 Cornell L. Rev. 445 (1977).

16. Michelman, *Formal and Associational Aims in Procedural Due Process*, in Due Process, Nomos XVIII, at 126 (J. Pennock & J. Chapman eds. 1977).

17. Stewart, *The Reformation of American Administrative Law*, 88 Harv. L. Rev. 1667, 1711–1813 (1975).

18. Summers, *Evaluating and Improving Legal Processes: A Plea for "Process Values,"* 60 Cornell L. Rev. 1 (1974).

19. There is other relevant legal literature, *e.g.*, Dauer & Gilhool, *The Economics of Constitutionalized Repossession: A Critique for Professor Johnson, and a Partial Reply*, 47 S. Cal. L. Rev. 116 (1973); Thibaut & Walker, *A Theory of Procedure*, 66 Cal. L. Rev. 541 (1978).

tion, not just the rationality of substantive results, must be considered when judging the legitimacy of public decision making.

I label approaches that reflect this perception "dignitary theories" of due process. Although the writers who make up this emerging school sometimes refer to values intrinsic to or inherent in the processes themselves,[20] it seems reasonable to interpret their concern instead as a concern for values inherent in or intrinsic to our common humanity—values such as autonomy, self-respect, or equality, which might be nurtured or suppressed depending on the form that governmental decision making takes. These values are the contemporary heirs to the legacy of *Hurtado* and the natural rights tradition.

THE APPEAL OF A DIGNITARY THEORY

INTUITIVE PLAUSIBILITY

At an intuitive level, a dignitary approach is appealing. We all feel that process matters to us irrespective of result. This intuition may be a delusion. We may be so accustomed to rationalizing demands for improvement in our personal prospects, in the purportedly neutral terms of process fairness, that we can no longer distinguish between outcome-oriented motives and process-oriented arguments. Thibaut and Walker's experimental work,[21] which tends to demonstrate that (at least under certain circumstances) people seek to maximize their personal involvement in decisional processes and that they gauge the fairness of processes by the degree of that participation,[22] may, after all, merely demonstrate that we generally regard control, or the opportunity for personal strategic behavior, as the best protection for our substantive concerns.[23]

Yet there seems to be something to the intuition that process

20. *E.g.*, L. TRIBE, AMERICAN CONSTITUTIONAL LAW 502 (1978) (citing Michelman, *supra* note 16); Saphire, *supra* note 13, at 120–21.
21. J. THIBAUT & L. WALKER, PROCEDURAL JUSTICE (1975); Walker, Lind, & Thibaut, *The Relation between Procedural and Distributive Justice*, 65 VA. L. REV. 1401 (1979).
22. J. THIBAUT & L. WALKER, *supra* note 21, at 1415–20; Walker, Lind, & Thibaut, *supra* note 21, at 1415–20.
23. I do not mean to imply that the studies by Thibaut, Walker, *et al.*, fail to distinguish between perceptions of means (process) and ends (outcomes). I do

Toward a Model of Dignitary Values / 163

itself matters. We *do* distinguish between losing and being treated unfairly. And, however fuzzy our articulation of the process characteristics that yield a sense of unfairness, it is commonplace for us to describe process affronts as somehow related to disrespect for our individuality, to our not being taken seriously as persons.[24] Imagine, for example, being excluded from voting. Disenfranchisement in a general election carries with it a loss of political power so minute that cold calculation should convince us that our personal franchise in practical, political terms is valueless.[25] But something—the affront to our self-image as citizens, our sense of the unfairness of exclusion—has led some of us to pursue this valueless privilege to participate in political decision making through every available court.[26] Involvement in the process of political decision making, through the exercise of a right to participation as a voter, seems to be valued for its own sake. The same may well be true for other processes.[27]

Avoiding Positivist Traps

The appeal of dignitary theory goes beyond simple intuition. A dignitary approach suggests a means to recognize and integrate the connection between substance and procedure without falling into one of the positivist traps previously described.[28] A dignitary theory can view the nature of the process claimant's substantive legal claim as irrelevant to the question of his or her

not, however, believe that they have been able to isolate perceptions of process that relate necessarily to some dimension of process other than its potential to provide a favorable outcome via either personal participation or the participation of an advocate committed to the claimant's cause. Indeed, their account of what is at work in a favorable or unfavorable perception of processes seems rather muddled. See Walker, Lind, & Thibaut, *supra* note 21, at 1415–20.

24. As Justice Brennan, writing for himself and Justices White and Marshall, put it in *Paul v. Davis*, "I have always thought that one of this Court's most important roles is to [protect] the legitimate expectations of every person to innate human dignity and sense of worth." 424 U.S. 693, 734–35 (1976) (Brennan, J., dissenting). For similar sentiments, see the cases collected in Saphire, *supra* note 13, at 121–24.

25. *See* J. Buchanan & G. Tullock, The Calculus of Consent (1962).

26. *See, e.g.,* Kramer v. Union Free School Dist. No. 15, 395 U.S. 621 (1969); Harper v. Va. Bd. of Elections, 383 U.S. 663 (1966).

27. Examples of other types of process exclusions are developed in Summers, *supra* note 18, at 1–30.

28. Chapter 3 *supra* at 145–51.

process rights. The issue is, instead, whether the challenged process sustains or diminishes an appropriate conception of human dignity. The statutory or common law characterization of the claimant's interest, or its relative social value as represented by the general pattern of positive norms, is perhaps evidence of the relative importance of dignitary values, and their protection, in differing contexts. But these sources can hardly be definitive. From the dignitary perspective, the search is for constitutional fundamentals, not legislative contingencies.

There is, of course, an element of finesse here. One meaning of substantive rights (rights to autonomy, equality, and self-respect) has been substituted for another (rights to a job, welfare payments, or the like). The difficult problem of delineating an appropriate judicial role in the determination of substantive values has been avoided simply by asserting that judicial definition of constitutionally significant dignitary concerns *is* the core function of due process adjudication. It remains to be seen whether dignitary theory can develop a persuasive case for that role. Persuasiveness will doubtless turn both on the degree to which the values asserted to be dignitary values can be seen to be at the core of our traditional conceptions of liberal democracy; and on the degree to which effectuation of those values, through constitutional adjudication, challenges contrary legislative judgments concerning legal process characteristics. For the legitimacy of *any* judicial revision of legislative judgments is a serious question in versions of liberal constitutionalism that permit more than a minimal state.[29]

29. Suffice it to say that I find unpersuasive the escapes from positivist traps suggested by Michelman, *supra* note 16, and by Tushnet, *The Newer Property: A Suggestion for the Revival of Substantive Due Process*, 1975 SUP. CT. REV. 261, 277–86. The former first suggests an allocation of roles between legislature and court—substantive rights definition for the legislature, procedural rights definition for the courts—that is premised on a supposed presupposition in the Supreme Court's implicit positivism that holds that substantive rights can only perform their office by setting bounds on zones of autonomy if procedures exist for effective implementation that are not themselves subject to legislative manipulation. Michelman, *supra* note 16, at 134. The Supreme Court (some Justices) may, indeed, (sometimes) hold this view, but it is hardly a coherent positivist position. Nor does it explain what underlies the presupposition limiting the legislature's legitimate province. Michelman's later suggestion that fake or quasi entitlements are sometimes found when the Court wants to require procedures in cases in which actual positive entitlements cannot be claimed, *id.* at 145–48, may again be

A Broadened Perspective

Closely connected with a desire to avoid positivist snares is a desire to broaden the range of due process inquiry. As detailed in chapter 3, the currently dominant due process approach is instrumentalist as well as positivist. The goodness of a procedure is determined by assessing its capacity for accurate fact-finding and for appropriate application of substantive legal norms to the facts as found. Claims to process protections become mediate or instrumentalist claims to facilitating structures for the protection of substantive rights.

There is no obvious reason, however, as the discussion of *O'Bannon* illustrates, why people should be more concerned with protecting their process rights with regard to existing substantive entitlements, than with protecting their participation in the processes by which substantive entitlements are defined.[30] Yet the Supreme Court has repeatedly denied that it is concerned, when interpreting the due process clause, with judging the appropriateness of the processes of legislative or quasi-legislative lawmaking, save as they approach the adjudicative mode.[31]

A Promise of Constitutional Coherence

The demand for accurate decision making seems to misdirect due process analysis. The due process clause is part of a

---

a way of describing the dominant jurisprudence, but it similarly avoids the critical question: What justifies an assertion of judicial power to constitutionalize administrative procedure? (I nevertheless think Michelman's analysis leads in a generally appropriate direction.)

Tushnet faces the problem squarely, recognizing that the issue is one of defining constitutional liberties. But the methodology he suggests is so wide-ranging—he calls it the "criteria of social importance"—that it belies his earlier claim to embrace substantive due process without *Lochnerian* excess. Tushnet *supra*, at 277–80. (For my approach to the same issue, see Mashaw, *Constitutional Deregulation: Notes toward a Public, Public Law*, 54 Tul. L. Rev. 849 (1980).)

30. *See generally* Cooper, *Goldberg's Forgotten Footnote: Is There a Due Process Right to a Hearing Prior to the Termination of Welfare Benefits When the Only Issue Raised Is a Question of Law?* 64 Minn. L. Rev. 1107 (1980); Comment, *Due Process Rights of Participation in Administrative Rulemaking*, 63 Cal. L. Rev. 886 (1975).

31. *See, e.g.*, Vt. Yankee Nuclear Power Corp. v. Natural Resources Defense Council, Inc., 435 U.S. 519, 542 & n. 16 (1978).

family of procedural protections contained in the Bill of Rights and made applicable to the states by the Civil War amendments. It is, therefore, at least arguable that its meaning should emerge by attention to concerns similar to those other protections. Yet the striking thing about protections such as jury trial, the prohibition against self-incrimination, or search and seizure restrictions, is that they make accurate decision making take second place to concerns about individual liberty. Why should accuracy be the sole concern of administrative due process? Why should it be a concern at all?

The Court has made use of accuracy as a constitutional value to reach results that many applaud—the protection of welfare entitlements in cases like *Goldberg* and *Yamasaki*, and the amelioration of potentially unjust effects by the rigid application of general rules in the irrebuttable presumption cases, to name but two categories. Yet if we approve of these cases, we surely must base our approval on some rationale other than improvement in the accuracy of administrative decision making. For *Goldberg* induces more errors than it corrects; *Yamasaki* involves a context in which accuracy is almost meaningless; and the irrebuttable presumption doctrine is unworkable. We are concerned with how bureaucracies treat individuals, but accuracy just does not capture that concern adequately. A dignitary theory that sought to articulate, defend, and effectuate a process-oriented conception of procedural due process just *might* discover, in its quest for the core conditions of individual dignity, principles that could both explain and limit individual demands for particularized official responsiveness.[32]

A dignitary perspective thus holds out the prospect of returning procedural due process to the family of individualistic concerns that are represented by constitutional values such as privacy, free expression, and religious freedom. It would also connect the methodology of administrative due process—a search for fundamental dignitary values—with the value matrix

32. For other attempts to deal with this issue, see Mashaw, *Conflict and Compromise Among Ideals of Administrative Justice*, 1981 DUKE L.J. 181; Tribe, *Perspectives on Bakke: Equal Protection, Procedural Fairness, or Structural Justice?*, 92 HARV. L. REV. 864 (1979); Tribe, *Structural Due Process*, 10 HARV. C.R.-C.L.L. REV. 269 (1975) [hereinafter cited as *Structural Due Process*].

that finds substantive due process expression both in the incorporation doctrine and in the Court's development of certain nonenumerated constitutional rights. It would, in sum, reconcile procedural due process analysis with the spirit of the Constitution.

THE CHALLENGE OF A DIGNITARY PERSPECTIVE

Recognizing that a dignitary approach to due process analysis has intuitive appeal, responds to contemporary concerns about a burgeoning administrative state, and tantalizes us with the prospect of a nonpositivist, yet coherent and satisfying, constitutional theory may propel our inquiry; but that vision leaves us far short of an account of what such a constitutional theory would propose, how it might be justified, and how it would evolve in the due process jurisprudence. Indeed, dignitary theorizing may fail at any of these points: (1) It may not be possible to elaborate a plausible set of process values. (2) If elaborated, these values may be impossible to support by satisfactory justificatory argument. And, (3) even if given a principled and coherent justification, the set of validated process values may yet fail us in application. On the one hand, a dignitary approach may go too far: a robust value matrix might demand more of administrative government than a world of scarce resources can admit. On the other hand, a dignitary approach might not go far enough: the set of plausible and justifiable values that can be forced into the mold of an adjudicable constitutional complaint might appear anemic in comparison with the issues that an elaborate due process jurisprudence confronts. Here again, dignitary theory might prove inadequate to the task.

Indeed, throughout its post-*Hurtado* history, the use of dignitary ideas in due process adjudication has seemed deeply problematic. Whether the fundamental value is adequate notice, grand jury indictment, freedom of contract, or the right to abort, the Court has had continuing difficulty explaining the source of the right it has enunciated. Often the opinions seem nothing more than the assertion of an intuition or of moral outrage.[33] And mere assertion suggests that the simple preferences

33. *E.g.*, Brown v. Miss., 297 U.S. 278, 286 (1935).

of an activist or a restraint-oriented majority are being made constitutional dogma. Yet the Court's few attempts at methodological rigor have fared little better. Justice Black sought refuge in a formalist incorporation doctrine[34]; Justice Douglas and Goldberg in some dimly perceived analogical method[35]; the current Court in scientism[36] and the rote recitation of precedent.[37]

Intuition has not and will not sit well with the commentators.[38] The Court's candid recognition that constitutional adjudication defines values is often sparingly praised on the way to turning such judicial candor into a fault. For the enunciation or denial of rights in this fashion seems to proceed from no unifying theory of individual dignity firmly connected to our constitutional tradition. If the Court is to rule on the basis of a moral or political theory of human dignity, then it must articulate and defend such a theory. But how is that abstract task to be accomplished responsibly in the context of deciding discrete controversies? Indeed, what are the chances that abstract political theory will provide the answers to the issues raised by specific cases?

I do not raise these problems merely to dismiss them. The argument that follows comes essentially to this: a dignitary approach to administrative due process does have some of the merits preliminarily ascribed to it. It can provide a theoretical grounding for the models of process that the appropriateness methodology employs by analogy and derives from tradition. It can explain the relevance of competent administration to the fundamental value of human dignity. It can provide a more satisfying basis for analyzing some of the issues that arise from our desire to maintain individual autonomy in an increasingly bureaucratic state. It can promote judicial restraint, while at the same time focusing and occasionally expanding judicial action.

But the model, as I portray it, will remain troublesome from

34. *See, e.g.,* Betts v. Brady, 316 U.S. 455 (1941) (Black dissent).
35. *See* Franklin, *The Ninth Amendment as Civil Law Method and Its Implications for Republican Form of Government: Griswold v. Connecticut; South Carolina v. Katzenbach*, 40 Tul. L. Rev. 487 (1966).
36. *Cf.* Roe v. Wade, 410 U.S. 113 (1973).
37. Lassiter v. Dep't of Social Servs., 452 U.S. 18, 26–27 (1981).
38. For a nice discussion of why not, see R.M. Hare, *Abortion and the Golden Rule*, 4 Phil. & Pub. Affairs 201 (Spring 1975).

a number of perspectives. Its core values do not necessarily include the versions of active, participatory, democratic public life
that inform the voluntarist strain of liberal democratic thought,
whether that voluntarism is the voluntarism of Rousseau,[39]
Arendt,[40] Barber,[41] or Nozick.[42] The model therefore will dis-
appoint some liberals and some conservatives alike. The rights
that emerge, including rights of participation, often are prudential and contingent. Indeed, I continue to believe, with Bentham, that most natural rights talk is "nonsense on stilts." The
question is not what rights are natural to persons, but what
rights persons must have to maintain a particular liberal-democratic polity. I can specify no algorithm for the unimpeachable
resolution of due process claims. I have not solved the problem
of how to combine political philosophy with constitutional adjudication. My arguments for a dignitary approach are marked
by the frustrating interplay of logic and contingency common
to all such efforts. I will not offer support to those who would
move constitutional analysis beyond liberty and toward community; my theory leaves the implementation of communitarian
ideals at a subconstitutional level. For I believe not all institution
building is or should be accomplished through constitutional
adjudication.

I will argue that the dignitary approach is both necessary to
and sufficient for an adequate jurisprudence of due process. It
is necessary because an acceptable jurisprudence must be able to
structure a conversation about public values that is both relevant
to our real concerns and consistent with our constitutional traditions. And as we have discovered, neither the model of competence nor the model of appropriateness has been equal to this
task. The dignitary model is sufficient because it provides a theoretical and historical grounding for the articulation of due
process values, and a methodology of adjudication that can address the crucial issues of legitimacy in the administrative state.

The chapters that follow will attempt to prove the sufficiency

39. J.J. Rousseau, Contrat Social (Nouvelle Ed. 1875).
40. H. Arendt, On Revolution (1965).
41. B. Barber, Strong Democracy: Participatory Politics for a New Age (1984).
42. R. Nozick, Anarchy, State and Utopia (1974).

claim twice. Chapter 5 will involve an argument from philosophic tradition. After canvassing some of the intuitively attractive candidates for due process values, I shall attempt to justify constitutionalizing those values by reference to the basic tradition of liberal democratic thought that underlies our constitution. The analysis produces a consensus set of values and then illustrates their application to some of the major cases that have punctuated the discussion of prior models. The methodology that emerges is an instrumentalist-balancing analysis, and to that degree is reminiscent of the model of competence. But in spite of these similarities, the dignitary model reveals very different core values and prudential concerns.

The second argument, in chapter 6, takes a quite different form. It attempts to provide a direct linkage between the central problem of nondomination in a liberal democracy and the customary forms of decision making in American governance. These forms are then shown to be heuristics that have a particular liberal-democratic content. With this recognition, it becomes possible to reinterpret the appropriateness model with explicit value dimensions. This reinterpreted appropriateness methodology—call it "dignitary appropriateness"—is then applied to many of the same issues examined in chapter 5, with similar results. Moreover, these applications suggest ways in which a dignitary theory can be integrated with ordinary legal reasoning to prevent every due process decision from becoming an essay on political philosophy. Procedural heuristics that *can* be justified are sufficient to the run-of-the-mine decision and to the maintenance of judicial hierarchy. Dignitary theory need be consulted directly only where the constitutional conversation is most intense and difficult.

A NOTE ON HUMAN DIGNITY AS A POLITICAL IDEAL

Before making these arguments extensively, it seems useful to attempt to distinguish the dignitary approach that will be elaborated here from other types of arguments that may be similar both in terminology and in the values to which they give peculiar prominence. The analysis that follows is an analysis of the conception of the individual that is affirmed by particular political structures and processes. It is concerned with human values as political ideals. "Dignity" is thus a particular *political* definition of personhood or citizenship.

This analysis should not be confused with a *psychological* analysis of the state of mind or well-being of individuals who confront or participate in legal institutions and processes. We are not exploring what processes make people *feel* dignified or have self-respect. The arguments do not attempt to generate behavioral hypotheses, which then might be tested through some variant of social science research. Rather we are attempting to specify what processes define people as dignified or self-respecting moral and political agents. The arguments therefore are about the values and ideals that our constitutional system should affirm. They can be tested only for their coherence within our peculiar constitutional tradition.

To affirm a politics is almost necessarily to affirm an epistemology and, therefore, some conception of human psychology. But these necessary linkages should not cause us to view as synonymous the questions, What processes make people feel fairly treated? and What processes within our political culture define individuals as autonomous and self-respecting moral agents? The first is a question about individual psychology; the second a question about political ideology. Although we cannot avoid consulting our feelings or intuitions as a source of ideas about procedural values, in the end our effort is to discover (or to construct) the process ideals that define a particular liberal-democratic constitutional culture.

5 / *Dignitary Process and the Liberal Tradition*

There are more calls for the abandonment of positivist, utilitarian, or instrumentalist perspectives and the construction of a dignitary constitutional theory (or for the elaboration of dignitary values) than there are taxonomies,[1] much less extended defenses, of the process concerns that would inform such a due process jurisprudence. Whether considering the literature, or viewing the question as opening up wholly virgin territory, the generation of a plausible group of dignitary-value candidates seems within our grasp. We can initially derive our proposed values intuitively, for they are rooted in common characteristics of liberal constitutionalism. A brief exploration of the prime candidates reveals, however, the need to pursue these intuitions in greater depth. The values that fit our intuitions are vague at the margins and potentially contradictory at the core. They only begin to suggest a usable constitutional theory.

After setting forth my intuitive candidates for a taxonomy of dignitary values in the first part of this chapter, I will then proceed to analyze the intuitive candidates in terms of the theoretical tradition of liberal-democratic political thought that underlies the United States Constitution. This theoretical analysis suggests that the intuitive candidates are of two general types. A

---

1. Summers and Saphire provide extended and overlapping taxonomies, Saphire, *supra* chapter 4, note 13, at 114–25; Summers, *supra* chapter 4, note 18, at 20–27. Michelman limits his candidates to revelation and participation. Michelman, *supra* chapter 4, note 16, at 127.

small set of process values—equality as implemented by majority rule, comprehensibility, and privacy—emerges as the core of a dignitary approach. Other candidate values—such as individualization, direct participation, and accuracy—remain important as support for the core principles but should be viewed more as prudential than as fundamental rights. Nevertheless, prudential concern with dignitary values may produce a nonconstitutional common law of administrative procedure that is attentive both to the crucial problems of legitimation in the administrative state and to the necessarily limited constitutional mandate of the judiciary in a democratic polity.

AN INTUITIVE STATEMENT OF PROCESS VALUES

EQUALITY

The demand that techniques for making collective decisions not imply that one person's or group's contribution (facts, interpretation, policy argument, and so on) is entitled to greater respect than another's merely because of the identity of the person or group is so ubiquitous and intuitively plausible that no extended defense of equality's candidacy seems appropriate. Yet equality is a notoriously slippery concept, and its procedural implications are puzzling.

First, the idea of equal respect and equal voice is strongly associated with majority rule: May's theorem demonstrates that if all persons are permitted to participate in all decisions under conditions that ensure that no one's identity or preferred outcomes have special status, and that each person has an equal chance to cast the decisive vote, then *only* majority rule can emerge as the decision rule.[2] Any judicial decision that imposes procedures contrary to those arrived at in the majoritarian political process accordingly carries some anti-egalitarian stigma, even if that intervention is itself premised on egalitarian concerns. The notion of equal respect therefore cannot carry us in a

2. May, *A Set of Independent Necessary and Sufficient Conditions for Simple Majority Decision*, 20 ECONOMETRICA 680, 683 (1952). My text provides a very free rendering of May's conditions. His proof is much more accessible in A. SEN, COLLECTIVE CHOICE AND SOCIAL WELFARE 71–73 (1970).

straightforward deductive fashion toward constitutional due process rules that supplant legislative judgments. The development of such rules must proceed prudentially from a concern with majoritarian tyranny.[3]

Second, building nonvoting decisional processes that protect equality in a prudential fashion is quite difficult. Formal and substantive equality often compete. The ability of both sides in a conventional adversary dispute to question a witness seems essential to formal equality. Yet such questioning may so increase the costs of litigation to certain parties—rape victims or malpractice defendants, for example—that they appear substantively disadvantaged. Weighted voting rules (constitutional amendments), special proof requirements ("beyond a reasonable doubt"),[4] presumptions (workmen's compensation coverage),[5] or one-sided appeal structures (criminal trials, public benefits decisions),[6] all violate or impinge upon formal equality; yet each may have at its base some notion of redressing substantive inequality.

The simple dynamics of processes may subtly advantage or disadvantage certain types of claims or claimants. Oral adjudicatory process, for example, may be a more powerful technique for exposing weaknesses, gaps, or uncertainties concerning a proposed decision than for portraying the general scientific or commonsense notions that would support it. Yet elimination of orality, or of cross-examination, or of the plodding, serial presentation of evidence normally associated with adjudication, may reverse substantive inequalities rather than redress an imbalance.

3. *See generally* B. ACKERMAN, SOCIAL JUSTICE IN THE LIBERAL STATE 301–13 (1980).

4. The due process clause requires that no person be convicted of a criminal offense unless every fact necessary to constitute the crime charged is proved beyond a reasonable doubt. *In re* Winship, 397 U.S. 358, 364 (1970).

5. Some workmen's compensation statutes establish presumptions that employees' claims fall within their provisions. 1 A. LARSON, THE LAW OF WORKMEN'S COMPENSATION § 10.33, at 3–120 (1978).

6. At least under federal law, the one-sided criminal appeal structure may be crumbling somewhat. The current trend appears to allow government appeals whenever the Constitution permits. *See* United States v. Wilson, 420 U.S. 332, 337 (1975); 18 U.S.C. § 3731 (1976). For an example in the public benefits arena, see the Social Security Act § 205(g), 42 U.S.C. § 405(g) (Supp. 1981).

Finally, we should note both the extended domain and the potentially limited power of process equality. The domain of concerns about equality reaches well beyond majority voting and adversary adjudication. Even in investigatory adjudicative processes formally involving only one party (for example, public assistance claims), we would be concerned that each person affected by a decision have equal effort (formal? substantive?) devoted to the accumulation of evidence and consideration of its import. For to do otherwise is to deny that one person's claim to the same subject matter is as valuable as another's. We similarly may be concerned about equal access to representative legislators, or to the legislative process, notwithstanding the admitted connection of the legislative process to majoritarian voting processes. Within this extensive domain, however, equality may be a thin protection. If we provided everyone confronting any administrative decision with the process made available to K in *The Trial*,[7] equality before the law could be maintained, but the protection afforded individual self-respect would be modest indeed.

PREDICTABILITY, TRANSPARENCY, AND RATIONALITY

Building on the last remark, it seems obvious that predictability, transparency, and rationality form a family of related process values that can make a worthwhile contribution to any process participant's[8] sense of self-respect. The participants' befuddlement is one hallmark of a decisional process that can be described as Kafkaesque. They know only that they seem to be involved in an important decision concerning their lives. But they have no idea what is relevant to the decision, who will make it, and, in the extreme case, what precisely the decision is about. Perhaps the only thing that becomes clear in such a process is that if and when a decision is made, the participants will not be given any understandable reasons for it.

Kafkaesque procedures take away the participants' ability to

7. F. KAFKA, THE TRIAL (W. Muir & E. Muir trans. E. Bulter rev. 1970).
8. When I refer to the participants in a decision-making process, I do not mean the decision *maker*, only the subjects of the decision and, perhaps, other contributors to the process.

engage in rational planning about their situation, to make informed choices among options. The process implicitly defines the participants as objects, subject to infinite manipulation by the system. To avoid contributing to this sense of alienation, terror, and ultimately self-hatred, a decisional process must give participants adequate notice of the issues to be decided, of the evidence that is relevant to those issues, and of how the decisional process itself works. In the end, there also must be some guarantee, usually by articulation of the basis for the decision, that the issues, evidence, and processes were meaningful to the outcome.[9] This reason giving is necessary, both to redeem prior promises of rationality, and to provide guidance for the individual's future planning. In this latter aspect, reason giving confirms the participant, even in the face of substantive disappointment, as engaging in an ongoing process of rational and self-regarding action.

Although these general remarks concerning this group of dignitary demands may appear to raise few problems, we should be clear about some of the questions that remain. Although random and unstructured processes obviously limit the purposiveness of participation and inhibit rational planning concerning other affected aspects of a participant's life, we sometimes prefer them to rigidly structured decisional rules. They emphasize the human—the emotional, eclectic, and intuitive—aspects of our personality. Opportunities to be engaged in predictable ways in purposive activity do not always increase our sense of self-worth. Certain familiar legal processes—for example, juries and hospital "God" committees—not only fail to give reasons, but are valued because they do not.[10] For sometimes the moral equality of litigants or supplicants can be maintained only by shielding from view the rationale for particular assessments of comparative worthiness.

Conflicts may also lurk somewhere between different aspects of our individual rationality. We sometimes view rationality as an intuitive process in which goals, means of achieving them,

---

9. Robert Summers has reached a similar conclusion in a discussion that appears to draw on, without expressly mentioning, dignitary values. *See* Summers, *supra* chapter 4, note 18, at 26–27.

10. G. CALABRESI & P. BOBBITT, TRAGIC CHOICES 57–62 (1978).

and states of the world constantly interact, each thereby reshaping our perceptions of the others. At other times rationality is captured by the instrumental paradigm of fitting means to ends. And in the latter case goals, at least, are fixed, coherent, and unambiguous. A demand that a process be rational thus fails to define the process ultimately desired. It leaves open the question, Rational in what way?[11]

PARTICIPATION

Participation is an obvious candidate for our set of dignitary process values. One constantly confronts the claim that the dignity and self-respect of the individual can be protected only through processes of government in which there is meaningful participation by affected interests.[12] Indeed, in my statement of process equality, I described such equality as equality of participation, and I described processes as predictable, transparent, or rational for their participants.

The basis for a connection between participation and self-respect may be variously explained. As our positivist-trap dialogue suggested, it has become traditional in the due process jurisprudence to make the connection only in circumstances in which the individual is attempting to defend some previously recognized right.[13] That is arguably a dignitary approach, but

11. Moreover, we must beware of demanding the impossible in the name of the rational. Kenneth Arrow's general possibility theorem, when applied to administrative decision making, indicates that under certain circumstances rationality in any sense may be unattainable. Suppose we chartered an administrative agency to regulate by license, permit, or order some potentially harmful behavior. Suppose further that we gave the agency a series of values to consider in arriving at its judgments, and required it to render reasoned judgments in the public interest. Arrow's theorem introduces into this familiar scenario the unfamiliar notion that if a small set of conditions is used to define what "consideration" and "public interest" entail—conditions so minimal that they can be expected to produce universal assent—then the agency will be unable to produce consistent decisions, and its attempts at reason giving will reveal it to be confused, devious, or both. *See generally* Spitzer, *Multicriteria Choice Preferences: An Application of Public Choice Theory to Bakke, The FCC and the Courts*, 88 YALE L.J. 717 (1979); Spitzer, *Radio Formats by Administrative Choice*, 47 U. CHI. L. REV. 647 (1980).

12. *See, e.g.*, E. REDFORD, DEMOCRACY IN THE ADMINISTRATIVE STATE 197 (1969).

13. *See* notes 84–86 and accompanying text *supra*, chapter 3.

with a substantive entitlements trigger.[14] Others would assert that participation is equally important in proceedings that function to develop the *content* of rights, rather than merely to enforce rights previously specified.[15] The latter claim—and it seems a persuasive one—suggests that our self-respect is called into question not only when our rights are affected by proceedings to which we are not admitted, but also when we are excluded from a process of social decision making that defines or elaborates the set of rights we all hold.

This point is extended by those who argue that participation increases self-respect to the degree that participation provides *control* over the process of decision making.[16] Loss of control, it is argued, is particularly damaging to self-respect in those circumstances in which rights are amorphous and decision making depends importantly on placing in context the events or norms that appear to be relevant to the issue to be decided. Such considerations may explain the strong appeal of the hearing requests in cases such as *Califano v. Yamasaki* (good faith of an applicant for waiver of recoupment) or *Paul v. Davis* (listing as an active shoplifter). It is in these situations that we are especially conscious of the need to explain and justify our actions and in which the loss of the opportunity to do so denies our self-worth. Indeed, the argument is pressed still further to urge that the legal system should universally employ broad principles and contextual processes, rather than objective rules and limited adjudicating discretion, in order to avoid inducing perceptions of injustice and loss of individual status.[17]

Like the more extreme positivist positions that it confronts, this latter form of participatory due process demand has important implications for the structure of substantive entitlements. In short the demand is for law without rules. If *this* is the direction in which a dignitary approach pushes the conceptualization of process, then there are equally obvious difficulties in structuring

14. Michelman, *supra* chapter 4, note 16, at 129–30. In fact, entitlements triggers might well protect dignitary concerns, provided that the entitlements conception is appropriately robust.

15. *E.g.*, Comment, *supra* chapter 4, note 30, at 898 & n. 47.

16. Such control theorists often do not, however, necessarily link control and self-respect. *See* note 23 chapter 4, *supra*.

17. *See* Thibaut & Walker, *supra* chapter 4, note 19, at 553–54; *Structural Due Process*, *supra* chapter 4, note 32, at 303–06.

constitutional adjudication of process rights around such a notion. Demands for participation begin to look like demands that the administrative state be dismantled; that all decisions instead be made by some combination of popular referendum, adversary adjudication, and negotiation to consensus.

The demand for participation might, indeed, be more modest if separated entirely from an entitlements conception, whether substantive entitlements are viewed as rule-bound and static or as principled and emergent. Such treatment of the participatory demand characterizes what Frank Michelman describes as nonformal processes, which evidence a human and moral concern. In his view, processes might pursue associational aims of which participation, having a part in the decision, is one. Michelman is particularly troubled by cases such as *Roth v. Board of Regents*.[18] There, reminiscent of our positivist traps dialogue, an untenured teacher on a year-to-year contract was not renewed for the next academic year. He demanded to have at least an explanation of the university's decision, but the president refused. The Supreme Court, noting that Roth's contract gave him no right to renewal, held that he had no right to any explanation or other process related to the renewal decision. In *Roth*, as in *O'Bannon v. Town Court Nursing Center*, the limitation of due process protections to the securing of existing formal rights seems somehow to miss the significance of the associational or communal interests that are at stake.

Although he describes the fraternal or communal ideal in ways that are intuitively plausible and attractive, Michelman yet despairs of converting ideals into rights:

> [A]n official whose explanations and interchanges have been *requisitioned* by someone who assertedly *owns* those elements of his behavior just will not be engaging in the kinds of acts which carry the interpersonal meanings that (possibly) we yearn for. If such a thing as a *right* to nonformalistic due process is conceivable, it must be a right of a sort of which we (or I) do not now have an adequate idea, a right existing outside the formalistic-positivist framework, a claim or drive or value having a mandatory quality, yes, but not ultimately dependent upon judicial coercion.[19]

18. 408 U.S. 564 (1972).
19. Michelman, *supra* chapter 4, note 16, at 127–28.

180 / *Dignitary Process and the Liberal Tradition*

To rethink participatory process rights in terms that make them meaningful at the level of self-definition or in terms of the desire for community may be, necessarily, to render them nonjusticiable.

PRIVACY

The intuition that privacy matters, that processes that protect privacy are better than those that do not, is reinforced by the few specific process protections embodied in the United States Constitution—the protections against self-incrimination and unreasonable searches and seizures. Moreover, in its attempts to provide a coherent framework for other, more substantive constitutional protections—protections surrounding procreative choices and the marital relationship—the Supreme Court has identified these specific process constraints with the more general notion of protecting privacy. Perhaps more than any of our other candidates, privacy has the jurisprudential advantage of some explicit instances of implementation.

But privacy raises different process concerns than the values previously canvassed in our intuitive taxonomy. Rationality and participation seem to demand additions to public decision processes—additions that will communicate and include, that will permit interchange, self-revelation, perhaps mutual understanding. And although, strictly speaking, equality of citizens with respect to public decisions may imply only majority rule, in our particular constitutional vernacular egalitarian concerns carry connotations of inclusion that make equality claims devices for demanding more extensive access to existing processes.[20]

Privacy, on the other hand, is in essence a demand to be let alone, to be respected as an autonomous being with legitimate claims to separateness. Moreover, if process rights are of the

20. This becomes most clear in the areas of criminal process protections, *see, e.g., Gideon v. Wainwright,* 372 U.S. 335 (1963) (requiring the states to provide counsel for indigent criminal defendants); and prisoners' rights, *see, e.g., Bounds v. Smith* 430 U.S. 817 (1977) (requiring prison authorities to supply inmates with law libraries or legal assistance). It is also reflected in the Fifteenth and Nineteenth Amendments of the U.S. Constitution, which proscribe the denial of suffrage on the basis of race or sex.

Hohfeldian[21] sort—that is, they imply a duty—then surely privacy sometimes will conflict with participation, rationality, even equality. If my legitimate demand on you is for participation or revelation, then your legal duty is certainly inconsistent with maintaining your right to privacy. Indeed, I may well seek to join you in a process of collective decision making, yet simultaneously seek to shield, through privacy claims, information that you deem highly pertinent to the correct resolution of our dispute. Many common rules of procedure and evidence seem to have this double aspect.[22] What conception of personhood can mediate this clash among dignitary values?

RESIDUAL CATEGORIES

Intuitive statement of the process implications of human dignity could go on. But we are nearing the point at which new characterizations of the theme can be reduced rather easily to one or to a combination of prior value categories. Thus, although I am attracted by additional formulations, such as humaneness, individualization, or appropriate symbolism, I am suspicious that they are largely proxies for combinations of values already declared. This is not to argue that further attempts at intuitive statement are useless. Combination is not mere repetition. It may provoke a synthesis of value attributes that would otherwise remain obscure. Thus, further thought in this area might be fruitful.

But for now, it seems sensible to view the exercise in intuitive taxonomy as ended. Its purpose has been to convince the reader that something prima facie plausible can be said for a dignitary approach. The precise formulation of the values posited is of minor importance. They can nevertheless serve as landmarks to prevent our inquiries into justification and implementation

21. *See* W. HOHFELD, FUNDAMENTAL LEGAL CONCEPTIONS AS APPLIED IN JUDICIAL REASONING, AND OTHER LEGAL ESSAYS 36–38 (1919).

22. For example, the Federal Rules of Civil Procedure allow broad pretrial discovery, but enable the subjects of such discovery to move for protective orders in cases of "annoyance, embarrassment, oppression, or undue burden or expense." FED. R. CIV. P., Rule 26(c). A prevailing rule of evidence proscribes the circumstantial use of character evidence in most trial situations. *E.g.*, FED. R. EVID., Rule 404 & Advisory Committee Note.

from becoming aimless wanderings among either abstract philosophical or particular procedural systems.

THEORETICAL DEFENSE

There are obviously some problems with our intuitions. The values enunciated do not have very definite shapes; they sometimes are internally contradictory, and they may be competitive. These features make them appear, at least superficially, poor candidates for constitutional implementation through the due process clause. For if we remain at the level of intuition, these values can only be asserted as desirable and attractive, eclectically developed in contingent contexts, and balanced against each other (and perhaps other values) in a continuingly intuitive fashion. Intuition may inform our concern. We may, with Justice Frankfurter, believe that the due process question is a question of fundamental fairness. But when Justice Black asks, "What's that?" and "Says who?" I, for one, would like to have something more to say.

Some theoretical defense therefore must be offered for translating moderately plausible intuitive claims into constitutional rights. Such a theory should define the core of our dignitary concerns, connect that core to a broader constitutional tradition, and point the way toward the means for practical implementation of dignitary values in the structuring of due process requirements. Can such a theory be devised? I think it can. There are several paths toward theoretical justification. None of the paths is simultaneously nonpositivist, noninstrumentalist, and nonutilitarian. Nor do the paths finally converge. Yet they traverse a common theoretical terrain and have points of tangency. They can lead us forward in our quest for a dignitary theory, while helping us to rethink and redescribe our proposed destination.

The moral and political theories that we most appropriately might employ to refine, reject, or support our intuitive taxonomy of process values are a family of theories that I will call the "liberal tradition." This tradition has at its core the notion that individuals are the basic units of moral and political value. It is within this tradition that limiting government by providing individual rights makes sense; and it is, of course, this intellectual tradition that has been most influential both at the formation and in the history of the American republic.

But liberal theories are not all alike. We may exclude Platonic idealism and Marxist materialism, as essentially illiberal and therefore inappropriate to the the American constitutional tradition, without getting very far toward an understanding of what that tradition entails. The liberal intellectual tradition has several major strands, no one of which has an exclusive claim to our attention. Each is an attempt to render a coherent account of individual rights, and each may to that degree inform our understanding of a dignitary perspective on process. Each has both eighteenth-century roots and modern spokesmen, and each may, therefore, seek to inform a process of constitutional adjudication that is oriented neither wholly to tradition nor wholly to contemporary concerns.

THE LIBERAL TRADITION

A description of the liberal tradition in a sufficiently short compass to meet our present needs, yet in a form that avoids presenting merely a cartoon, is no easy matter. Liberal ideas have emerged in social and political contexts[23] from which they can be extracted only with substantial loss of meaning. Describing the logic of liberalism in some sense falsifies it.

The basic liberal movements fall into three ancestral categories—Lockean, Benthamite, and Kantian. I shall discuss the first two very briefly, merely to demonstrate the possibility of arriving at dignitary process values from these positions. But since the first maintains little attraction for the modern liberal imagination and the second, even if properly understood, has many of the defects suggested by the discussion in chapter 3, we need not tarry long. The Kantian tradition will receive more extended treatment because it has an intuitive connection with a digni-

---

23. And religious and juridical ones as well. *See generally* R. TUCK, NATURAL RIGHTS THEORIES (1979).

tary approach to process and because John Rawls's Kantian political theory has had a powerful influence on contemporary legal thought.

Locke and the Entitlements Conception. Some variation of Locke's ideas, at least as embodied in a general Whig conception of governance, influenced the structure of constitutionalism in America.[24] But imbedded in Lockean political theory is a deep contradiction between individual proprietorship over life, liberty, or property and majoritarianism—a contradiction that can be resolved in two ways. The first is to choose majoritarianism, a choice that, as previously noted, is strongly connected to the dignitary ideal of equal respect. This choice also entails a commitment to positivism and to just those revelatory and associational processes generated by majoritarian governance.

The alternative approach emphasizes entitlement. In this view, as Robert Nozick recently has reinterpreted it, persons and property emerge with rights attached.[25] Given that such rights have a possessive character and are attached to particular individuals, society has no claim on individually held property or liberty. To Nozick, taxation is theft. He, therefore, views even a minimal or guardian state as an undesirable, but inevitable, response to individual insecurity. In his view, the state has no positive (redistributive) functions, because such functions necessarily would invade the rights of individuals. The state's only role is to protect individual liberty and acquisitions.

In this radical libertarian perspective, it seems logical to presume that procedures for dispute resolution would be classified easily as either legitimate or illegitimate. Legitimate procedures would include only those that could be seen to produce no errors (and therefore invade no one's substantive rights)[26] or that had been agreed to by a process of free negotiation among the affected parties.[27] Both types of legitimate process protect au-

---

24. *See generally* B. BAILYN, THE IDEOLOGICAL ORIGINS OF THE AMERICAN REVOLUTION 22–54 (1967); G. WOOD, THE CREATION OF THE AMERICAN REPUBLIC, 1776–1789, 3–45 (1969).

25. R. NOZICK, ANARCHY, STATE AND UTOPIA (1974).

26. *Id.* at 106.

27. *See id.* at 101–02.

tonomy. The former emphasizes rationality, the latter participation. Here are dignitary processes in a robust form.

Yet, because either type of legitimate procedure often is unavailable or extremely expensive, the practical difficulties of a radical libertarian conception of process seem overwhelming. In an attempt at overcoming these difficulties, Nozick, for example, tells a metaphorical tale concerning the growth of a minimal state (including machinery for dispute resolution) that avoids the necessity (and obvious impracticability) of individual consent to all procedural arrangements by invoking the "invisible hand" of "voluntary association." But in this metaphor voluntariness breaks down, if not everywhere, at critical points. In the end Nozick's explanation of state sovereignty, the final unification of competing protective agencies, is a pure power play based on social necessity.[28]

But the libertarian theorist cannot relinquish insistence on consent in the face of social necessity. Once the necessities of social order are admitted, there is no obvious theoretical stopping point when trading the claims of individual liberty for the demands of social necessity: thereafter, argument is only about the facts. And given the reinterpretation of liberalism in this century, to emphasize the social preconditions for meaningful exercise of individual rights,[29] if the libertarian wishes to retain a Lockean posture of natural entitlements, he had better hold fast to the demand for individual consent to processes that can rearrange rights coercively. Otherwise natural rights rapidly disappear in a positivist conception of substantive entitlements and procedural rights. This is the land of Charles Reich's "New Property"[30]; a land that William Van Alstyne[31] has shown to be heavily mined with positivist traps.

Finally, it is clear that processes in Nozick's system merely are the means for protecting substantive entitlements. In this particular brand of instrumentalism, a robust set of dignitary process rights depends on the acceptance of its similarly robust theory of

28. *See id.* at 108–10. Nozick describes this event as the inevitable development of a "de facto monopoly." *Id.* at 109.
29. *See, e.g.,* J. DEWEY, LIBERALISM AND SOCIAL ACTION (1935).
30. Reich, *The New Property*, 73 YALE L.J. 733 (1964).
31. Van Alstyne, *supra* chapter 4, note 15, at 452–70.

natural rights in acquisitions, and its limitations of collective action to minimal or guardian state functions. That suggestion can be viewed only as quaint.

Bentham,[32] *Mill, and Utility.* It is tempting to exclude utilitarianism as inconsistent with the individualist starting point of a dignitary or liberal theory. The utilitarian, after all, asks not, "What rights do individuals have?" but, "What maximizes social welfare?" In some sense utilitarianism is the antithesis of an individual rights perspective. But, on reflection, the temptation to ignore approaches maximizing utility should be rejected. Utilitarians can be as concerned with the happiness induced by process as with the benefits that flow from accurate results. Neither should utilitarianism be rejected out-of-hand because it demands a *social* accounting. That accounting is, after all, one in which each individual counts as one: my happiness is as important as yours, and vice versa. There is in the utilitarian social welfare calculus strict equality of persons (indeed, so far as one can tell, all sentient beings). Moreover, the calculation is not meant to suggest that society itself has an organic existence. By "social welfare" the utilitarian means *only* the sum of individuals' welfare. Finally, as a matter of intellectual history, it seems inappropriate to exclude the author of *On Liberty*[33] from the liberal tradition, on the ground that he also wrote *Utilitarianism.*[34] Indeed, even Bentham seems to have entertained some notion of an indirect means by which utilitarianism might yield especially strong forms of moral claims—claims that might then override obedience to positive law.[35]

The question, then, is what the utilitarian has to say about individual rights. Or perhaps more aptly, to what extent can a utilitarian approach yield a justification for individual rights? Within the general utilitarian framework, there seem to be three basic methods of approaching this problem. One is Mill's

---

32. The use of Bentham is figurative. Although he is now more familiar to us, the eighteenth-century roots of utilitarianism in American constitutionalism lead more directly to others. *See generally* G. WILLS, INVENTING AMERICA (1978); *see also* B. BAILYN, *op. cit. supra* note 24; G. WOOD, *supra* note 24.

33. J.S. MILL, ON LIBERTY (C. Shields ed. 1956) (1st ed. London 1859).

34. J.S. MILL, UTILITARIANISM (S. Gorovitz ed. 1971) (1st ed. London 1863).

35. H.L.A. HART, ESSAYS ON BENTHAM: STUDIES IN JURISPRUDENCE AND POLITICAL THEORY (1982).

method in *On Liberty*. The idea is to separate the individual and the social. Calculations of social welfare have no place within the sphere of individual thought and action, that is, thought and action having no substantial consequences for other persons.[36] The individual is free to pursue his own desires, however misinformed or repugnant. Only when he acts in society by taking action affecting its members is he subject to constraint on the basis of calculations of social welfare.

There are, of course, well-known objections to this approach. The principal one is the indeterminateness of the line between individual and social action. Another is the absence of any justification, other than *social* welfare, for drawing such a line. Note, however, that this approach does yield at least one dignitary process restraint, some notion of individual privacy that is beyond social invasion because it is necessary to social welfare. The problem, of course, is that the right is so fragile that it might as well be called an "interest"—which may later be balanced against others.

A more satisfying move toward generating protected individual rights is made by the so-called Rule Utilitarians.[37] Their basic argument is that certain individual rights or protections so often maximize social welfare that they should have the status of rules. The use of these rules, rather than de novo social welfare calculations when making decisions, is believed to enhance overall welfare because the rules are likely to be wrong less often than unguided and contingent attempts to maximize social welfare.[38] The rules, of course, establish only prima facie rights. They may be overridden by a convincing demonstration in particular cases that social welfare demands an exception. Nevertheless, even prima facie rights, rights that merely prevail when the social welfare calculation is uncertain, may be quite robust in the face of pervasive uncertainty.

What sorts of rights should have the status of rules in a utili-

36. "The only part of the conduct of anyone for which he is amenable to society is that which concerns others. In the part which merely concerns himself, his independence is, of right, absolute." J.S. MILL, *supra* note 33, at 13.

37. This is not to say that rule utilitarianism is necessarily a better moral theory. For a recent discussion of the difficulties with rule utilitarian approaches, see D. REGAN, UTILITARIANISM AND CO-OPERATION 83–93 (1980).

38. *See generally* Harrod, *Utilitarianism Revised,* in 45 MIND 137 (new ser. 1936).

tarian moral universe? Here there can be much disagreement, but two principles seem straightforward. First, the rules must be few in number. Otherwise the basic feature of utilitarianism would be lost.[39] Second, rules should be developed only when exceptions are thought to be rare and the conduct proscribed (or required) relates directly and powerfully to the core notions of pleasure and pain.

A common example of a utilitarian rule might be a prohibition against slavery. Although they are often taxed by nonutilitarians with the claim that their moral stance permits even such abominations as slavery, modern utilitarians have given a persuasive argument for rule utilitarianism in this context. R. M. Hare, for example, admits that he can hypothesize a situation in which slavery would do more good than would the abolition of slavery. But he further argues that, try as he might, he cannot construct a *believable* scenario for such an outcome. Moreover, because the condition of slavery produces a reign of terror—the slave (having no legal rights) lives in constant fear of pain from the master's caprice, neglect, or vengefulness—a clear prohibition on slave status seems to Hare consistent with a well-considered utilitarian position.[40]

The utilitarian might take a similar view of wholly arbitrary procedures. The state bureaucracy that combines general power with absolute discretion becomes as the master to the slave. A reign of terror ensues. The citizen lives in constant fear of pain, and any movement toward predictability and transparency will produce substantial social welfare gains. The Kafkaesque total bureaucracy should clearly be proscribed.

As one moves away from the limiting case toward the types of procedural issues normally confronted in American legal life, the place of utilitarian rules becomes highly problematic. Bureaucracies as we know them have limited jurisdictions, discernible (although sometimes vague and conflicting) substantive pol-

39. Rule utilitarianism has thus been severely criticized as undermining the central notion of utilitarianism—that one must always act to maximize human happiness. *E.g.*, Smart, *Extreme and Restricted Utilitarianism*, in THEORIES OF ETHICS 171 (P. Foot ed. 1967); Stout, *But Suppose Everyone Did the Same*, 32 AUSTRALIAN J. PHIL. 1 (1954) (offering a defense to this criticism).

40. Hare, *What is Wrong with Slavery?* 8 PHIL. & PUB. AFF. 103 (1979).

icies, and relatively standardized procedures. Uncertainty is not terror, and the possibilities for contingent justification of limited discretion abound.

Here lies the domain of the third and dominant utilitarian methodology, an unfettered social welfare calculation, with all the well-known difficulties inherent in that intellectual exercise.[41] A calculation of costs and benefits concerned with the impact of process *directly* on the happiness of affected persons would, for example, remain concerned with the potentially greater happiness to be had from allocating public resources to a multitude of worthwhile ends other than procedural reform. The methodology yields a priori no support for any particular process or process value. It can say only that, ceteris paribus, processes should produce pleasure rather than pain or, perhaps more likely, should cause as little pain as possible. We must consign this approach to the same dustbin as the *Mathews v. Eldridge* three-factor analysis if we ever are to develop a convincing set of process rights.

Kant and Rawls. Thus far liberal theory has seemed to point the way toward an anemic and fragile set of process rights— majority rule, some domain of privacy, and the absence of complete arbitrariness. Revelatory and participatory process values might emerge only as possible incidents to the maintenance of substantive entitlements in a minimal state, or from general considerations of social welfare. In addition to their other weaknesses, neither of these latter approaches seems to define man as a political actor in a fully satisfactory fashion. The entitlements approach subsumes politics in the market and implies that liberty and human dignity are defined in economic terms.[42] Utilitarianism subsumes the right in the good. Even when it converts the pleasure principle into a moral duty, it falls short of demanding that we recognize the moral integrity of others—their

41. *See* Urmson, *Utilitarianism: The Philosophy*, in 16 INTERNATIONAL ENCYCLOPEDIA OF THE SOCIAL SCIENCES 224, 225 (1968).

42. *Cf.* Dworkin, *Is Wealth a Value?* 9 J. LEGAL STUD. 191 (1980) (criticizing contemporary economic analysis of law theorists for implying that social wealth is a social value—*i.e.*, a thing worth having for its own sake).

right to pursue their own happiness, the general welfare notwithstanding.[43]

The Kantian strand of the liberal tradition might perhaps be more satisfactory as a basis for constructing natural rights. Kant's approach is a priori and categorical; it seeks to reveal the moral imperatives imbedded in the structure of normative rationality. Kant thus does not create interests that can easily be balanced away. Moreover, the well-known second formulation of the basic Kantian moral command compellingly characterizes the core value of liberal thought, that each person be treated as an end, never merely as a means.[44] Can this ideal provide a basis for a dignitary approach to due process?

Edmund Pincoffs has suggested as much.[45] He applies what he calls a "Kantian injunction" to the issue in *Board of Regents v. Roth*[46]—whether a nonrenewed teacher on an expired term contract is entitled, by virtue of the due process clause, to some

---

43. *See, e.g.,* B. ACKERMAN, *op. cit. supra* note 3, at 100–03, 342–45.

44. A few words may be in order here concerning Kant's categorical imperative and the formulas he derived from it. In his attempt to explicate the foundations of morality, Kant formulated a basic moral command—*i.e.,* a categorical imperative. Against this command the morality of all subjective, individual principles of action (in Kant's terminology, maxims) could be judged. Reasoning that only those maxims are moral that a rational being could conceive as being valid bases of action for all other rational beings, Kant stated his categorical imperative as follows: "Act only according to that maxim by which you can at the same time will that it should become a universal law." I. KANT, FOUNDATION OF THE METAPHYSICS OF MORALS 39 (L. Beck trans. 1959) (1st ed. Riga 1785). In order to focus the application of the categorical imperative, Kant proceeded to reformulate it in four ways: (1) "Act as though the maxim of your action were by your will to become a universal law of nature." *Id.* (2) "Act so that you treat humanity, whether in your own person or in that of another, always as an end and never as a means only." *Id.* at 47. (3) Act in accord with "the idea of the will of every rational being as a will giving universal law. . . . [E]verything must be done from the maxim of [the] will as one which could have as its object only itself considered as universal laws." *Id.* at 50. (4) "Act as if [you], by [your] maxim, [are] at all times a legislative member in the universal realm of ends. . . . [A]ct as if your maxim should serve at the same time as the universal law of all rational beings." *Id.* at 57 (on the "realm of ends," *see* notes 48–51 and accompanying text *infra*). The reader should note that each of these formulations is really a restatement of the basic imperative, and its equivalent in meaning, if not in focus.

45. Pincoffs, *Due Process, Fraternity, and a Kantian Injunction,* in DUE PROCESS, NOMOS XVIII, at 172 (J. Pennock & J. Chapman eds. 1977).

46. 408 U.S. 564 (1972).

kind of explanation or hearing concerning the board's failure to renew his contract. Pincoffs proceeds:

> [I]f there are no very persuasive arguments why Roth should not be given reasons, are there any arguments why he should—or are we to leave it that it is just intuitively obvious that he is morally (even if not legally) entitled to reasons? Are we to say that of course he should be given reasons—and a chance to contest them—out of simple decency? Or that in an ideal community he would be given reasons? Or that to refuse to give him reasons and an opportunity to contest them would be unthinkable? None of these remarks would be very helpful. None of them gives reasons for the giving of reasons; all seem like ways of avoiding the kind of account which must be given to those who are impressed with the need for official efficiency, for getting on with whatever the task may be. . . .
>
> Somewhat to my own surprise, I find that I am driven, in my analysis of the moral rights and duties that obtain between Roth and his president to the second formulation of the Kantian categorical imperative; the formulation that commands us never to treat anyone—including ourselves—as a mere means. Think of the Kantian command as being justified and at the same time clarified by the examination of a number of varying paradigms of treating persons as mere means to some end. One paradigm that might be offered is precisely the case in hand. If the president is assessed—and assesses himself—solely on grounds of his efficiency in attaining the complex end of an adequate educational opportunity for those who are qualified to take advantage of it, then he regards himself as a mere means, and at the same time regards Roth and his colleagues as mere means to the attainment of educational opportunity. . . . [I]f Roth is not informed of his fault, he is treated as a mere means; he is eliminated, like a faulty machine part, from an organization that will henceforth, supposedly function better without him, and in that [sic] no further thought is given to Roth's interest in correcting his own performance. . . .
>
> But [Roth's] being owed reasons is but a small distance—if it is any distance—from his being owed a hearing in which he can examine, and challenge, what is said by the president—in which he can participate in the decision that concerns himself. . . .
>
> It is not necessary, then, to suppose that there is value in sheer participation. Participation may be instrumentally valuable, but instrumental to the achievement of a moral purpose that is itself impossible to describe in instrumental terms, the purpose of treating a man not as a mere means but as an end in himself. This is not to say

that there is no intrinsic value in participation. I would prefer to say that there may be, but that the moral value of participation turns on its relation to a moral end. This relationship of instrumentality is not the same kind as that between the president's raising money and educational opportunity for all. We might say that participation is an instrument by which the valuation of persons as ends in themselves is expressed. It is as if the Kantian principle were determinable in any number of ways, but participation is one of the ways in which it may become determinate. It does not follow that mere participation is of value (though it may have value), but rather follows that participation is morally valuable to the degree that it makes determinate the moral principle that we should never treat a man as a mere means.[17]

Now it is this type of reasoning from first principles of human dignity or moral integrity that seems most likely to generate cognizable claims of right within a dignitary theory of due process. As Pincoffs's analysis demonstrates, extensive procedural demands may be justified by an argument that includes consideration of prudential concerns for other social goals. Direct application of the Kantian categorical imperative, in which dignity may be said to consist of being treated as an end in oneself rather than as instrumental to the ends of others, may thus yield a robust set of procedural rights. Presumably, Roth may demand, as at least a Kantian moral right, a process designed to preserve and enhance his particular goals in life.

The attempt to apply Kantian injunctions in Pincoffs's fashion leads, however, to an apparent contradiction. If frustrating Roth's process claims by balancing them against resource constraints, and hence implicitly against the claims or purposes of others, is a failure to treat Roth as an end in himself, then Roth legitimately seems entitled to demand any process that he deems necessary to the pursuit of his purposes in life. But what is to be said to Roth's colleagues who object to spending their time pursuing Roth's purposes? Are they not being used as mere means? May they not wield the categorical imperative to demand privacy from Roth's incessant pursuit of participatory governance? Where is the principle of limitation that would adjust competing claims or ends?

The problem lies, I believe, in the use that Pincoffs makes of

47. Pincoffs, *supra* note 45, at 175–79.

the second formulation of the categorical imperative. The injunction to treat persons always as ends in themselves is derived from the universalization requirement of Kant's categorical imperative.[48] Like the basic imperative, the second formulation must be read as related to an objective or universal realm of ends or moral persons.[49] So construed, the injunction relates not to frustrating any person's goals or purposes in life, but to frustrating that person's exercise and development of a good will.[50] Each person thus is an end in himself *because* each person participates in, or strives for, objective moral goodness. The injunction to respect that participation or striving can—indeed should—be limited by some notion of which actions or claims relate to the dignity of a rational being. Other claims are not universal.

But if in theory we have rescued Kant from the incessant and competitive claims of the self-realizing ego, we have not thereby specified a determinate perspective on process claims. Indeed, the rescue operation seems doomed. For when we put the question—What is the good will against which actions and claims are to be measured?—we get two equally unhelpful answers. In the last part of *Foundation of the Metaphysics of Morals*,[51] and in the second *Critique*,[52] we seem to be told that the kingdom of ends—the reality of the moral self rather than its historically contingent appearance—lies always beyond our vision. It is a conceptual ideal necessary to explain the *possibility* of our notions

48. *See* note 44, *supra.*

49. "[A]ll rational beings stand under the law that each of them should treat himself and all others never merely as means but in every case also as an end in himself. Thus there arises a systematic union of rational beings through common objective laws. This is a realm which may be called a realm of ends (certainly only an ideal), because what these laws have in view is just the relation of these beings to each other as ends and means." I. KANT, *supra* note 44, at 52. Kant adverts to the realm of ends expressly in his fourth formulation of the categorical imperative. *See* note 44 *supra.*

50. "Morality . . . consists in the relation of every action to that [individual, personal] legislation through which alone a realm of ends is possible. This legislation, however, must be found in every rational being. It must be able to arise from his will, whose principle then is to take no action according to any maxim which would be inconsistent with its being a universal law." I. KANT, *supra* note 44, at 52.

51. *See id.* at 50–52, 60–64.

52. I. KANT, CRITIQUE OF PRACTICAL REASON (L. Beck trans. 1956) (1st ed. Riga 1788).

of moral worth and our striving for goodness, but it is not available for comparison with the phenomenal world. The first answer thus says that our quest is inevitable, but the goal is beyond our reach.

The second answer comes from Kant's famous examples, the applications of the categorical imperative. But this answer is unsatisfactory, because the examples are famous non sequiturs. For Kant, the requirement of universalization of moral maxims excludes suicide, and all lying, whereas it requires charity. In one essay he even purports to derive rules of etiquette at dinner parties from the categorical imperative.[53] But to Kant's readers these "obvious" applications always have been troublesome.[54] They merely seem to dress up in philosophic costume the conventional morality of eighteenth-century Konigsberg.

In order to rescue Kant from the second criticism—that, in application, the categorical imperative owes almost everything to place, time, and person, and almost nothing to objective theory —we must embrace the first. The categorical imperative was not meant to be *directly* applied to the phenomenal world to generate rules of conduct or moral claims. Rather, it provides an ideal toward which the rules of those who formulate the moral rules of the phenomenal world can strive. It specifies a hypothetical condition for the existence of individual moral agency.

From this perspective the wisdom and subtlety of John Rawls's approach to rendering Kant more determinate in his *A Theory of Justice*[55] is thrown into sharp relief. The original position[56] might be viewed as an approach to the kingdom of ends;

53. I. KANT, ANTHROPOLOGIE, PRAGMATICALLY CONSIDERED 185–91 (Dowdell trans. 1978).

54. *See, e.g.,* C.D. BROOD, FIVE TYPES OF ETHICAL THEORY 129–31 (1934) (arguing that Kant's examples do not illustrate his categorical imperative). For sympathetic attempts to interpret Kant's moral thought and to explain the relationship between its abstract principles and its concrete examples of moral duty, see, *e.g.,* M.J. GREGOR, LAWS OF FREEDOM (1963); H.J. PATON, THE CATEGORICAL IMPERATIVE (1947).

55. J. RAWLS, A THEORY OF JUSTICE (1971).

56. The original position is a hypothetical situation that Rawls posits. It forms an initial status quo from which a group of rational and mutually disinterested people reach a set of agreements that provide the basis of a just society. All persons in the original position enjoy fundamental equality. *Id.* at 11–22, 118–92. *See generally* Dworkin, *The Original Position,* in READING RAWLS 16 (N. Daniels ed. 1975).

the veil of ignorance[57] as a technique for protecting the universal or good will from the clash of contingent purposes that punctuate the phenomenal world. The choices of the disembodied, rational wills posited by Rawls are universal by definition, and the pursuit of the principles of justice by a rational placeholder, who does not know where he will end up in the social scheme, necessarily treats all rational beings as ends in themselves.

Rawls is more than incidentally committed to the satisfaction of Kant's imperative.[58] To treat anyone as a mere means is to deny the importance of his ends in life and, at the same time, to undermine his basis for self-respect. In *A Theory of Justice* the idea of self-respect plays a critical dual role. It is the intuitive bedrock upon which many of Rawls's psychological assumptions about acceptable bargains are based, and it is also a test of the moral legitimacy and relative desirability of the principles and institutions that emerge from the process of contracting.

Rawls generates two basic principles of justice from the original position of self-interested neutrality. The first is a principle of strict equality with respect to basic liberties. The extent of this set of liberties is unclear, but it includes for Rawls at least universal suffrage with majority rule; freedom of conscience (moral and religious), speech, and assembly; and freedom from arbitrary arrest as defined by the rule of law. Restrictions on these basic liberties are permissible only in the interest of increasing the amount of liberty experienced by all. Thus, an expanded set of universal and preferred rights might, for example, be put beyond the reach of majority rule. But Rawls views this set of rights as indeterminate. Any number of constitutional regimes might satisfy the principle of equal liberty. The important feature is equality. Rawls sees no sufficient reason for any contractor to forego equal liberty; for, in his view, this strict equality is so related to self-respect that (barring extreme circumstances) no one would forego equal liberty for social or economic advancement.

57. The veil of ignorance is a condition Rawls imposes upon participants in the original position: none of them knows anything about him- or herself, such as social status or natural abilities, that could differentiate him or her from the other participants. J. RAWLS, *supra* note 55, at 12, 136–42.

58. *See id.* at 251–57; Rawls, *Kantian Constructivism in Moral Theory,* 77 J. PHIL. 515 (1980).

The second principle relates to problems of economic and social position. Here Rawls rejects strict equality on the grounds that the self-interested, but temporarily ignorant, contractor need not forego the possibilities for material advancement that inequality could provide for every person, even the worst off. All he need do is ensure that should he end up as the worst off, he would nonetheless be better off than under a regime of strict equality. This insight leads to Rawls's second principle of justice, which requires (a) that inequalities be attached to positions and offices available to all under conditions of fair equality of opportunity, and (b) that advances in the position of better-off persons be limited by the requirement that the position of the worst-off be maximized.

This principle might, like the first principle, be satisfied by a large number of constitutional and legislative arrangements. Certain approaches to social arrangements, however, would be proscribed. Slavery and other arbitrary classifications relating to personal legal status would be illegitimate, as would attempts to maximize total or average utility. Rawls further believes that the operation of this second principle, by reducing extremes of social and economic position and reinforcing bonds of social fraternity, supports the priority of the first principle. Liberty becomes more desirable as basic economic needs are assured, and more closely associated with self-respect as extremes of wealth and position are eliminated.

This rather straightforward statement of Rawls's two principles of justice provides little of the subtlety, insight, or interconnectedness of his arguments. I am here concerned, however, only with those aspects of Rawls's theory that could give a firmer foundation to intuitive notions of dignitary process rights.

We may begin by excluding, tentatively, consideration of the second principle; for if process rights merely are fungible parts of what Rawls calls "primary goods"—all those things it is rational to desire because they are instrumental in achieving particular goals in life—then they can form no part of a constitutionally preferred set of rights.[59] Constitutional preference

---

59. Nor, as Frank Michelman demonstrates, does the second principle generate a set of insurance or welfare rights having special constitutional significance. Michelman, *In Pursuit of Constitutional Welfare Rights: One View of Rawls's Theory of Justice*, 121 U. PA. L. REV. 962, 967–97 (1973).

implies that these rights not be overridden by majority vote, and Rawls's system permits no trades of basic liberties[60]—majority rule included—for other, lesser primary goods. Basic liberties are by definition things that we want no matter what other things we also have or desire. Hence, unless process rights beyond majority rule can be given a place in the set of basic liberties that might be adopted, they cannot be allowed to restrict the basic liberty of majority rule.

That due process claims should be considered liberties rather than mere goods is not surprising. We are accustomed to thinking of Bill of Rights protections in liberty terms. But the conception of process rights as Rawlsian liberties does not lead easily to the conclusion that those rights should have constitutional protection.

The clearest notion of process rights in Rawls's theory applies to legislative processes. He argues, at least some of the time, that equal participation—one-person-one-vote, majority rule, offices open to all—is essential to the notion of equal liberty. However, when Rawls moves beyond voting to concern himself with the application of legal rules, he connects that function directly to the rule of law. Such a connection primarily provides support not for process values in adjudication, but, in Rawls's own words, for a system "reasonably designed to ascertain the truth."[61] The rule of law, for Rawls as for Locke, is not itself a concept of liberty, but rather a means of implementing such liberties as are available. The notion is both limited and instrumental: unless the law is reasonably clear concerning the citizens' rights and duties, and is administered through a rational process reasonably designed to produce accurate (and therefore regular and consistent) applications, there can be no secure expectations with respect to equality of access to the basic liberties.

This is not to suggest that Rawls's views of due process are necessarily inconsistent with the notion of process values. The values most closely connected with the rule of law—predictability, transparency, and rationality—can be instrumental *both* to

60. Although Rawls includes liberties among his social primary goods, J. RAWLS, *supra* note 55, at 62, he later establishes, by what he calls "the priority of liberty," that "liberty can be restricted only for the sake of liberty itself." *Id.* at 244.

61. RAWLS, *supra* note 55, at 239.

correct results and to the support of self-respect. Indeed, one might argue that because the Rawlsian concept of justice is directed toward the preservation of the primary value of self-respect, the pursuit of correct results in the well-ordered or just society may be indistinguishable from the pursuit of dignitary values. Yet Rawls clearly does not conceive of a good adjudicatory process as independently or directly supporting the citizens' sense of self-worth. Regularity of application is enough for a theory concerned primarily with the justice of substantive claims.

We must beware of making more of the demand for dignified or self-respecting adjudicatory process on the basis of Rawls's theory than Rawls makes. It cannot, for example, be asserted that a thinker who gives the primacy Rawls does to self-respect would necessarily applaud its pursuit through judicial elaboration of the due process clause. For Rawls is also concerned with institutions, and he clearly views judicial review as a move away from equality of political participation. In at least some of his discussions of liberty, the countermajoritarian difficulty is a stark reality. He admits that bills of rights and judicial review might be developed in ways that maintain equal liberty. But there is no strong argument here for the inclusion of process rights in constitutional arrangements—beyond the dictates of equal political liberty and the rule of law.

Perhaps the strongest case that comports with Rawls's theory for constitutionalizing process values in pursuit of self-respect is this: in a less than well-ordered state, in which legislation results from bargaining rather than from a rational attempt to implement the two principles of justice, a process of rational constitutional adjudication *might* legitimately restrain or supplement majoritarian institutions. And as a part of the judicial activity tending to promote the ultimate achievement of the just state, the court *might* find it beneficial, even necessary, to impose process restraints on administrative decision making. Moreover, it *might* be useful in such a situation to construct process requirements in ways that not only promote attention to the rational ends of administrative decision making, but that also support a sense of self-respect otherwise promoted inadequately by the existing organization of society.

We might, for example, construct a basis for reason-giving as a due process requirement by proceeding in this prudential way. At least in the Kantian-Rawlsian, perfectionist version of liberalism, human dignity and self-respect are rational constructions. Kant emphasizes the dual role of reason in moral action: reason is the will's tutor as well as its handmaiden, both the means by which the good will is formed and the means for constructing good actions in daily life.[62] As with Rawls,[63] at least one can say that Kant would view as immoral institutional arrangements that interfered with either function of rationality. Pincoffs's analysis is thus on firmer ground when he hinges Roth's need for information on his need to be able to regulate his own future behavior. Processes that are wholly uninformative, yet potentially meaningful, constrain individuals in their endeavor to act as free and rational beings. Such processes, at some level of opacity or seeming arbitrariness, combined with substantial state involvement in our lives, would tend to undermine the bases for conceiving of the individual, in political terms, as an autonomous moral agent entitled to self-respect.

A fundamental demand for rational processes of social decision making is thus a fair implication from Kantian moral theory. But the individual's right to know the reasons for official action need not imply an extensive right to processes that would require the public agency to behave rationally. That the agency or official is mistaken or foolish in some—even many—cases may thwart our desires, but it need not impair our capacity to understand what has happened and to receive whatever instruction is appropriate to the occasion. For a process to be rational in this sense is only for it to be *comprehensible*—a much thinner sense of rationality than the Benthamite accuracy-seeking process, which other dignitary theorists have found inadequate.

THE LIBERAL CONSENSUS

Some interesting implications arise from this modest foray through classical and contemporary liberal thought. It seems

62. I. KANT, *op. cit. supra* note 44, at 10–11, 29.
63. This idea is captured in Rawls's theory by the notion of reflective equilibrium. *See, e.g.,* J. RAWLS, *op. cit. supra* note 55, at 20, 49–51.

clear that we were correct to be concerned about intuitive claims to process. If we view those claims as claims to personal autonomy, to doing what one wants, then we must (if we are to be coherent) make liberalism's classic move (from Locke to Mill to Nozick) to separate the private from the public sphere. Dignitary claims then take on the character of substantive restraints on state power. Acceptable characteristics of processes mediating interpersonal or intergroup conflicts would be either consensual (in the private sphere) or, when the processes are designed to further public purposes, subject to protected zones of privacy. It appears that claims to *participation* in public processes must take the form of utilitarian-instrumentalist claims to equal respect. No matter which form the claims take, mainstream liberal thought gives them only a limited determinate content: (a) equally weighted voting under conditions of majority rule; (b) equal application of legal rules; and (c) the avoidance of incomprehensibility.

This is not to say that ideals like participation in public process or opportunities for revelation make no contribution to realizing the ultimate liberal value of individual self-respect. It is merely to say that they do not seem to be a part of its core conditions. Participation and revelation contain contradictions and raise counterarguments that suggest that they can be pursued only in a prudential fashion—by weighing them against other values. They cannot be asserted as strong constitutional rights, to be respected in every context on pain of transforming the body politic into an illiberal regime.

Those in quest of a richer set of dignitary due process requirements will have to move beyond the basic tenets of liberalism, or construct a complex *prudential* argument that renders additional protections necessary to the implementation of the core values—majority rule, equal application of legal rules, thin rationality, and privacy. Both approaches seem misguided to me. For I do not believe that fraternity can be mandated by law without an unacceptable loss of individualist liberal values. Nor do I believe that much of administrative procedure should be made constitutional through prudential due process requirements. There are, indeed, rich possibilities for constructing prudential legal rules that attempt to implement basic liberal-democratic process values. But as the next section of this chapter seeks to demonstrate, the process of developing such rules is sufficiently problematic to destroy almost any claim that these instrumental constructions are the special province of the *judiciary* through *constitutional* interpretation.

A PRUDENTIAL APPROACH

A prudential approach asks, What is necessary, given the contingencies of modern government, to effect the liberal state's promise to construct a legal order that supports privacy, equality, and comprehensibility in public decisional processes? To ask is not, of course, to answer, but the way the argument proceeds is quite familiar.

One begins with the notion that dignitary promises are not easily kept. The clearest decisional-process implication of equality—majority rule—requires support from several directions if it is to provide more than formal legitimation of public decision making. First, much majority rule is mediated, rather than immediate—we have a representative, not a direct, democracy. Second, the electoral process is subject to many well-known forms of corruption—concentrations of power, information gaps, and so on. Third, the voting process, whether at referendum or within representative assemblies, has some basic theoretical problems—often described as voting paradoxes or agenda difficulties—which demand attention.[64] Fourth, the output of the mediated voting process must be realized by administrative action, which may undermine effectuation of those electoral preferences that reach the stage of implementation.[65]

Rationality, even in the thin sense of comprehensibility, is similarly subject to constant challenge. In part, the challenge proceeds from the weaknesses of the guarantee of equality via majority rule. At the legislative level, majority rule is the legitimizing rationale for particular policy choices. We are to under-

64. *See generally* B. ACKERMAN, *op. cit. supra* note 3, at 289–93; Kramer, *Some Procedural Aspects of Majority Rule,* in DUE PROCESS, NOMOS XVIII, at 264 (J. Pennock & J. Chapman eds. 1977).

65. *See* Ackerman & Hassler, *Beyond the New Deal: Coal and the Clean Air Act,* 89 YALE L.J. 1466 (1980); Stewart, *supra* chapter 4, note 17, at 1682–87.

stand the output of the legislative process as simultaneously making substantive choices and supporting equality.[66] But to the extent that the difficulties of effecting equality through majoritarianism have undermined the connection between policy choice and electoral preferences, that rationale seems implausible.

Additional problems emerge at the level of administrative implementation. Instrumentally rational pursuit of legislative policy confronts the ambiguity and incoherence of legislative goals and the uncertainties of fact-finding. Administrative articulation of a rationale instrumentally relating goal X to state-of-the-world A hardly provides the assurances of rationality necessary for responsible self-regulation when the citizen had presumed that goal Y was intended and that situation B obtained. There are also serious problems with structuring rational processes of decision making when more than a few decision makers are involved. Bureaucratic decision making obviously should be consistent across deciders; a process in which *who* decides matters—perhaps more than the articulated public policies or the facts—is an obvious example of arbitrariness, and hence, from one perspective, of irrationality.[67] If the substantive outputs of administration seem contradictory, or explicable only in terms of the undisclosed propensities of different deciders, then we become, as Kafka's K, the objects of the personal caprice of state officials.

Thus, rich possibilities begin to emerge for developing prudential legal rules demanding both legislative specificity and accuracy-seeking administrative processes combined with reason giving. Indeed, at the prudential level, reasonable accuracy emerges as a peculiarly salient instrumental value. A demand that administrators accurately find the facts upon which their implementing action is predicated supports comprehensibility, equal application, *and* the effectuation of policies adapted under conditions of majority rule.

66. *See* Kuflik, *Majority Rule Procedure,* in DUE PROCESS, NOMOS XVIII, at 296, 321–22, (J. Pennock & J. Chapman eds. 1977); *cf. id.* at 323 (positing various justifications for majority rule, some reflecting concern for correctness of decisions, others for equality and procedural fairness).

67. *See* J. MASHAW, C. GOETZ, F. GOODMAN, W. SCHARTZ, P. VERKUIL, & M. CARROW, SOCIAL SECURITY HEARINGS AND APPEALS 42–48 (1978).

We should be clear, nevertheless, that however plausible
—even compelling—the arguments for constructing prudential
structures to support core demands for equality and rationality,
implementation will not be straightforward. A concern for rationality, for example, leads to concerns about inconsistency and
arbitrariness. Yet the routines that make consistency possible
in bureaucracies are among our prime examples of irrational
behavior—the wooden inability to respond to differences in
context. We thus seem to confront a choice between the irrationality of bureaucratic control and the irrationality of official
discretion.

Similarly, when we return to the question of support for majoritarianism, we might think that the vagueness and mediate-
ness of electoral decisions, plus the possibilities for corruption
and agenda manipulation, demand direct participation by affected interests when administrators formulate implementating,
subsidiary norms. It is equally sensible to argue the opposite,
that more of this kind of direct participation will in fact skew
policy away from the desires of the general electorate and toward the demands of special interest groups, thus lessening the
effectiveness of general arrangements that sustain equality of
voting power.[68]

Interpretive mysteries also afflict the application of privacy
constraints and the important prudential demand for reasonable accuracy. We may be clear that familial and individual privacy should be protected by evidentiary privileges. For the burdens of public revelation may destroy the bases for mutual trust
or personal autonomy. But we are far from sure what should
count as a family relationship, or what remedial measures would
best protect the underlying values of the self-incrimination restraint, while leaving intact the value of reasonable accuracy.
Moreover, this latter value hardly can be implemented without
attending to the question, Reasonable accuracy about what? The
possibility of legal security that accuracy supports surely has
some relationship to the importance of the interests at stake in
any particular decision process.

We need not pursue the whole litany of problems and potential solutions to appreciate that in the prudential realm much

68. *See, e.g.,* T. Lowi, The End of Liberalism 68–72, 85–93 (1969).

turns on one's sense of highly uncertain social, political, economic, and psychological factors. This is not to say that all these factors will never point in the same direction. A decisional process that is neither consistent nor capable of finely textured individual judgments is not faced with the dilemma of choosing which of these ends to pursue at the expense of the other. Yet, when we *are* faced with this choice, the mere demand that the official behave with sufficient rationality to provide an understandable legal order does not of itself determine which horn of the dilemma will be chosen, or whether some compromise between systemic and intuitive rationality might not turn out to be prudent. In some circumstances we might even wish to abandon transparent rationality entirely, either because the decision is too poignant (the draft lottery) or the reasons too distressing (allocation of life support systems).[69] Prudential systems may balance and accommodate values in an *almost* infinite variety of ways.

Notwithstanding these difficulties, the preceding discussion may point the way toward a sensible strategy for implementing dignitary values when constructing administrative procedures. In outline, the argument proceeds as follows. First, from the perspective of liberal theory, process values have a rough hierarchy—equality (as embodied in majority rule), thin rationality (comprehensibility), and some set of privacy constraints have been seen to be more fundamental to the preservation of a political morality based on individual self-respect (that is, liberalism) than are other values. These values therefore have strong claims to implementation via judicial review for constitutionality. Second, additional prudential or derivative values (individualization, direct participation, accuracy, and the like) present prima facie constitutional claims for realization. They are the means for giving the basic values a content that realistically confronts the social context of the individual self. None of these claims is absolute. Each may be defeated by the recognition that the challenged process is explicable either as one of the means for achieving the value asserted, or as a trade-off among competing values. Notwithstanding the weakness of these claims as constitutional standards, they may nevertheless, because of their

69. G. CALABRESI & P. BOBBIT, *supra* note 10, at 57–62.

prima facie status, have powerful effects as principles of statutory construction.

Thus far, then, it would appear that we have labored long and hard, sometimes tediously, to bring forth an approach to constitutional claims that is as objectionable as it is familiar. It not only relies on a fundamental values analysis, it then permits balancing of the purportedly fundamental. I would argue, nevertheless, that there are significant differences between this theory and, for example, the two-tier formula of fundamental and other values that has previously been so influential in equal protection analysis,[70] and, to a lesser degree, in due process analysis. First, the criterion of fundamentalness, which I have elaborated, has a claim to more than intuitive plausibility. It is rooted in the consensus elements of liberal political thought, a philosophic tradition that nearly all would agree provides the ideological bedrock for the construction of American constitutional theory. Second, as the next section of this chapter seeks to demonstrate, this theory of dignitary process values is capable of a reasonably straightforward application to some of the major administrative due process problems that have confronted, and will continue to confront, the Supreme Court. More important, that application seems to solve those problems in coherent and convincing ways.

SOME HYPOTHETICAL APPLICATIONS

Perhaps the simplest way to proceed is by example—to consider a series of claims and how they might be analyzed. I shall take as examples some now familiar cases that illustrate three focal points of continuing concern about the processes of the administrative state: (1) the application of general rules to individual cases without the opportunity to supply a circumstantial context; (2) limits on direct participation in processes for the formation of rights; and (3) the protection of welfare state entitle-

70. *See, e.g.,* San Antonio Independent School Dist. v. Rodriguez, 411 U.S. 1, 17, 40 (1973); Gunther, *The Supreme Court, 1971 Term—Foreward: In Search of Evolving Doctrine of a Changing Court: A Model for a Newer Equal Protection,* 86 HARV. L. REV. 1 (1972); *Developments in the Law—Equal Protection,* 82 HARV. L. REV. 1065 (1969).

ments. The application of the dignitary approach to these questions is not always without problems, but neither is it particularly elusive.

GENERAL RULES AND INDIVIDUAL CASES

Imagine a substantive context modeled loosely on *Califano v. Yamasaki.*[71] The case before the Court involves recoupment of wrongfully paid AFDC benefits. The federal statutory standard, let us assume, provides for recoupment except where the refund would create undue hardship and the recipient has received the benefits in good faith. Assume further that state X has taken the position, as a matter of regulatory policy, that recipients who received improper payments because of their failure to report changes in earnings cannot satisfy the good faith standard. The claimant, who admittedly received improper payments because of a delay in reporting increased income, requests a hearing in which to demonstrate good faith. She offers to prove that illness during the relevant time period prevented notification of the welfare department concerning the changed circumstances. The request for hearing is denied because of the previously announced policy.

The welfare recipient has two plausible due process claims. First, if her proofs were accepted, she would be seen not to have acted in bad faith when she failed to report increased income during the relevant time period. To deny the recipient an opportunity to make those proofs excludes crucially relevant evidence from a process purportedly designed to illuminate the issue of good faith. The refusal to consider individual circumstances thus seems *irrational.* The second due process claim is that because the hearing process refuses to hear her excuse, although it hears excuses from persons overpaid for other reasons, there is an obvious *inequality* in access to hearings among potentially affected persons.

How might the state's case proceed? Its defense must begin by elaborating the constitutional content of rationality and equality. The state's equality defense is straightforward and de-

71. 442 U.S. 682 (1980).

terminative. There is no special rule for *this claimant's* case. The attempt to compare her position to the cases of others to whom the rule does not apply is really an attack on the rationality of the rule, not the equality of the process; it must be dealt with as such.

We turn then to the rationality claim. Here again the core value has been respected. The process is rational in the sense that it gives reasons. The claimant's case fits under the rule. The decision is thus transparent and comprehensible. When the claimant says more, that the process is irrational because it produces errors due to overgeneralization, her claim becomes a claim to reasonable accuracy and must be evaluated from a different and more prudential perspective.

The state might begin its defense against the reasonable accuracy challenge by noting the relationship of the contested rule to consistent decision making. Wholly discretionary judgments by a number of hearing officers concerning the good faith of persons who fail to report income changes almost certainly would lead to inconsistent, and in that sense arbitrary or irrational, administration of the good faith test. Orderliness and equality in administration are promoted by developing some clear rules that can be applied consistently by multiple decision makers in subsequent decisional processes. Indeed, it is not clear how an agency that gave free reign to its adjudicatory personnel to decide cases on individualized bases *could* pursue a policy of assuring reasonable accuracy. In a system of individualized judgments on an issue such as good faith, clear evidentiary rules may be the only means for controlling the subjectivity of decision making. Moreover, the failure to report earnings does seem clearly and directly related to the good faith issue. Using such behavior as a proxy for subjective good faith is unlikely to be grossly inaccurate.

The state's defense need not prevail. The plaintiff might yet demonstrate that the choice between systemic and contextual rationality was unnecessary. Perhaps there is no basis, in experience or otherwise, for the judgment that administration would be inconsistent under the general standard. Perhaps the state could have allowed individualized determinations without introducing objectionable levels of decider subjectivity and, there-

208 / *Dignitary Process and the Liberal Tradition*

fore, of potential arbitrariness. But, obviously, the going will be tough.

A critic of the results of this example might argue that if that's the way the theory works, it justifies obvious irrationality. Good faith, the critic might proceed, clearly implies *individualized* judgment. I would reply as follows: either the critic means to say that there is only one way to conceptualize rationality in administration, or he means to say that *under this statute* only a single perspective is permissible. The former meaning is too obviously false to require discussion. The latter argument may be a good one, *but it is not a constitutional argument.* It is a challenge to the authority of the agency under the statute. The question then becomes a question of statutory interpretation, of what protections are afforded by the positive law.

At the level of statutory construction many other questions also are relevant: the general structure of the statute, the language of other related sections, legislative history, and so on. At this level one can imagine a quite common scenario in which the prima facie case for individualization will carry the day. The general statutory structure is, after all, one in which a rigid general rule—recoupment—may be relaxed by reference to a waiver standard—good faith—that appears designed to permit individualization. In these circumstances it seems perfectly plausible to decide that the administrator has misconstrued the statute by failing to give appropriate weight to the statutory value of individualized determination in the waiver process. Yet because it would be a nonconstitutional ruling, a judicial construction of this point would not preclude majoritarian reversal or modification of that judgment. Judicial review based on a generous positivism—one informed by attention to dignitary process values—may be simultaneously protective and modest.

I do not, however, want to argue that individualized judgment can never be a constitutional requirement, only that such a requirement should not proceed from the simple fact that rules overgeneralize. *Stanley v. Illinois,*[72] for example, certainly provides an appealing case for granting a request for individualized hearing as an aspect of due process. To be deprived of the

72. 405 U.S. 645 (1972). See also discussion *supra,* chapter 1 notes 91–95.

custody of one's child because the legislature has declared that all unwed natural fathers are just not fit parents seems terribly harsh. And the statute seems resistent to generous positivist interpretation. Yet to remit the state to a different procedure—a hearing on Stanley's fitness that considers both his circumstance and his child's—one must surely say more than (as the irrebuttable presumption cases do) that the results of the legislative characterization will sometimes be wrong. The Court must instead be prepared to assert that preservation of natural familial ties is so important to the individual's sense of self, to the maintenance of individual autonomy and self-respect, that the state can allocate familial rights and enforce familial duties only on the strongest showing of necessity and through the most cautious and elaborate of decision processes. In short, the Court must assert and defend a substantive constitutional right to which the requested process is instrumental, if not essential. That theory of substantive rights, of substantive due process, will serve then to organize the constitutional conversation about the functions and requirements of individualization in that and other substantive contexts.

LIMITS ON PARTICIPATION

Imagine again Roth's case.[73] The term contract of a nontenured state college professor is not renewed. The teacher claims he had a due process right to a statement of reasons and an evidentiary hearing before being fired.

As in the example based on *Yamasaki*, the plaintiff has no very plausible *equality* claim. So far as we know, everyone on a term contract gets the same process—some form of evaluation and judgment. The fundamental problem relates to the *rationality* of the process. For all Roth can tell the judgment is based on whim. Because he is provided no reason, Roth is treated as a being for whom reasons are unimportant, for whom legitimacy and power are synonymous. And if that is Roth's position, then he is an infinitely manipulable means for realizing whatever secret ends the power wielders may have in mind.

73. Roth v. Bd. of Regents, 408 U.S. 564 (1972). See also dialogue in chapter 3 at 146–51.

The question is what the state college may say in defense. How can the failure to provide a reason be consistent with support for the value of thin rationality? There are, of course, institutions whose acts carry their reasons with them—legislative promulgation of statutes, draft lotteries, and jury verdicts, for example. These are institutions established to exercise discretion in the absence of, or outside of, revealed legal criteria. To be subject to their power is not to be subject to general principles from which reasons can be derived to explain decisions in specific cases. To understand these institutions is to understand that their legitimacy lies instead in processes of selection or operation that support individual liberty and that render reason giving irrelevant. But that is not Roth's situation. Presumably the college president has a reason. Roth should be entitled to it (if he wants it) at a constitutional minimum.

As we saw in the previous example, however, a reason alone may or may not be satisfactory. There is still the question of what counts as a reason—another way of stating the argument for *substantive* rationality. And lurking in the background is our prior concern with how the rationality principle, once loosed on the administrative process, stops short of requiring that administrative judgments be absolutely correct in all cases.

Suppose, for example, the college president's letter says that Roth is not rehired because "I don't like you." Is that a reason? Of course. It is a reason that analogizes the president to the legislature. If Roth has a claim in these circumstances, it will relate to the authority of the president, under the governing legislation, to hire and fire on the basis of personal preference. And should the president get past that hurdle, to the authority of the legislature to make the exercise of public power private.[74]

More often we would expect the president to give reasons such as, "It is necessary to cut back our staff by five percent"; or, "Better qualified candidates are available to us"; or "Your teaching (research and the like) has not been of a quality that justifies retention." These are also, obviously, rational answers. They give reasons; they are not internally contradictory. Yet Roth may certainly want more. To each of the president's reasons we can

74. *See, e.g.*, Carter v. Carter Coal Co., 298 U.S. 238 (1936).

imagine him saying: "Why me?" "How better qualified?" and, "What precisely are my shortcomings?"

These are again perfectly reasonable sorts of questions. Moreover, assuming that some answers are forthcoming, they lead to a further round of queries of the "How do you know that?" sort. And in the next iteration, Roth can be expected to begin asserting that certain facts are wrong, or have been considered out of context, and to start demanding some further process for testing facts and placing them in proper perspective. Does a right to reasons or to a reasonably accurate process carry him that far?

At the level of stating a claim, the answer is yes. But the possibilities for adequate defense by the state are so substantial that one is hard pressed to imagine that Roth would prevail. The reasonableness of declining further process could be established from a number of directions: the impact of such processes on the resources available for the principal mission of the school; the effects of contentious processes on the willingness of supervisory personnel to act on their convictions in replacing existing staff; the low probability that hearings will illuminate, rather than misdirect, decision making that is subjective, incremental, comparative, and synthesizing. Any of these reasons might support the reasonableness of limiting the public aspect of the decisional process to the simple provision of a reason. Nothing in the college's statutes and regulations, or in Roth's contract, leads him to expect additional legal security for the position he holds. Roth would surely have difficulty analogizing his interest in retaining a job at a particular college to Stanley's interest in avoiding disqualification from exercising the custodial role of a parent for his natural child, or indeed to any interest of similar constitutional significance.

This limited participation may make Roth feel doubly excluded—excluded not just because of his nonretention, but because of the minimal role he was allowed to play in formulating the institution's policies and in assessing their applicability to his case. Yet, assuming that there was compliance with applicable statutes and regulations, there seems no convincing basis for a constitutional participatory right in this context. Participation in policy formation at Roth's college may be an interest of all within (students, faculty, staff) and many outside it (neighbors, alumni, applicants). Yet the exclusion of some potential interests is hardly a sufficient threat to political equality to justify restructuring the university's authority system.

Roth's disappointment at an *application* of some policy does not heighten his claim to participation in policy *formation*. His claim to further participation in the process of application could succeed therefore only by defeating the reasons for process limitations that seemed pretty certain to overwhelm that same claim when viewed as a demand for additional safeguards of the rationality of the process. I can see no reason to believe that those countervailing interests are of any lesser weight when a claim to increased participation is at stake. In this prudential weighing of interests the state will almost certainly prevail if it is given the most modest presumption of regularity.

DEFENDING WELFARE STATE ENTITLEMENTS

The foregoing examples suggest the basic approach of the dignitary theory of process values. There is strong protection for the core values: reason giving, majority rule, and certain privacy protections. Participation, accuracy, and individualization are additional process values that support human dignity and self-respect. But they are more likely to be realized as aspects of statutory construction than as constitutional rights. Given their multiple meanings and potential conflicts, prudent legislatures and administrators might have many excellent reasons for not supporting certain aspects of these values more strongly when designing some particular form of public decision making. What is at stake for a party demanding additional or substitute processes is important to a dignitary theory as a *constitutional* matter only insofar as the Court is prepared to give that party's *substantive* interest independent constitutional significance.

How, then, do these principles apply in the arena that started the due process revolution and within which it has arguably had its greatest significance—defense of the benefits provided by the welfare state? Let us revisit *Goldberg v. Kelly, Mathews v. Eldridge*, and *O'Bannon v. Town Court Nursing Center*. Will the modesty of the dignitary approach require us to reverse *Goldberg* although affirming *Eldridge* and *O'Bannon?* There are surely strong reasons for believing that the answer is yes. For the AFDC system in *Goldberg* was indeed reasonably accurate, gave reasons, conformed to the legislative mandate, and involved only money. The same was true of the *Eldridge* disability benefits scheme. Can we imagine the *O'Bannon* plaintiffs, whose basic medical support was not even threatened, sustaining their claim to increased participation by elaborating a substantive constitutional right to preservation of a particular nursing home placement or to maintenance of their emotional well-being?

Analysis tends to confirm the suspicions that these capsule statements and questions suggest. As presented to the Court, *Goldberg* and *Eldridge* involved only the timing, not the existence, of a hearing check on bureaucratic routines. Moreover, these routines were, so far as anyone could demonstrate, reasonably accurate. Chapter 3 suggested some ways in which AFDC determinations might be feared to be more error-prone than disability determinations. But there was no evidence presented that either AFDC or DI administration was wildly erratic, or that either failed to conform to the general ideals of the rule of law. Both systems surely make errors.[75] And, given the protective purposes of the two programs, I certainly can see a responsible court construing either or both titles of the Social Security Act to presume that aid be continued for terminated recipients pending completion of the existing statutory hearings, when such hearings are requested. Such a decision would protect both AFDC and DI claimants, while permitting Congress to decide more explicitly where it intended to place the risk of error pending a hearing.

O'Bannon was at base an attack on the rationality of the statutory presumption that state decertification implied low-quality nursing home care. Yet surely that scheme was a reasonably accurate means for implementing the congressional desire not to support inadequate nursing home care with federal third-party payments on behalf of elderly and poor recipients. Unless the desire to stay in a particular home, however understandable,

---

75. For a much more extended treatment of the accuracy issue in the disability system see J. MASHAW, ET AL., SOCIAL SECURITY HEARINGS AND APPEALS (1978) and J. MASHAW, BUREAUCRATIC JUSTICE (1983).

even poignant, can be given some independent constitutional significance, I do not see how the Court could reach a result like *Stanley* in a case like *O'Bannon*. Nor does the statute seem hospitable to a generous construction that would build in a waiver of certification clause, although stranger constructions of congressional legislation certainly are not unknown.

Lest these results seem too distressing, let me be clear about what is *not* being said here. It is not being asserted that welfare state beneficiaries have *only* those process rights provided by statute. Had the statutes in question in these cases not provided hearings or other circumstantial guarantees of trustworthiness of the judgments made; had the regimes in question been ones of simple discretion giving free reign to the caseworkers' moral preferences and personal instincts;[76] then due process reform, including perhaps a structured right to hearing, would have been in order. If basic legal security is to be maintained, and with it the possibility of individual choice and individual moral responsibility, such lawlessness must be proscribed. But this was not the situation portrayed in *Goldberg* or *Eldridge* or *O'Bannon*.

Moreover, it surely remains open for the Court to elaborate a special doctrine applicable to income support (and perhaps other welfare state benefits) that would increase the constitutional protections afforded interests in those benefits. As the Court's desperation language in *Goldberg* suggests, it may be sensible to say that welfare recipients, along with the criminally accused, are in peculiarly precarious positions. Manipulation of the power to withhold basic sustenance, like manipulation of the power to punish, poses special dangers for the maintenance of individual liberty. And, as in the criminal context, this special danger can be combated only by making the government bear large risks of error in the private individual's favor.

Although I do not wish to argue here for this special doctrine

---

76. For examples of such regimes and their correction by due process adjudication see, *e.g., Holmes v. N.Y. Hous. Auth.,* 398 F.2d 262 (2d Cir. 1968); *Hornsby v. Allen,* 326 F.2d 605 (5th Cir. 1964); *Sun Ray Drive-in Dairy, Inc. v. Or. Liquor Control Comm'n,* 16 Ore. App. 63, 517 P.2d 289 (1973). Local AFDC administration has sometimes operated in a similar fashion. *See* Mashaw, *Welfare Reform and Local Administration of Aid to Families with Dependent Children,* 57 Va. L. Rev. 818 (1971). But these instances result from disregarding federal statutory and regulatory requirements, not from applying them.

for recipients of income support, it is worth noting what that doctrine need not entail. First, this is not the dignitary approach smuggling Charles Reich's new property in through the back door.[77] The argument would not be that welfare benefits must be accorded formal protection because they are like airline route certificates or television broadcast licenses in the modern administrative state. The argument instead would be that protection should be provided this special form of property because of the vulnerability of the population seeking access to it to the personal domination of the dispensers of largesse. It is after all no accident that public welfare made a major contribution to the demise of the Democratic party's machine in New York City, or that negative income tax plans (by other names) have foundered in the Senate Finance Committee because of their social and political effects on white political power in the South.

I also want to be clear that, if based upon the dignitary considerations I have been discussing, special procedural protections for subsistence welfare rights need not entail provision of subsistence welfare as a substantive constitutional right. The danger to be avoided is bureaucratic manipulation of individuals via control of the conditions of access to governmental programs of subsistence. The possibility of such manipulation is reduced as the difficulty in denying eligibility by an exercise of pure discretion is increased. Procedural rules making decisions more transparent, consistent, and accurate clearly reduce the discretion of low-level deciders. The constitutionally relevant danger disappears entirely, however, when there is no program to administer. Hence the right to welfare state benefits is not a necessary part of the constitutional legal security supported by this hypothetical extension of the dignitary theory of due process.

A PRELIMINARY ASSESSMENT: THE DIGNITARY
MODEL AND CLAIMS OF FRATERNAL ASSOCIATION

These hypothetical cases, and others, could be further developed and analyzed. Enough has been said, however, to provide an idea of how dignitary theory can be applied in practice.

77. Reich, *supra* note 30.

There is also at least some indication from these examples of potential strengths and weaknesses. Although we began with a robust set of intuitive claims, the approach has proved rather restrained. While avoiding initial positivist traps, this theory nonetheless may refer many process issues to the construction of the positive law. A "generous positivism" might be the appropriate label under which to proceed in further elaborating prudential process protections having their fundamental basis in the liberal ideal of individual self-respect. For those who, in pursuit of dignitary values, would vigorously constitutionalize administrative processes and who distrust prudential elaboration of constitutional rights, the challenge is clear. Some basis beyond traditional liberal theory is required to justify the pursuit.

That liberal theory fails to provide a robust vision of process values will not surprise many. The conventional criticism of individualist moral and political ideas—a criticism elegantly and forcefully stated by Robert Paul Wolff in *The Poverty of Liberalism*[78]—explains the procedural barrenness of liberal theory. As Wolff puts it, individualistic notions of political rights are at war with man's basic sociability. We are fundamentally social beings, not individuals. Indeed, the concept of an individual is coherent only in the context of social existence. Our fundamental demands are not for separateness, but for community. We want not merely to be left alone, but to be related to others in significant ways. For Wolff an individualistic foundation for a philosophy of politics is about as informative as an explanation of the harmony of a string quartet that begins with the thesis that the musicians are competing with each other to produce a solo.

Wolff's account, whether viewed as an account of individual psychology or social reality, has some persuasive power. To send Roth away with a reason sufficient for him to understand what has occurred to him may be enough to protect his individuality, but it seems a meager response nevertheless. A liberal polity that defines moral action in this atomistic fashion seems not to recognize the social preconditions of individuality. From a communal, or fraternal, perspective it makes more sense to imagine that what Roth really wanted when he asked for a "reason" was a

---

78. R. WOLFF, THE POVERTY OF LIBERALISM (1968).

"conversation." His interest was not just in a statement, to internalize as he might, but in a relationship in which he both knew and was known. For it may be that we cannot, after all, ever know ourselves except as mediated and reinforced by association with others.[79]

Once these arguments are accepted, demands for participation take on life and force. Notions of equality and rationality that seem somehow sterile when they are interpreted as creating equal rights to pull a voting machine's lever and to receive a reason from an official are energized when they are conceived as promoting an ongoing dialogue in a community of equals.[80] And it is this conception that seems to motivate much of the dignitary theory literature—a conception that Frank Michelman recognized in describing his discussion as a discussion of associational aims in due process.[81]

Yet for Wolff to suggest that liberal thought ignores demands for community surely is incorrect. A careful reading of the history of liberal ideas should rather describe the central problem liberal thinkers have set for themselves as the development of appropriate means for mediating the competition between individualistic and associational drives—a problem resolvable in a variety of ways, none of which forgets the duality of human nature.[82] Indeed, the communitarian perspective of the Scots moral sense school seems to have strongly influenced Thomas Jefferson[83] and James Wilson.[84] Gordon Wood finds an undifferentiated communitarian ethic permeating the intellectual atmosphere at the founding of the American republic.[85] But these constitutionally significant communitarian ideas lead in a familiar direction—utilitarianism. The moral posture of the

79. *See* R. UNGER, KNOWLEDGE AND POLITICS 191–235 (1875).

80. As Bruce Ackerman has asked, "What would our social world look like if no one ever suppressed another's questions of legitimacy, where every questioner met with a conscientious attempt at an answer?" B. ACKERMAN, *supra* note 3, at 4.

81. Michelman, *supra* chapter 4, note 16.

82. *See* Kronman, *Book Review*, 61 MINN. L. REV. 167, 181–83 (1976) (reviewing R. UNGER, *op. cit. supra* note 79).

83. G. WILLS, *supra* note 32, at 200–06.

84. W. McWILLIAMS, THE IDEA OF FRATERNITY IN AMERICA 193–94 (1973); G. WILLS, *supra* note 32, at 250–51.

85. G. WOOD, *supra* note 24, at 53–59.

individual—benevolent action—translates at the community level into the promotion of the greatest good for the greatest number.[86] The integration of the individual into the moral community is achieved by internalizing the good of the community as a maxim of individual moral action.[87]

Wolff therefore must be suggesting some transformation of our ideas that goes further—that recognizes the separate reality and claims of community, but presumably maintains the reality of individual freedom.[88] I have no clear vision of this theory.[89] What due process claims such a theory might entail must await the event. Indeed, in a world both genuinely communal and genuinely individualist, adjudicable dignitary claims to process just might be beside the point. For one might easily imagine such a theory leading to a rather conventional distinction between private realms of fraternal self-realization and public realms of decision making subject to the restraints of liberal constitutionalism. In such a state, a liberal legal order would protect the opportunity for fraternity, but would not attempt to transform society into community.

As I stated previously, I am not dismayed by the limitations of a noncommunitarian conception of the due process clause (or of American constitutionalism in general) or by the ultimately prudential character of much of the analysis that a dignitary conception of due process invites. For I believe, with the liberal tradition I have described, that we should give ourselves laws primarily through nonjudicial institutions of private and public ordering, and that the compromised character of public life necessarily limits the degree of constitutionalization that will accommodate our constantly shifting needs to mediate the clash of individual and group interests.

86. G. WILLS, *supra* note 32, at 248–55.

87. *See* H. SIDGWICK, THE METHODS OF ETHICS 387–89 (7th ed. 1907).

88. Wolff provides only a possibility theorem on the conceptual coherence of a community value. R. WOLFF, *op. cit. supra* note 78, at 163–95.

89. For an exemplary attempt at such a theory, see R. UNGER, *op. cit. supra* note 79. I suspect such a theory would follow Rousseau in the sense that Frank Michelman describes in *Politics and Values or What's Really Wrong with Rationality Review?* 13 CREIGHTON L. REV. 487 (1979). But as Michelman has also told us, *supra* chapter 4, note 16, translating this vision into a demand for procedural review is much more complicated than using it to explain our discomfiture at rationality or efficiency as a constitutional standard for valid substantive legislation.

Moreover, I am rather encouraged by the way in which a search for first principles and a sketch of their application incorporates the valuable insights of prior models of due process adjudication. In particular the dignitary approach seems to explain much of what is valuable in the model of competence and to present those values in a more plausible and convincing way. Attention to accuracy is obviously important. It relates to our most general due process demands for a reasonably stable, coherent, and therefore comprehensible legal order. Such a legal order cannot survive legal decision making that is arbitrary, that ignores what is or can be known about the physical and social world in which we attempt to plan our actions and achieve our goals.

This demand for competent fact-finding need not—and from a dignitary perspective, does not—cause us to imagine that all legal decision making is simply some form of accuracy-seeking implementation of prespecified legal rules. The reinterpreted prudential demand for reasonable accuracy includes ideas of coherence and of the relation of fact-finding to transparent value propositions. Yet it demands neither absolute correctness nor the explanation of residual error in some intuitive or pseudoscientific calculation of social welfare. Whether administration is reasonably competent can be based on a rough judgment about its comprehensibility without undermining the basic methodological approach. There is no claim here to auditing the social welfare balance sheet, only to protecting the fundamental preconditions of moral agency and individual self-respect.

Of equal or greater importance, the dignitary model explains our concern to respect the positive law. Majority rule is integrated into the set of dignitary values that are of interest to individuals. Judicial deference therefore is not the abdication, but the fulfillment of the judiciary's accepted constitutional mission of protecting individual rights. Yet, unlike the positivist traps that beset the model of competence, there is here no logical implication of universal judicial abdication. Majority rule's support for individual perceptions of equal citizenship need not *always* trump other dignitary values. For the substantive right that due process protects is not some contingent substantive claim embodied in positive law, but the fundamental individual right to legal arrangements that preserve the preconditions for moral agency and self-respect. Majority rule with universal suffrage is but one of those preconditions. It must somehow be accommodated to others where, in specific situations, they compete.

From what has been said it seems also to follow that the dignitary model, unlike the prior models, is not embarrassed by the relationship of substantive and procedural claims. The basic value of individual self-respect is obviously substantive. Yet at its core it is noncontroversial. The maintenance of individual liberty is what the American Constitution is preeminently about. To say that due process analysis proceeds from this substantive basis carries none of the implications of judicial usurpation that have long been associated with the term "substantive due process." The substantive agenda is neither hidden, as in the model of appropriateness, nor is it misdirected to general social welfare considerations, as in the model of competence.

Despite these many virtues one nevertheless might remain skeptical of the model of dignitary values. Constitutional adjudication hardly seems the place for leisurely reflection on the philosophical sources of American constitutionalism or cautious deduction of the implications of liberal-democratic theory for run-of-the-mill due process claims. Litigants generally appear in court to demand bits and pieces of adjudicatory process—some kind of hearing—in Judge Friendly's phrase.[90] These specific demands seem to connect in myriad ways to intuitively plausible dignitary values. Sorting out what the claim is really about is hard enough, without then hoping to assess carefully the way that support for this value by that process will sustain the ultimate values of human dignity and self-respect. For a dignitary model to work at the level of adjudication requires some rules of thumb.

The problem is still more difficult. The need for simple touchstones reminds us of the dynamics of precedent making and model building that seemed to plague and distort the model of appropriateness. Perhaps here too the desire for efficiency and the need for simplification will overwhelm the search for

90. Friendly, *Some Kind of Hearing*, 123 U. Pa. L. Rev. 1267 (1975).

fundamental ideals that motivates the dignitary methodology. A bastardized dignitary model, one whose dynamic is controlled by ordinary legal discourse and developed in ordinary legal institutions, easily might become as perplexing, contradictory, and divorced from its root ideas as have the models of appropriateness and competence in their application. Or alternatively, why should we not imagine that activist judges, impatient with theoretical limitations and prudential ambivalence, will consult the core ideal of human dignity in a wholly intuitive fashion and constitutionalize their own visions of a good society?

These are sensible and important questions that can only be resolved by observing the theory in action over time. No confined set of hypothetical applications like the ones I have made will convince those who instinctively distrust philosophizing as a technique for practical decision making. Yet we might approach these practical issues obliquely by another exercise in theory. For a concern with making dignitary theory operational at the level of ordinary legal discourse reminds us that the model of appropriateness has further claims on our attention. That model, more than any other, is the model of ordinary legal reasoning. It responds most easily to the particularity of adjudication and to the need to begin analysis with some set of simple models or metaphors of process—court, legislature, private ordering—that are part of the characteristic intellectual equipment of persons trained in law. The model of dignitary theory cannot hope to dislodge images as deeply imbedded as these in the legal imagination.

Yet, remember that the heuristics generated by the model of appropriateness (court, legislature, contract, and so on) failed to provide convincing analogies for any of the critical administrative due process issues that we have just discussed. They failed because although apparently value laden, they were divorced from any articulation and defense of their implicit normative position that might justify a choice among competing analogies. The question on our agenda thus is set: Might it be possible to combine appropriateness and dignity, as we have dignity and competence, to deepen, explain, and reorient the model of appropriateness, while retaining something of its ease of application?

6 / *Dignitary Appropriateness*

We now require an act of translation—a rebuilding of the conventional methodology of appropriateness on a foundation of liberal dignitary ideals rather than on an obscurantist traditionalism that no longer holds our allegiance. If successful, this new vernacular will presumably help resolve some of the puzzling issues of administrative due process that we have encountered in the Supreme Court's prior jurisprudence. We shall, therefore, reinterpret some classic cases in the jurisprudence of administrative process in terms of our new model of dignitary appropriateness. Only after observing the methodology in action can we determine, at least tentatively, whether it satisfies the symbolic and regulative criteria that chapter 1 suggested for methodological adequacy.

THE DIGNITARY BASES OF APPROPRIATENESS

Is there some set of processes appropriate to the dignitary ideals of a liberal-democratic polity? Can the forms, images, or metaphors of process that have been generated by the model of appropriateness (legislation, adjudication, contract, and the like) be given some explanation beyond tradition, analogy, precedent, or perhaps judiciomorphism—explanations that will connect the interpretation of these forms to dignitary ideals? If this can be done, then our primary objection to the model of ap-

propriateness—its failure to explain its basic theoretical underpinnings in a fashion that is consistent with modern liberal requirements for legitimation (generality, transparency, and rationality)—will have been answered.

A successful grounding of appropriateness models in liberal
theory would not imply that every due process case would demand an extended means-ends inquiry linking decision process
and political ideal. Rather, the demand of a rational bureaucratic legal order is only that such an analysis be possible. Once
accomplished it may yield a set of acceptable forms of process
that can be wielded as prototypes or rules of thumb, heuristics to
be employed as analytic guides when considering particular issues of the legitimacy of specific institutions or practices. These
prototypes would thus become the appropriate forms to which a
synthetic methodology compared the contingent, historical
structures generated by diverse administrative activity. A more
fundamental analysis from first principles, something resem-
bling the approach of chapter 5, would then be required, as is
traditional in American constitutional adjudication, only in the
face of substantial novelty.

This act of translation seems feasible. From basic ideas of
liberal-democratic governance and social relations one can construct a logic of collective decisional forms. Those forms can be
articulated in a fashion that will permit close comparison of the
elements of the ideal types and the features of existing decision
processes. The basis for legitimacy in the model of appropriateness can thus be transformed from the *fact* of tradition to a reasoned linkage between decision processes and the fundamental
liberal ideal of individual dignity. Moreover, as the discussion
proceeds it will appear that a modernized methodology for appropriateness analysis helps to explain much of the prior administrative due process jurisprudence and to justify the usually deferential, yet occasionally interventionist, posture that the Court
has historically adopted. But do not be misled. This transformation of the idea of appropriateness, whatever its interpretive insights, does not leave us with some infallible algorithm. We
emerge instead with rather familiar legal analytic tools and with
all too familiar defects. A revised model of liberal appropriate-

ness may structure constitutional argument more in accordance with our basic political ideals, but it will not often decide the cases for us.

AN ATTEMPT AT LIBERAL TRANSLATION

Suppose we were to ask what the appropriate collective decision processes were for a liberal-democratic state of substantial size and advanced technological development. The reader may be uneasy that I am about to launch into a major treatise of potentially staggering proportions. Fear not. The approach instead will be to take some conventional ideas and move them rapidly toward their implications for institutional forms. The movement will be too rapid for some. As a philosophic inquiry it is woefully inadequate. My basic purpose is to provide a more satisfactory basis for due process adjudication in a state whose basic political ideals are relatively stable, not to develop a more perfect political theory.

Let us begin by restating the basic value of *liberal* governance in terms of a general prohibition: State power shall not be used to subject any person to the will of another. This ideal can never be wholly realized. Nevertheless, collective decision processes in a liberal state must employ techniques that sharply constrain *personal* domination. *Democratic* governance implies broad opportunities for participation in collective decisions. It simultaneously implies that individual autonomy can be limited by the legitimate, that is, democratic expression of public values. Democracy thus presupposes both opportunities for cooperation in collective choices and inevitable conflicts of interest concerning the choices to be made. Finally, *advanced technology and substantial size* suggest a degree of interdependence necessitating frequent resort to collective action and the likelihood that decision making will have to be delegated to specialized institutions, rather than be carried out in a committee of the whole.

From the liberal perspective, there are essentially two techniques through which the state may exercise power, while avoiding the legitimation of personal domination. The first is *consent*; the second, the use of *impersonal rules* or principles. Consent may, of course, take several forms—actual agreement to a decision (*negotiation* to consensus) or agreement to a set of institutional rules that then generate decisions. In a democracy these latter rules usually involve *voting*, whether in town meetings, political caucuses, elections, referendums, or representative assemblies. *Impersonal decisions* may also be produced through two different institutional mechanisms. One employs general consensus principles (due care, reasonableness, fairness, and the like) that are applied in concrete situations by decision makers who are neutral as to the benefits and costs that flow from their particular decisions (*adjudication*). The other is the instrumentally rational implementation of collective decisions. In the ideal case such rules would be stated in wholly objective terms and would therefore be subject only to the contingent determination of the facts necessary for the accurate application of the rule (*administration*).

These basic decision processes—negotiation, voting, adjudication, and administration—might be thought to emerge from a simple two-by-two matrix illustrated by Table 1. On the horizontal axis are the normative ideals—consent and impersonality; on the vertical, alternative positive conceptions of democratic social life—cooperation and conflict. (But they appear as cooperation and conflict in mediate forms. We are dealing with a social reality lying somewhere between total war and perfect love; in those situations legal forms are irrelevant.)

The logic of the matrix is fairly straightforward. Negotiation, for example, is a successful decision process only where some element of cooperation is present in a social relationship—where joint action is recognized as increasing the returns to all partici-

Table 1

Positive \\ Normative	Consent	Impersonality
Cooperation	Negotiation	Administration
Conflict	Adjudication	Majoritarian Voting

pants. But simple joint maximizing is hardly enough to make negotiated agreement legitimate. Such agreement must proceed from the consent of parties whose wills are free from major restrictions on autonomous choice—impediments such as fraud and duress, which are known to the civil law as the "vices of consent." Alienation, false consciousness, class domination, and the like, are ever-present threats to the reality of consent in many contexts. But these problems need not trouble us here. The question for us is what collective decision processes are implied by liberal-democratic theory in the context of social relations that seem constantly to oscillate between cooperation and conflict.

The coalescence of conflict and consent yields adjudication. This process emerges most clearly in arbitral tribunals. There the parties find themselves unable to agree on a just distribution of the values in question but able to agree on a third-party decision maker. Before the proceeding begins, they consent to the fairness or legitimacy of the distribution that the arbitral tribunal will make. Consent to the decisions of courts of compulsory jurisdiction is, of course, more problematic. Yet the nearly universal use of courts in liberal-democratic politics attests to a social logic—Martin Shapiro's "logic of the triad"[1]—that strongly reinforces the notion that metasocial bargaining (in some appropriately sanitized original position) would generally produce agreement on some group of triadic judicial institutions for the peaceful resolution of some indeterminate set of limited and focused social conflicts. The quasi-consensual bases of adjudication are reinforced by the common use of superficially noncontroversial, and therefore consensual, social norms, such as fairness, reasonableness, and the like.

Decisions involving broader social conflicts, conflicts that render the appropriate norms for decision making problematic, are rather more difficult to legitimate by an appeal to consent. The domination (perhaps tyranny) of the majority is acceptable within a liberal-democratic polity, not because the persons who lost consented to the process or to the product, but because majority rule avoids *personal* domination. The majority could have

---

1. M. Shapiro, Courts: A Comparative and Political Analysis (1981).

been composed of anyone, including the losers. Majority rule is strictly impersonal concerning the opportunity for dominance. Each person has the same chance to be the social decision maker. Therefore, as long as majoritarian voting avoids substantive decisions that close off crucial, individual avenues of moral agency (freedom of expression, religion, family life, association), the voting *process* maintains a political egalitarianism essential to both liberal autonomy and democratic governance.

Administration—the accurate application of rules—appeals, not to the impersonality of a conflict-resolving process, but to the impersonality of the rules. Administrators in the typical case implement social decisions; they shape the world in the image of social policies or goals previously decided. Those goals may be the product of any of the legitimating processes that we have discussed. But whether agreed to or impersonally given, those rules represent an exogenous social decision that is no longer at issue. It is in this sense that administration is cooperative; it implements a socially approved goal. And, as such, the authority exercised is not the personal authority of the administrator—indeed of anyone.

Whereas the foregoing discussion may explain something of the derivation of what I claim to be the paradigmatic decision processes of a liberal-democratic polity, these processes have been portrayed in a highly abstract form. One step toward reducing the level of abstraction might be to provide a somewhat more extended discussion of four of the defining attributes of these processes: their dominant legitimating values, their characteristic structures, their cognitive styles, and their orientations toward questions of fact and questions of value. The sketches of these attributes will be sufficient to explore the relationship of pure process types to questions of process appropriateness.

1. Negotiation. Negotiation is *the* legitimate process for classical liberals. Of all processes, negotiation leading to consent, or consensus, seems to support individual autonomy most directly. Submission to another emerges through consent; consent thus transforms potential domination into cooperation. Collectivities also act and make decisions but, ideally, only through an ongoing process of mutual accommodation or negotiation to consensus. Such a decision structure is very loose jointed. It might be described as a market or a network. And because negotiation concerns how to shape individual and collective action in the market, or social space, of the immediate or remote future, the cognitive style of the activity is strategic. By that I do not mean that negotiation is characterized necessarily by posturing or haggling, but rather, that planning for future action and future contingencies is being accomplished.

Planning should not be thought to have connotations of comprehensiveness. In negotiation, planning is oriented toward shaping the facts, the contingent reality, of particular parties for a particular future time. The values of the negotiating parties, what they hope individually to realize through agreement, may facilitate or retard consensus; but strictly speaking, agreement on basic values is irrelevant to the legitimacy of the obligations that have been undertaken so long as coordinated action (who will do what, when, and with what rewards) can be established. And of course the broader public values that might emerge from extensive, decentralized, consensual activity can hardly be anticipated.[2]

Negotiation is thus both a strong protection for autonomy and privacy and a powerful support for individual participation in the direction of collective action by small groups. It also supports what some might call "strong democracy," an ongoing dialogue of citizens concerning issues of public moment and collective interest. Nevertheless, because I am extremely skeptical of the capacity to move this idea of public citizenship much beyond the scale of the small community, my working assumption is that negotiation to consensus in fact implies rather indirect forms of participation in broad-based collective choice. The collective values that emerge from multiple instances of decentralized consensual activity may literally have been intended by no person or group. They will be the values of a group that has insufficient

2. For a view of negotiation emphasizing its orientation toward questions of normative values, particularly where negotiation substitutes for adjudication, see Eisenberg, *Private Ordering through Negotiation: Dispute-Settlement and Rulemaking,* 89 HARV. L. REV. 637 (1976).

cohesiveness to make the metaphor of the general will meaningful as a legitimating idea in political discourse.

   2. Majoritarian Voting. Voting operates where there is agreement that collective decisions should be made, but irreducible
conflict persists over what they should be. It may be more precise to view majoritarian voting processes, the usual democratic
form, as supporting citizen *equality*, or as the impersonality of
authority, a sort of negative liberty that contributes only as a necessary condition for the more positive-sounding citizen autonomy.[3] Indeed it is customary to limit the domain of majoritarian
decision making in the interest of maintaining a larger scope for
autonomous individual action.

   Notice, however, that equality in the sense of equal chances
to be the decider can be maintained by a lottery—a "Ruler for a
day" (or perhaps for an instant) system. The use of voting rather
than lotteries thus tells us something about the cognitive style
and orientation of voting processes. Voting is an expressive activity, and it is precisely the expression of majority sentiment
that would not be captured by a lottery. Voting is thus democratic in a way that lotteries are not. Majority rule attempts to
preserve equal chances to decide, while aggregating expressions
of preferences by the voter participants. Collective values are
thus created through conscious collective choice.

   There are reasons to believe that preference aggregation by
voting is a deeply compromised activity,[4] and that nondomination in majority rule voting is more appearance than reality. But
let us not be carried away by the distressing theorems of the public choice fraternity. Voting is only the end of a process of discussing, bargaining, logrolling, and agenda setting that diffuses
as well as concentrates power. These social realities perhaps help
explain why the vote seldom appears trivial to those who do not
have it.

   3. The axiomatic social-choice literature makes these points with great rigor.
See generally A. SEN, COLLECTIVE CHOICE AND SOCIAL WELFARE (1970); Sen, *Social
Choice Theory: A Re-Examination*, 45 ECONOMETRICA 53 (1977).
   4. *See, e.g.*, Levine & Plott, *Agenda Influence and Its Implications*, 63 VA. L. REV.
561 (1977).

3. Administration. Administration is the process of realizing stated values in a world of contingent facts. The legitimating ideals of administration are accuracy and efficiency. Administrators are to discover and undertake those actions that will be instrumental to the achievement of specified ends, without, of course, forgetting that no particular goal or end exhausts the collective demand for a good life. Administrators are to do the job assigned in a cost-effective fashion. Because values are specified, administration is oriented toward facts—some concrete or historical, What is the world like? some probabilistic, What actions in that world will cause it to conform to the goals that have been stated? Answering these sorts of questions implies an investigative turn of mind. Doing so efficiently generally requires division of labor and hierarchical control—in short, bureaucracy.

I do not believe values can be fully specified in legislation, contracts, or charters; facts are created as much as found. Indeed, I have written whole books[5] asserting that administrative implementation is a creative process. Yet it surely makes a difference to the maintenance of the possibility of liberal autonomy (and to democratic participation) that officials have discretion bounded by stated and general policies, structured by hierarchical authority, exercised in a procedurally regular fashion, and reviewed for rough conformity to some paradigm of instrumental rationality.

4. Adjudication. Whereas administration seeks to implement chosen values, adjudication seeks to resolve conflict by choosing the value(s) to be preferred.[6] The paradigmatic adjudicatory situations are civil and criminal trials. In the civil trial, for example, a property dispute, "The smell of your turkey farm is driving me mad," confronts, "I was here first." The turkey farmer's neighbor has a valid complaint, *provided* his conduct in locating nearby was reasonable and he is not being overly sensitive. The turkey farmer, on the other hand, has a right to carry on a legitimate business, *provided* she does not unreasonably burden her neighbors.

5. J. Mashaw, Bureaucratic Justice (1983).
6. *See generally* Fiss, *The Supreme Court, 1978 Term—Forward: The Forms of Justice,* 93 Harv. L. Rev. 1 (1979).

The questions posed by such disputes obviously go beyond "Who did what?" to "Who is to be preferred?" when specific interests and the public values to which they are connected conflict. This entitlement-awarding goal gives a distinctive cast to adjudication. First, the legitimating value of the process is fairness. Institutions making such judgments, if they are to be socially effective, must be perceived as fair in their procedure and in their substantive results. Procedurally this perception will require equality of access to a neutral tribunal—that is, one that is not biased in favor of one of the parties. Substantively, the tribunal's judgments must respond to recognized or emerging social values. For it is the function of the tribunal to *interpret* or *construct* these values in the context of deciding disputed claims of right.

Table 2 summarizes these processes as we have just described them. They are both familiar and foreign: familiar because they represent the dominant collective decision processes that we observe; foreign because we tend to observe them in rather compromised forms. Contracting in mass markets and subject to multitudinous regulatory constraints may not look much like autonomous individuals negotiating to consensus; the connection

Table 2

CHARACTERISTICS

	Legitimating Values	Typical Structure	Cognitive Style	Orientation to Facts/Values
Negotiation	Consent	Network or Market	Strategic Planning	Facts
Voting	Democratic Participation	Representative Assembly	Preference Aggregation	Values
Administration	Instrumental Rationality	Bureaucracy	Investigative	Facts
Adjudication	Fairness	Neutral Tribunal	Interpretive	Values

PROCESSES

between citizen votes and governmental policies often seems to be some set of key political actors whose voice in the collective polity far exceeds everyman's; administrators repeatedly seem to be making broad value choices, not just finding facts; and adjudication is constrained increasingly by technical legislation or administrative rules that exclude a search for fairness in individual cases. Courts sometimes look like mere implementers, whereas administrators combine the value-defining powers of courts and legislatures. Contracts seem to be given in standardized form by dominant public and private entities, whereas legislation is often negotiated to consensus before it is formally voted.

THE IDEAL TYPES IN ACTION

When attempting to resolve administrative due process cases, courts often are troubled by precisely this apparent lack of fit between political ideals and political reality. The substantive due process decisions, for example, that invalidated regulatory legislation during the early part of this century did so in the name of liberty of contract.[7] The Court believed, for a while, that it was inappropriate to vote (legislate) the terms of contracts, particularly labor contracts—a view that was surely explicable for a generation that not only revered markets, but that could remember a civil war fought over the issue of free versus slave labor.

The courts have also been confronted with claims that sought to protect the value-creating function of elected representatives from the propensity of those representatives to delegate value choices to administrative agencies. The nondelegation doctrine, which requires that administrators only fill in the details of statutes, not make basic choices, and which is honored primarily in the breach, thus mediates a struggle between voting and administration for recognition as appropriate processes for policy choice. Recent scholarship[8] and the recent opinions of certain Supreme Court Justices[9] have demanded a reinvigoration of the

7. *E.g.*, Lochner v. N.Y., 198 U.S. 45 (1905).
8. *E.g.*, J. ELY, DEMOCRACY AND DISTRUST 131–34 (1980).
9. Indus. Union Dep't v. Am. Petroleum Inst., 448 U.S. 607, 672–88 (1980) (Rehnquist, J., concurring); Am. Textile Mfrs. Inst. Inc. v. Donovan, 452 U.S. 490, 543–48 (1981) (Rehnquist, J., & Burger, C.J., dissenting).

democratic ideal by active utilization of the nondelegation constraint. And an emerging public choice literature views the shifting of responsibility from elected representatives to bureaucratic structures as the politician's most successful technique for remaining on all sides of most issues.[10] The implication is that the delegation of value choices to administrators creates an antidemocratic administrative state.[11]

Similarly the continuing tension between administration and adjudication explains many of the developments in the administrative law jurisprudence of the last two decades. These events are conventionally described in process terms as involving movement from adjudication to rulemaking as the preferred vehicle for policy development.[12] That description is accurate so far as it goes. The promulgation of general rules clearly involves administrators in perceptible value choices as they translate vague principle into administrable policy. It is this perception of value choice that is in part responsible for the renewed interest in the nondelegation doctrine. I should prefer, however, to characterize the shift in administrative technique as a movement from incremental, decentralized, and contextual interpretation of basic values to systematic, centralized, and instrumentally rational implementation of administrative policies. The movement from adjudication to rulemaking is, thus, a movement from considering individual circumstances in the light of social context to making general welfare calculations expressed as general rules. Such policies are then *applied* to individual cases (in that limited sense, adjudication continues) wholly in terms of the predetermined rules. The demand for a process—a hearing—which punctuates the administrative law jurisprudence, is thus in part a demand to substitute individualized fairness for impersonal social welfare.

Consider, for example, some of the specific cases that give rise to the so-called participatory model of administrative law

10. M. Fiorina, *Group Concentration and the Delegation of Legislative Authority* (Prepared for the Conference on Social Science and Regulatory Policy, Sponsored by the Regulation Program of the National Science Foundation, Jan. 1982); *See also,* J. ELY, *supra* note 8, at 111.

11. There are significant reasons to doubt this story. *See* Moran & Weingast, *Congress as the Source of Regulatory Decisions,* 72 AMER. ECON. REV. 109 (1982).

12. *See, e.g.,* Scalia, *Vermont Yankee: The APA, The D.C. Circuit, and the Supreme Court,* 1978 SUP. CT. REV. 345 (1979).

discussed in chapter 1. In those cases challenges to administrative decision processes were sometimes framed as an attack on agency rulemaking power, sometimes as a protest against the use or development of bright-line standards in the course of adjudication, sometimes as an attack on the adequacy of rulemaking processes, and sometimes as a claim to procedural due process. Yet at the heart of each controversy, whatever its formulation, lies a conflict between a view of adjudication as a straightforward fact-finding process emphasizing accuracy and efficiency (bureaucratic rationality), and a view of adjudication as a value-realizing process tied inextricably to the deservedness of the affected parties (what I will here call "moral judgment").

In cases such as *National Petroleum Refiners Association v. FTC*,[13] *United States v. Storer Broadcasting Co.*,[14] and *FPC v. Texaco, Inc.*,[15] for example, the complaining parties attacked the power of the agency to adopt rules that restricted the scope of inquiry in subsequent adjudicatory proceedings. In *National Petroleum Refiners* the Federal Trade Commission had adopted a rule requiring service station owners to post octane ratings for gasolines on all retail gas pumps. In *Storer Broadcasting* the Federal Communications Commission had adopted a rule specifying that it would not serve the public interest to grant television licenses to entities that currently had five licensed outlets. In *Texaco* the Federal Power Commission had adopted a rule that certain clauses in contracts for the sale of natural gas would preclude the issuance of certificates for interstate pipeline transmission of the gas. Affected parties in all three cases claimed that they were statutorily entitled to trial-type hearings about whether their practices or proposed operations were unfair, deceptive, or not in the public interest under the relevant statute. It followed, they argued, that agencies could not foreclose by rule full adjudicatory exploration of the fairness or suitability of the behavior in question. The reviewing courts disagreed, stating simply that effective administration often demands the particularization of general standards through rulemaking. To find that the agencies lacked the asserted rulemaking power, the

13. 482 F.2d 672 (D.C. Cir. 1973).
14. 351 U.S. 192 (1956).
15. 377 U.S. 33 (1964).

courts reasoned, would interfere with the efficient discharge of their regulatory tasks.

Having lost the battle on agency *power* to adopt bright-line rules foreclosing subsequent adjudicatory exploration of value questions, the proponents of adjudicatory procedure attacked the standard rulemaking process under the Administrative Procedure Act as insufficiently adjudicatory. The claim in cases such as *Florida East Coast Railway v. United States*[16] may be vulgarized as stating simply, "If we cannot challenge the relationship between the values underlying these rules and our particular situation in proceedings applying the rules, we should at least have an adversary proceeding to discuss those issues at the rulemaking stage." The Supreme Court firmly rejected this request for judicialization of rulemaking and, in *Vermont Yankee Nuclear Power Corp. v. Natural Resources Defense Council, Inc.*,[17] admonished the Court of Appeals for the District of Columbia Circuit to remember that the Administrative Procedure Act established the maximum procedural requirements that Congress was willing to have the courts impose on agencies in conducting rulemaking proceedings.

Complaints about inappropriate agency choices between rulemaking and adjudication may also run in the opposite direction. In *NLRB v. Wyman-Gordon Co.*[18] and *NLRB v. Bell Aerospace*[19] the Supreme Court rejected the argument that the National Labor Relations Board should not do its administrative policy making in individual adjudicatory proceedings. The inappropriateness claim lurking in these cases might be characterized: "The board should not be permitted to determine that we have behaved unfairly in a proceeding directed against us where the grounds for any such finding have nothing to do with our blameworthiness. If the board wants to make general policy in the form of prophylactic rules, it should do so in a proceeding that signals that effective administration, not our individual culpability, is the topic under discussion."

We may contrast the preceding cases with a line of cases that

16. 410 U.S. 224 (1973).
17. 435 U.S. 519 (1978).
18. 394 U.S. 759 (1969).
19. 416 U.S. 267 (1974).

is considerably less deferential to the agency's or the legislature's choice of decision-making procedure. These contrary cases are the irrebuttable presumption cases, and include *Bell v. Burson,*[20] *Stanley v. Illinois,*[21] and *Cleveland Board of Education v. LaFleur.*[22] In *Bell,* for example, Georgia had adopted legislation barring from the highways persons who had been involved in accidents and had no liability insurance. The plaintiff, a driver suspended under the statute, claimed that the state had deprived him of due process of law by adjudicating his fitness to retain his license without a hearing. The Supreme Court agreed. In *Stanley,* Illinois law provided that children of unwed fathers become wards of the state upon the mother's death, thereby presuming that the father was unfit to raise the children. The Court held that due process required an individual determination of an unwed father's fitness. Similarly, in *LaFleur,* the Court held unlawful a school-board rule requiring all pregnant teachers to take maternity leave five months before the expected birth. The Court held that a pregnant teacher was entitled to an individual determination of her continuing fitness to teach.

The first interesting aspect of these cases is this—they are contrary to the well-entrenched administrative law doctrine, illustrated in the *Storer-Texaco* line of cases, that bright-line rules may be employed to foreclose adjudicatory exploration of particular issues. That the challenged rules were in some cases adopted by state legislatures rather than by administrators merely deepens the puzzle. Indeed the Court has even applied the irrebuttable presumption doctrine to congressional legislation—the species of lawmaking toward which conventional separation of powers theory would have the Court exercise its greatest judicial restraint.

The irrebuttable presumption decisions thus not only fail to comport with cases like *Storer Broadcasting,* they also fit uneasily within the general mold of constitutional law doctrine. If a bright-line rule may not replace a general principle unless the rule perfectly effectuates the principle, then most legislation and regulation, state and federal, is unconstitutional. Apparently

20. 402 U.S. 535 (1971).
21. 405 U.S. 645 (1972).
22. 414 U.S. 632 (1974).

recognizing this, the Court appears to have abandoned irrebuttable presumption analysis without ever cogently explaining the grounds for either its original use or its ultimate rejection. Yet the juxtaposition of the traditional administrative law jurisprudence and the irrebuttable presumption cases cries out for some meaningful response. When is it necessary to engage in an individual inquiry into deservedness, and when may a rule transform the adjudicatory inquiry into efficient, fact-seeking implementation?

We may make some progress in understanding these two seemingly incompatible lines of decisions by characterizing them in terms of a competition between the prototypes of bureaucratic rationality (administration) and moral judgment (adjudication). If the adjudication purports to allocate benefits and burdens on the basis of individual deservedness, the moral judgment model is more appealing. If the decision process does not directly or indirectly raise deservedness issues, a rule-bound and fact-oriented bureaucratic process will suffice. Viewed in this manner, *Stanley*, for example, is clearly distinguishable from *Storer Broadcasting*. A rule that deems one an unfit parent has very different individual deservedness implications from a rule that forbids certain concentrations of communications ownership, regardless of who the owners are. Storer Broadcasting may think that the concentration rule is silly, but it can hardly view the rule as defamatory.

Contemporary controversy over the constitutionality of the legislative veto seems another useful occasion for thinking through the problem in terms of models of process firmly grounded in liberal-democratic ideology.[23] To be sure, legislative vetoes of administrative regulations superficially mix legislative with executive power—the model of voting with the model of implementation. But on reflection the mix is in a direction that supports our liberal ideals of electoral value choice (voting) and agency implementation (administration) without demanding—as a reinvigorated nondelegation doctrine would—that we forget the uncertainties that beset the legislative task or

23. Much of the commentary is collected in *INS v. Chadha*, 103 S. Ct. at 2797, note 12 (dissenting opinion of Justice White).

that the legislative choice of the degree of delegation is itself a value choice. Legislation plus administration plus the possibility of legislative veto of quasi-legislative rules seem designed to ameliorate the real world difficulties of making voting meaningful in a technologically advanced administrative state. And in making that attempt, the legislative veto seems to pose no threat to the values of nondomination imbedded in either majority rule or bureaucratic rationality as liberal-democratic ideals.

Approaching the question in this way may help us distinguish instances of legislative veto that do pose such a threat. When the Congress acts to deprive certain named aliens of a favorable exercise of discretion by the Immigration and Naturalization Service,[24] one wants to respond, with Justice Black in *McGrath*, that the action smacks of attainder. But smacks of falls short of is. For attainder in our jurisprudence requires punishment, and withdrawal of a favorable exercise of discretion not to deport does not qualify.

Yet this type of individualized, highly contextual decision, based explicitly on considerations of character and personal situation, is surely dangerous in the hands of a legislative institution. The liberal ideal of protecting the individual from politically motivated personal law cries out for the interposition of process, if not judicial, then judicialized, within an administrative institution. It is just such a process that the dignitary-based model of appropriateness both demands and justifies. In so doing it demonstrates once again the need for the due process clause as a residual shield. Further, and more important for our purposes, this analysis portrays a shield that although traditional in form —adjudication—can be deployed from a position that responds not just to tradition, but also to the fundamental principles of a liberal-democratic legal order.

ASSESSING LIBERAL-DEMOCRATIC APPROPRIATENESS

Of Doubts Allayed and Doubts Rekindled

One could proceed to organize more of the jurisprudence in this way, to identify mistakes and to applaud successes. But

24. See, *e.g., Id.*

enough has been said to provide a basis for returning to our initial question: How is the model of appropriateness connected to fundamental liberal-democratic ideas of American constitutionalism? The answer is now to some degree obvious. We can interpret the Court's jurisprudence as a search among familiar liberal-democratic processes for *the* process that fits particular substantive activities. In periods when the emphasis of substantive law in particular areas shifts rapidly from private to public (negotiation to voting), or the general form of public law shifts from principle to rule (adjudication to administration), stress may generate substantial litigation concerning the appropriateness of the transitions. This litigation may be accompanied by a judicial insistence on old forms until the new ones become familiar and established. But because all the processes that are contending with each other for recognition are compatible with a liberal-democratic ideology, any pattern of judicial invalidation passes fairly rapidly to a pattern of judicial legitimation.

The conceptual scheme does not itself, of course, produce judicial restraint in its application. We might imagine legislators and administrators making large numbers of mistakes when assigning decisions to appropriate processes. Conceptually such mistakes might be of three sorts: (1) using an illegitimate process; (2) assigning a substantive issue to the wrong process category; and (3) mixing the categories. Indeed, put in this way the possibility for mistakes, or at least judicial perception of mistakes, seems nearly limitless. Use of this deductive, taxonomic approach to appropriateness as a decision rule rather than as an interpretive heuristic might thus produce a highly interventionist judicial posture.

But the derivation of categories of appropriate process in terms of ideal types must be sharply distinguished from application of the taxonomy that has been generated in either constitutional adjudication or in legislative or administrative drafting. Judicial review identifying deviation from, or mixing of, ideal types as constitutional error would rapidly be perceived as a form of constitutional madness. For it is far from clear that any one type supports the liberal-democratic values that it purports to uphold. In practice we find the processes that we have been discussing only in compromised forms because in theory they are defective or incomplete. These types are ideal, not perfect.

The ease, for example, with which neoclassical economics finds market failures attending consensual commercial activity casts grave doubt on whether we are, when negotiating and contracting with each other, able to get what we really want from the transactions to which we consent. Consent and self-determination are indeed linked, but the linkage is enormously complex. Moreover, these problems do not evaporate when negotiation takes place in nonmarket contexts, as a vast literature on informed consent in noncommercial settings amply attests.[25] Similar stories can be told about the ambiguity of the relationship between voting and democratic participation, between adjudication and community values, and between administration and rational implementation of social goals. But I will not discuss here the bases for skepticism about the four processes that might flow from the literature of welfare economics, public choice theory, organization theory, or legal realism. The point is simple and familiar—each process tends to forget something critically important about human personality or about organizational limits. As a normative matter, we are unlikely to subscribe fully to the implications of any of these processes. It is not, therefore, distressing that as an empirical matter we find them to be seriously incomplete descriptions of our present governmental reality or that courts view the matter as one of prudential judgment rather than categorical assignment.

From the perspective of interpretive methodology, the determination that a decision is allocable to any particular process model is obviously to construct reality, not to find it. Judicial justification of the application of such simplified constructions on the ground that some particular decision necessarily implies one or another particular decision process will strain our credulity to the breaking point. We would see the courts defending liberal autonomy in this fashion (for example, the Old Court in the New Deal) as themselves the oppressors, imposing on us some unified and simpleminded vision of a complex and compromised social reality. A convincing and unique characterization of appropriate legal form simply does not flow from laying partic-

---

25. *See, e.g.,* J. KATZ, EXPERIMENTATION WITH HUMAN BEINGS (1972); R. BURT, TAKING CARE OF STRANGERS (1979).

ular facts alongside a four-cell taxonomy of constitutionally approved processes.

Consider, for example, *Bishop v. Wood*.[26] A police officer was removed from a local police force, apparently because his superiors believed him unreliable. He objected to his removal on due process grounds. The officer argued that he was not removable under state law except for cause and that cause implied a right to defend his conduct in an evidentiary proceeding after specific notice of his alleged faults. The state responded that, in fact, public employees served at will and could be terminated without any formal adjudicatory process. This dispute about the character of public employment was argued by the parties, and decided by the Supreme Court, in terms of whether the police officer had a property interest in his job that required due process protection. Because the Supreme Court agreed that state law made public employment employment at will, it agreed with the state that there was no property interest requiring a termination hearing to establish the facts.

Beneath the property analysis, however, lies a contest between competing visions of the appropriate conception of public employment. One vision, the one that prevailed in *Bishop*, is a vision of contract negotiation. Parties enter into and exit from employment relations by mutual consent. Where consent is lacking there is no employment relation. The other is a vision of employment as a status conferred by statute and premised on good behavior. Termination, implying unacceptable behavior, is a deservedness or entitlements judgment that demands adjudication. Clearly both of these visions are plausible constructions of the reality of public employment.

It is, of course, possible for the Court via an appropriateness analysis to go about constructing the world in terms of one or the other of these competing categories, but as we have seen there is no obvious way to convince a skeptic of the legitimacy of that activity. In a mixed economy public employment can have both contractual freedom and statutory entitlement dimensions. Moreover, these characteristics might be mixed or synthesized in any number of ways in an attempt to accommodate our sense

26. 426 U.S. 341 (1976).

that neither pure contractual freedom nor pure statutory entitlement is a sensible way to structure the peculiar relationship
created by an employment contract with the sovereign power
that stands behind all contracts and determines the limits of
their enforceability.

In short, an analysis of *Bishop v. Wood* in appropriateness
terms demonstrates that our rational deductive approach to appropriateness analysis could merely reproduce a degenerate category of the traditional empirical version. We are wielding abstract categories in a world that can be described in terms of all
or of none of them. We are, apparently, no closer than we were
before to the discovery of some underlying rule of recognition
for determining which category is appropriate. We can explain a
case like *Bell* or *Stanley* as one in which procedure is made to
follow—to be appropriate to—substantive function. But that
merely poses our dilemma: If we take our appropriateness judgment to be a statement about the nonconstitutional positive law,
we cannot answer Justice Rehnquist in his bittersweet mode
when he asks how we knew what the substantive function truly
was without considering the evidence of the procedure that the
positive law provided for executing it. On the other hand, if we
take our explanation to be an explanation in terms of the proper
constitutional characterization of the function, we have made a
statement about substantive due process for which we must provide a justifying argument. Which are we to be, positive or natural lawyers? And, if the answer is some prudential combination
of both, what could that mean?

SYMBOLIC APPROPRIATENESS

Yet to address this supposed dilemma squarely is to begin to
see the considerable virtues of the reinterpreted model of dignitary appropriateness. For the Court need not wield these formal
categories to second-guess legislative or administrative process
choices. It can seek instead to understand what choice has been
made and to assertain whether that choice has been implemented in a reasonably coherent fashion. In *Bell* the state statute
seemed to have employed an individualized fault standard with-

out the appropriate adjudicatory decisional form. The case was, in effect, remanded to the legislature either to take out the fault standard or to put in an appropriate hearing process. In *Bishop* the positive law was found to make continuing consent the substantive norm; hearings were, therefore, beside the point.

A number of the Court's recent rulings begin to make sense when viewed in this fashion. Reconsider two examples we have previously encountered. The first is *Califano v. Yamasaki*,[27] holding that recoupment of overpayments from Social Security disability beneficiaries who had requested a waiver on equitable grounds, could not be accomplished without some form of oral hearing to consider the special circumstances that the claimant alleged. The Court bent itself into a pretzel to apply the *Eldridge* accuracy standard, finding first that the Congress intended *perfect* fact-finding and then that orality was essential to accuracy. Neither finding is at all convincing.

How much simpler, and truer to the circumstances, to have said merely that the Congress seemed to have intended the waiver standard to include considerations, such as subjective good faith, that demanded individualized moral judgment. Attempting to make those judgments about often barely literate, and always impaired, beneficiaries, as questions of fact on the basis of pieces of paper was a very peculiar form of administration. And attempts to transform the decision into an accuracy-seeking form of administration through objectification of the criteria for judgment failed to carry out the individualized waiver program the Congress had in mind.

Similarly, in *O'Bannon v. Town Court Nursing Home*[28] the apparently callous and conceptually incoherent ruling that nursing home residents had no relevant interest in the shutting down of their homes might have been explained in appropriateness terms. The Medicare-Medicaid legislative-regulatory scheme employs relatively objective standards for qualification of nursing homes. Nothing in that scheme made it possible for the relevant administrators to certify a home that failed to meet those

27. 442 U.S. 682 (1979).
28. 447 U.S. 773 (1980).

standards because the residents were satisfied and wanted to remain there. A rational bureaucratic system, not a judgment involving individual special circumstances, was being implemented, and only some demonstration that that system was incompetently designed or managed would have provided a basis for judicial invalidation of the existing decision process.

So far so good, but these examples are by now probably provoking additional questions of the following sort: (1) Doesn't the methodology we are describing simply fall into the second positivist trap? Due process adjudication has become simple statutory interpretation. And, (2) Why is it so clear that the legislative intent in the *O'Bannon, Bell,* and *Yamasaki* statutes was as we have described it? Surely other stories can be told about such complex statutes, stories that might suggest quite different results.

Consider the second question first. Statutory interpretation is not foolproof. But let us not kid ourselves that the real issue here is whether the Court can discover *the* correct story. There is no correct story, or there are many. The Court, with the parties' assistance, will ultimately construct an approved version of what is going on. Remember that the stories that make up the set of relevant choices are about decision-making modes that are acceptable techniques of liberal-democratic governance. The Court's construction, therefore, will either, by its reasoned approval, transform the scheme into a constitutionally acceptable process or, by its reasoned disapproval, require that a coherent and explicable choice be made by others.

On the way to that construction, the Court can establish a meaningful conversation about the appropriate modes of governmental action. It need not require simpleminded storytelling that unifies complex statutes around simple models of decision making. I can certainly imagine the state of Georgia, for example, making a compelling argument that the scheme challenged in *Bell* was an attempt at synthesizing administrative and adjudicative modes of proceeding. The first step, administrative suspension of the financially irresponsible driver's license on the occasion of a mishap, pursued a general welfare goal—identifying poor traffic risks and getting them temporarily off the road. But the statute also presumed a later adjudication that would deter-

mine whether individual suspensions were fair by allocating individual responsibility for particular accidents. Indeed, this is almost precisely the sort of compromise scheme that the Court
approved in *Mathews v. Eldridge*.[29]

To require that more complex arguments be made in order
to escape a preliminary classification would also provoke discussion of the real substantive issues in many cases. The *O'Bannon*
plaintiffs really have a claim that relates to the substantive standards adopted by federal and state agencies to regulate the quality of nursing homes. In the residents' view those regulations
should take account of patient satisfaction in addition to objective criteria concerning the required number of nurses' aides
and square feet of floor space per resident. To grant the residents a hearing would merely be a device for insinuating such
considerations into the scheme without ever confronting directly
the regulators' substantive authority under the statutes either to
be informed by or to exclude them. And that is the question that
should be confronted. Posed as a procedural issue, the Court is
asked to make a choice between either (1) limiting the regulators' substantive discretion to some uncertain degree (granting a
hearing that can be used as a bargaining chip in negotiation) or
(2) providing unfettered administrative discretion to use exclusively objective regulatory standards, without ever hearing arguments addressed pointedly to either of those outcomes.

As for falling into positivist traps, the answer is again, "Yes,
but . . . ." For one thing, by attempting to ensure transparent
and coherent implementation of the substantive law, the Court
at least promotes the basic dignitary value of legal comprehensibility. More important, it seems to me, this is a positivist trap that
holds the Court in precisely the right grip. To escape the judge
must assert that there is a constitutional value beyond legislative
will that justifies judicial intervention. And, that assertion, in order to persuade us of its acceptability, must be defended in
terms that connect it to a coherent vision of liberal-democratic
constitutional values. Rather than an assertion that some form of

29. *See* Mashaw, *Conflict and Compromise among Models of Administrative Justice*
1981 Duke L.J. 181.

246 / Dignitary Appropriateness

action simply *is* structured in terms of a particular form of process or allocation of decisional power, the Court must declare that it *should be* so structured because of the ideas of individual autonomy and dignity that inform the constitutional order. On some occasions these assertions may be textually based and easily defended. For example, the legislature cannot choose to impose individualized punishments except in impeachment proceedings because the Constitution prohibits bills of attainder. That is not to say that the reach of the attainder idea is always clear, but that the value assertion—no punitive legislative adjudication—is relatively nonproblematic. On other occasions such assertions will be deeply troublesome as, for example, the Court's contraception[30] and abortion[31] decisions have been. The zone of privacy, and therefore of consent, from which majoritarian voting, administration, and adjudication have been banished in these cases is not easy to spot in the constitutional text. Yet, surely physical autonomy is of the essence of individual moral agency. The boundary between private and public action may be difficult to discern, but the Court could defend *no* border only by forfeiting a (perhaps the) central liberal ideal.

Thus, although the attempt to articulate the boundary in scientific terms in *Roe v. Wade* may be less than persuasive, the general debate is a debate about the right questions. It is about the nature and extent of individual liberty in the context of a collective, if no longer communal, life. However impoverished some aspects of the *Roe v. Wade* dialogue, it is vastly superior, for example, to *Stanley v. Illinois.* For *Stanley* merely declares *to be* adjudicatory what the state had determined to be administrative. It asserts that the general rule establishing the unsuitability of natural parents is irrational because it might be overgeneral. But that is true of all rules. If rules relating to parental fitness cannot be categorized in potentially overgeneral ways, then surely the reason that they cannot be must have something to do with the *substantive* issue that the rules decide. The opinion in *Stanley* never begins the discussion of what that reason is or how it might be linked to a particular form of process.

30. Griswold v. Conn., 381 U.S. 479 (1965).
31. Roe v. Wade, 410 U.S. 113 (1973).

SYMBOLISM AND EFFICACY

Structuring constitutional argument in the right way will not lead to universally acclaimed results. Legal methodology can usually provide only a framework for discussion that focuses on asking and answering the right questions—that promises some prospect for producing an acceptable form of constitutional conversation. Yet this methodological contribution should not be stated too modestly. On the symbolic dimensions of methodological aptitude the dignitary model that we have been elaborating has considerable promise. It is grounded in the traditional ideals of individual liberty that infuse the basic structure of the Constitution and the Bill of Rights. It recognizes the demands for collective action that pervade the modern administrative state and it connects majority rule to liberal ideas of nondomination. Its taxonomy of appropriate processes, justified by relation to the basic presuppositions of liberal democracy, can also structure debate concerning the comprehensibility of various everyday procedural designs.

The vision that has been offered responds to the usual and, from a liberal-democratic perspective, the relevant concerns about the legitimacy of judicial review by casting that review, ordinarily, in the tentative form of statutory interpretation. But positive law is not the ultimate authority. Interpretation is informed by certain prima facie dignitary claims that are embodied in process heuristics. Where these metaphors are inadequate, the forms of government action are also constrained by a modest list of fundamental dignitary values that, as we saw in chapter 5, unify substantive interests in autonomy with the procedural preconditions of moral agency.

REGULATIVE APTITUDE

How likely is it that this complicated, balanced, often prudential methodology will produce behavioral consequences that are themselves acceptable? Will legislatures, administrators, or private parties be able to discern from these heuristics a synthetic demand for dignitary protections that yields clear guidelines to follow when creating or evaluating administrative structures? Will this complicated model of due process adjudication speak with sufficient clarity to chill the adversary ardor that has given due process cases numerical prominence, indeed a not altogether pleasant ubiquity, in an increasingly litigious society?[32] Does this revised methodology promise surcease from inefficient administrative adaptations brought on by vague, threatening (and occasionally interventionist) judicial pronouncements? Does it also provide adequate protection from the dangers of personal domination that lurk in administrative discretion? Well, not quite. Rather, it all depends.

To begin with a modest virtue, the proposed methodology could hardly speak with *less* clarity than the contemporary three-factor test. A less coherent jurisprudence than that elaborated in chapter 3 is difficult to imagine. Moreover, by giving a principled foundation and some determinate content to the models and metaphors of process that are bandied about in the traditional appropriateness mode, some additional clarity seems to be produced. Finally, the model locates issues—reveals them as issues of substantive policy and agency authority, as issues of structure and process, as issues of constitutional principles, or as problems of statutory interpretation—with considerably greater facility than the other models we have examined. Whether these apparent communicative virtues will persist over time in a dynamic legal system that features decentralized issue framing, legal argument, and adjudication is anybody's guess.

But assuming the model somewhat clarifies the jurisprudence, should we then expect better self-application and less due process litigation? It is difficult to know. On at least one theory of the determinants of litigation,[33] vagueness (or other reasons for poor information about probable outcomes) should explain why lawsuits go to trial rather than to settlement. For it is only when adversaries have different estimates of the outcome of the case that compromise will not be reached. Yet it is difficult to credit the application of this model to much due process litigation. The explanation assumes situations in which there are di-

32. *See generally* J.K. LIEBERMANN, THE LITIGIOUS SOCIETY (1981).
33. *See* Priest & Klein, *The Selection of Disputes for Litigation*, 13 J. LEGAL STUD. 1 (1984).

visible stakes, few repeat players, and full internalization of the costs and benefits of litigating by the parties to the lawsuit. Jobs, welfare benefits, and civil commitments, on the other hand— the grist for the due process mill—often present themselves as indivisible stakes. Governments and organizational plaintiffs are constant repeat players who can be expected to have litigation strategies stretching far beyond the individual case. And both plaintiffs and defendants are often playing the game with other people's money.

Under these circumstances it is the relationship between the expected value of appropriable gains and out-of-pocket costs, not variance in predicted outcomes, that can be expected to drive litigation. And, if that is true, then it is also probably true that only a set of rules that forces the expected value of due process litigation toward zero for one side will stem the tide. We are dealing, after all, with an increasingly litigious society that is, as chapter 1 details, rife with administrative decision making. Nothing said previously suggests a set of rules that drastically favors either the government defendent or the private plaintiff in every conceivable context (or in even most of the contexts) where due process disputes arise. I have argued repeatedly that retraint in constitutionalizing procedure is fully justified. But most statutes are sufficiently ambiguous to provide multiple occasions for claiming that administrative implementing processes are inconsistent with legislative intent. If a drastic skew in favor of plaintiffs or defendants is what is required to stop useless litigation, this book provides no good prospect for relief.

There are questions about institutional design that *should* be litigated and relitigated, for they involve essential legal relations that will always fit uncomfortably within my categorization of the appropriate forms of liberal-democratic governance. The issue of dependency in particular is a perennial and poignant problem for liberal politics. For many forms of dependency seem to demand a paternalistic control that liberal autonomy rejects. To rationalize paternalism within a liberal polity, paternalism must be presented in therapeutic, rehabilitative, or educational forms that promise only temporary limitation of individual autonomy, a reversion at the earliest possible moment to self-command, and necessary assistance in making the transition. The institutions through which the state's paternalistic purposes are carried forward thus have a double aspect that generates, and should generate, a profoundly ambivalent reaction. On the one hand, these institutions purportedly seek to establish or rekindle those traits that are the psychological or cognitive preconditions for life in a liberal society. On the other, they are organs of control and conditioning that sharply limit freedom, that seek to suppress or change the individual will.

No wonder, then, that the courts have been uncertain, tentative, and contradictory when confronted with due process issues pitting dependent families against social welfare workers,[34] students against their teachers,[35] inmates against their custodians,[36] patients against their doctors,[37] and children against their families.[38] And no wonder that the Court's disposition of these sorts of cases over the last dozen or so years has raised the loudest and most critical outcry. For, whatever the ruling in a particular case, it will be seen either as destroying those forms of authority that are the preconditions for a stable liberal-democratic polity, or as abandoning the most fundamental precepts of liberal autonomy.

The conceptual models that we have constructed provide no deft jurisprudential move that will make these problems go away. The control being exercised in these instances is not based on consent, or on voting processes including the dependent class, or on bureaucratically rational or value-assigning adjudicatory decisions. The control is instead premised on the authority of natural relations (the family) or the superior, and ultimately unfathomable, competence of the helping professions—primarily physicians, but also social workers, educators, and penologists. A jurisprudence that refuses to legitimate or to displace such authority in general terms—that views obligatory help as

34. *Compare* Goldberg v. Kelly, 397 U.S. 254 (1970), *with* Wyman v. James, 400 U.S. 309 (1971).
35. *Compare* Goss v. Lopez, 419 U.S. 565 (1975), *with* Ingraham v. Wright, 430 U.S. 651 (1971).
36. *Compare* Wolff v. McDonnell, 418 U.S. 539 (1979), *with* Bell v. Wolfish, 441 U.S. 520 (1980).
37. *Compare* Parham v. J.R., 442 U.S. 584 (1979), *with* Vitek v. Jones, 445 U.S. 480 (1980).
38. *See generally* Burt, *The Constitution of the Family*, 1979 SUP. CT. REV. 329.

sometimes necessary, but always suspicious—is about the best that we can expect. If rules were promulgated with sufficient clarity to stop the litigation, that would almost surely signal some form of grave jurisprudential mistake.

Indeed, much of this discussion has been animated by a perspective quite different from this pursuit of doctrinal clarity. Due process adjudication has been viewed not only as a dispute-resolving process through which conflict is more efficiently managed, but as an important creative activity through which we discover what sort of governance we have and what we want it to be. Due process litigation has been portrayed as a constitutional conversation that has been going on since 1855. And it has been suggested that due process cases satisfy a deep social need to debate and to come to terms in some authoritative fashion with the evolving structure of government. In that sense this discussion conflates the symbolic and the regulative aspects of due process doctrine, but not around a reform program that would necessarily result in a radical reduction in the incidence of litigation.

Uncertainty concerning how much due process litigation is enough mirrors uncertainty concerning the characterization that should be given the functional effects of due process adjudication. If the due process decisions of the last dozen years have inserted expensive hearing rights in various programmatic contexts that have disabled administrators from pursuing worthwhile social goals, and simultaneously failed to provide adequate protection for individual interests, then surely the results have been dysfunctional. The existing empirical literature, however, hardly allows us to reach such a confident negative conclusion about the regulative effects of the recent jurisprudence. For it appears that the effects have been more complex and their normative evaluation more controversial than the high-cost/low-return picture just presented.

Welfare administration has been fairly extensively studied and provides an apt illustration of both complex regulative effects and normatively ambiguous consequences. The *Goldberg* requirement of extensive pretermination hearings has not produced a huge, or even a very substantial, increase in the number of hearings held. Yet the demand for formal legality represented by *Goldberg*, and supplemented by other substantive welfare decisions, has within a decade transformed AFDC from a decentralized, discretionary, and informal program into one characterized by formal rules, limited low-level discretion, and authoritative centralized supervision.[39] From the perspective of welfare recipients, these changes have increased security of expectations, while reducing invasions of privacy and personal coercion by caseworkers. They have also drastically limited recipients' abilities to obtain consideration of contextually relevant individual differences and have probably increased the frustrations and bewilderment associated with bureaucratic paperwork requirements. From the perspective of top-level managers, these changes have facilitated hierarchical control, which may be employed to emphasize either the benevolent purposes of public assistance or a cautious, budget-conscious desire to minimize payments to ineligible and to marginally qualified beneficiaries. As benefits determinations based on formal rules have been made routine, the social work profession has been driven from the program and, in William Simon's characterization, the work force of low-level eligibility technicians has been proletarianized.

So, has formalization of welfare, in part at least as a response to due process demands, been a good thing? I am tempted to say yes. The personal domination of the coercive caseworker has been replaced by general rules susceptible to political control. From a liberal perspective that is an unambiguous gain. But if what was really wanted was individualized attention based on consensus values *and* freed from the risks of arbitrary personal domination, the transformation to formalism may seem a hollow victory. The ability of administrators to use the new hierarchy to constrain awards, and the loss of social work professionals as natural allies in political struggles over the extent and level of income support, might reinforce this bad-bargain view from the recipients' perspective. Moreover, the purported benefits of consistent administration, increased security and autonomy, may be contingent on political will and managerial competence. James Jacobs's study of Stateville prison,[40] for example, sug-

---

39. This discussion is based on Simon, *Legality, Bureaucracy, and Class in the Welfare System* 92 YALE L.J. 1198 (1983).

40. J. JACOBS, STATEVILLE: THE PENITENTIARY IN MASS SOCIETY 105–99 (1977).

gests that absent those two ingredients, hearing rights may simply destabilize the existing authoritarian power structure and transfer domination from one set of oppressors (guards) to another (gangs).

I am, of course, prepared to argue that ideas have some power to constrain these more dysfunctional effects—that a jurisprudence structured around demands for appropriateness, competence, and dignity will instruct as well as command. Moreover, because this marriage of legal techniques and substantive values recognizes administration as a fully legitimate means of implementing liberal-democratic ideals, it has a much better chance than a traditionalist approach (focused on judicial or quasi-judicial hearing processes) to influence administrators to accept independent responsibility for the pursuit of liberal-democratic governance.

7 / *Beyond Constitutional Adjudication*

This has been a book on constitutional adjudication. Its purpose has been "liberal" in a modern, reformist sense. I have attempted to move the constitutional conversation about administrative process beyond both traditional legal methodology and the narrow utilitarianism of the Supreme Court's contemporary accuracy-seeking vision of procedural adequacy. Yet in a more profound sense my analysis and conclusions are deeply conservative and therefore "liberal" in the historical and philosophical meaning of the term. My purpose has also been to lay a firmer foundation for protecting individual rights through due process adjudication—rights that are in my view to be asserted and defended as fundamental preconditions for individual dignity and self-respect. Because they are fundamental, these rights are also few in number and limited in scope. My complaints about contemporary doctrine have thus more often been complaints about the Court's process of reasoning about due process rights than about its failure to find that constitutional rights to hearings exist.

The foundation laid in the constitutional jurisprudence by a liberal, dignitary approach will support many political houses —some beautiful, some perhaps grotesque. For construction of the principal living space, from subfloor to parapets, I have often urged reliance on the positive law. Yet this is precisely the law that due process adjudication continuously challenges—that those attentive to due process jurisprudence see only as it is bathed in the harsh glare of disappointment and distrust, the dual wellsprings of constitutional litigation. It therefore seems necessary to say something more about that law; to suggest how I can utter such phrases as "generous positivism"; to justify in some fashion my belief in a subconstitutional dialogue about the forms of American administrative governance that is not the dialogue of disparagement, frustration, or despair.

Let me therefore provide three moderately cheerful sketches of subconstitutional positive law in the American administrative state. These sketches describe experience with (1) the participatory ideal in administrative policy formation; (2) the defense of welfare state entitlements; and (3) the mandatory use of general rules that limit official discretion. Each concerns one of the critical issues that gave rise to the due process revolution and later to disappointment with the reemergence of something akin to the old order during the reign of the Burger Court. They are stories embodied repeatedly in the cases and hypotheticals that have populated this discussion, and on which I focused in the concluding pages of chapter 5. Moreover, these descriptions suggest that legislative and administrative institutions, like courts, are concerned with the dignitary values that due process adjudication should support. Each sketch also suggests that these institutions, often in conjunction with *statutorily* based judicial review, possess a creativity, a responsiveness, and a capacity for complex experimentation with decision structures that a more ambitious constitutionalization of administrative processes cannot duplicate—indeed, that it might easily stifle or retard.

THE PARTICIPATORY IDEAL IN ADMINISTRATIVE POLICY FORMATION

The central domestic concerns of modern government—steering the economy, controlling externalities, and maintaining some semblance of distributional equity—can be addressed only by institutions combining technical competence with centralized responsibility.[1] But such institutions seem remote, perhaps unapproachable. The inner workings of vast administrative agen-

---

1. For a general critique of efforts to decentralize large portions of federal governmental programs see Mashaw & Rose-Ackerman, *Federalism and Regulation*, in THE REAGAN ADMINISTRATION'S REGULATORY RELIEF EFFORT: A MID-TERM ASSESSMENT (G. Eads & M. Fix eds. 1984).

cies are obscure; their policies proceed from an expertise that may also harbor not a little trained incompetence. This is surely one of the bureaucratic problems that makes a major contribution to our sense of unease about the administrative state.

Thus, for example, when the Supreme Court tells us in the *Vermont Yankee*[2] case that the participation of environmentalists in developing general policies for licensing nuclear reactors is justified neither by the Administrative Procedure Act nor by the Constitution, we may be alarmed, particularly if we abhor nuclear energy. Once again, we may say, the massive bureaucracies of the government and the power companies have steamrollered the opposing private interests without heeding even their calls for caution and restraint.[3]

That reaction is mostly nonsense—or perhaps more charitably, nostalgia. Listen to the description of the bare bones of the nuclear regulatory process as it is stated in the Supreme Court's opinion.

> Under the Atomic Energy Act of 1954, 42 U.S.C.A. § 2011 *et seq.*, the Atomic Energy Commission was given broad regulatory authority over the development of nuclear energy. Under the terms of the Act, a utility seeking to construct and operate a nuclear power plant must obtain a separate permit or license at both the construction and the operation stage of the project. In order to obtain the construction permit, the utility must file a preliminary safety analysis report, an environmental report, and certain information regarding the antitrust implications of the proposed project. This application then undergoes exhaustive review by the Commission's staff and by the Advisory Committee on Reactor Safeguards (ACRS), a group of distinguished experts in the field of atomic energy. Both groups submit to the Commission their own evaluation, which then becomes part of the record of the utility's application. The Commission staff also undertakes the review required by the National Environmental Policy Act (NEPA), and prepares a draft environmental impact statement, which, after being circulated for comment, is revised and becomes a final environmental impact statement. Thereupon the three member Atomic Safety and Licensing Board conducts a public adjudicatory hearing, and reaches a de-

2. Vt. Yankee Nuclear Power Corp. v. NDRC, 435 U.S. 519 (1978).
3. *See* Mitchell, *Participation of Private Interest Representatives in Nuclear Power Plant Licensing Proceedings*, 13 IDAHO L. REV. 309 (1977).

cision which can be appealed to the Atomic Safety and Licensing Appeal Board, and, in the Commission's discretion, to the Commission itself. The final agency decision may be appealed to the courts of appeals. The same sort of process occurs when the utility applies for a license to operate the plant, except that a hearing need only be held in contested cases and may be limited to the matters in controversy. . . .

In December 1967, after the mandatory adjudicatory hearing and necessary review, the Commission granted petitioner Vermont Yankee a permit to build a nuclear power plant in Vernon, Vt. Thereafter, Vermont Yankee applied for an operating license. Respondent Natural Resources Defense Council (NRDC) objected to the granting of a license, however, and therefore a hearing on the application commenced on August 10, 1971. Excluded from consideration at the hearings, over NRDC's objection, was the issue of the environmental effects of operations to reprocess fuel or dispose of wastes resulting from the reprocessing operations. This ruling was affirmed by the Appeal Board in June 1972.

In November 1972, however, the Commission, making specific reference to the Appeal Board's decision with respect to the Vermont Yankee license, instituted rulemaking proceedings "that would specifically deal with the question of consideration of environmental effects associated with the uranium fuel cycle in the individual cost-benefit analyses for light water cooled nuclear power reactors." The notice of proposed rulemaking offered two alternatives, both predicated on a report prepared by the Commission's staff entitled "Environmental Survey of the Nuclear Fuel Cycle." The first would have required no quantitative evaluation of the environmental hazards of fuel reprocessing or disposal because the Environmental Survey had found them to be slight. The second would have specified numerical values for the environmental impact of this part of the fuel cycle, which values would then be incorporated into a table, along with the other relevant factors, to determine the overall cost-benefit balance for each operating license.

Much of the controversy in this case revolves around the procedures used in the rulemaking hearing which commenced in February 1973. In a supplemental notice of hearing the Commission indicated that while discovery or cross-examination would not be utilized, the Environmental Survey would be available to the public before the hearing along with the extensive background documents cited therein. All participants would be given a reasonable opportunity to present their position and could be represented by counsel if they so desired. Written and, time permitting, oral statements would be received and incorporated into the record. All persons giving oral statements would be subject to questioning by the Commission. At the conclusion of the hearing, a transcript would be made available to the public and the record would remain open for 30 days to allow the filing of supplemental written statements. More than 40 individuals and organizations representing a wide variety of interests submitted written comments. On January 17, 1973, the Hearing Board held a planning session to schedule the appearance of witnesses and to discuss methods for compiling a record. The hearing was held on February 1 and 2, with participation from a number of groups, including the Commission's staff, the United States Environmental Protection Agency, a manufacturer of reactor equipment, a trade association from the nuclear industry, a group of electric utility companies, and a group called Consolidated National Intervenors who represented 79 groups and individuals including respondent NRDC.

After the hearing, the Commission's staff filed a supplemental document for the purpose of clarifying and revising the Environmental Survey. Then, the Hearing Board forwarded its report to the Commission without rendering any decision. The Hearing Board identified as the principal procedural question the propriety of declining to use full formal adjudicatory procedures. The major substantive issue was the technical adequacy of the Environmental Survey.

In April 1974, the Commission issued a rule which adopted the second of the two proposed alternatives described above.[1]

A New England town meeting this is not. Groups and interests were heard through spokesmen and coordinating institutions, not by individuals giving voice to individual concerns. But neither is the question of how to regulate the terminal end of the nuclear fuel cycle the equivalent of the question whether an additional marina should be built in Essex, Connecticut.

These composite voices will be heard. For subsequent *substantive* judicial review will police their consideration and the agency's response.[5] Participation is not dead because the Su-

---

4. Vt. Yankee Nuclear Power Corp. v. NDRC, 435 U.S. 519, 525–30 (1978).
5. NDRC v. NRC (Vt. Yankee III), 685 F.2d 459 (D.C. Cir. 1982); rev'd 103 S. Ct. 2246 (1983). *See also,* Scalia, *Vermont Yankee : The A.P.A, the D.C. Circuit, and the Supreme Court,* 1978 SUP. CT. REV. 345 (1978); Raymond, *A Vermont Yankee in*

preme Court denied the opponents a trial as an aspect of due process. Participation is instead lively, robust, and significant in the NRC process. The list of nuclear projects stopped, relocated, modified, and almost endlessly delayed attests to the significance of public participation. Moreover that participation is all a function of the positive law constructed jointly by the Congress through the Atomic Energy Act and the National Environmental Policy Act, the NRC through its procedural regulations and licensing practices, and the courts through their construction of these organic statutes, agency regulations, and the general provisions of the APA.[6]

This story of subconstitutional pursuit of the participatory ideal can be played out in a similar vein across the vast range of federal programs and activities: the (ill-starred) Community Action Program[7]; the enormously complex set of participatory devices attached to federal projects pursuant to the Intergovernmental Cooperation Act[8]; the Food and Drug Administration's development of a Chinese menu of processes that may be chosen by firms attempting to obtain approved new drug applications[9]; the inclusion of outside contractors in the development of Consumer Product Safety Rules[10]; the National Highway Traffic

---

King Burger's Court: Constraints on Judicial Review Under NEPA, 7 B.C. ENV. AFF. L. REV. 629 (1979); Nathanson, *The Vermont Yankee Nuclear Power Opinion: A Masterpiece of Statutory Misinterpretation*, 16 SAN DIEGO L. REV. 183 (1979); Stewart, *Vermont Yankee and the Evolution of Administrative Procedure*, 91 HARV. L. REV. 1805 (1978); Byse, *Vermont Yankee and the Evolution of Administrative Procedure*, 91 HARV. L. REV. 1823 (1978); Breyer, *Vermont Yankee and the Courts' Role in the Nuclear Energy Controversy*, 91 HARV. L. REV. 1833 (1978).

6. *See, e.g.,* Porter, *The Need for Finality in the Administrative Process: Problems in Licensing Nuclear Power Facilities*, 17 WAKE FOREST L. REV. 25 (1981); Hennessey, *The Nuclear Power Plant Licensing Process*, 15 WM. & MARY L. REV. 487 (1974).

7. Urban and Rural Community Action Programs, 42 U.S.C. § 2790–2837 (1976 & Supp. IV 1980); *see, e.g.,* D. MOYNIHAN, MAXIMUM FEASIBLE MISUNDERSTANDING (1969).

8. Intergovernmental Cooperation Act, 42 U.S.C. § 4231–4233 (1976 & Supp. IV 1980); OMB CIRCULAR NO. A–95, REVISED (41 Fed. Reg. 2052) (1976).

9. *See* Formal Evidentiary Public Hearing, 21 C.F.R. §§ 12.1–.159; Public Hearing before a Public Board of Inquiry 21 C.F.R. §§ 13.1–.50; Public Hearing before a Public Advisory Committee 21 C.F.R. §§ 14.1–.174; Public Hearing before the Commissioner 21 C.F.R. §§ 15.1–.45; Regulatory Hearing before the Food and Drug Administration 21 C.F.R. §§ 16.1–.119 (1982).

10. *See* Consumer Product Safety Act, 15 U.S.C. § 2054(c) (1976).

Safety Administrator's *sixty* iterations of notice and comment on automobile passive restraint standards[11]; the nationwide public hearings conducted by the Social Security Administration before adopting its vocational guidelines for assessing disability claims[12]; the electoral processes of the Agriculture Department when adopting product marketing orders.[13]

The list could go on and on; I have not even touched upon the rich variety of state and local administrative schemes for citizen and interest group involvement. The conditions of modern life may not make the participation just described as satisfying as (at least our image of) the town meeting. It may not cure our nostalgia for the *polis.* Yet the basic point remains: there is abundant external participation in the formation of governmental administrative policy. Attempts to constitutionalize this variety and abundance of participatory opportunity—to capture it somehow as a determinate constitutional right that goes beyond participation in electoral politics—are unlikely to yield greater satisfaction.

Indeed, constitutionalization may stifle participation in useful and meaningful forms. It is but one anecdote, but we should perhaps remember that *Goldberg v. Kelly* imposed procedures on (then) HEW that were nearly identical to those the department itself had issued in a notice of proposed rulemaking.[14] We should also remember that in complying with the Court's mandate, the department deleted from its final rules[15] the provision of free claimants' representatives, which the Court had in *Gold-*

11. *See generally* State Farm Mutual Ins. Co. v. DOT, 680 F.2d 206 (D.C. Cir. 1982).

12. Disability benefits are administered under Titles II and XVI of the Social Security Act. *See* 42 U.S.C. § 401–433, 1381–1383c (1976 & Supp. III 1979); Public hearing process described at 43 Fed. Reg. 55355 (1978).

13. Procedure for Conduct of Referenda to Determine Producer Approval of Milk Marketing Orders to Be Made Effective Pursuant to Agricultural Marketing Agreement Act of 1937 as Amended, 7 C.F.R. § 900.300–.311 (1982); Orders Regulating Handling of Commodity, 7 U.S.C. § 608(c)(s) (1976 & Supp. V 1981).

14. *Compare* Goldberg v. Kelly, 397 U.S. 254, 270–71 (1970); *with* 45 C.F.R. § 205.10, 34 Fed. Reg. 1144 (1969); 45 C.F.R. § 220.25, 34 Fed. Reg. 13595 (1969).

15. Revocation at 35 Fed. Reg. 10591 (1970); final rule at 36 Fed. Reg. 3034 (1971).

berg ruled to be constitutionally unnecessary. In accepting the
Court's vision of good process, the agency removed the provision that I believe was the single most important innovation that
could have been made for the protection both of the claimants'
substantive rights and of their sense of control over the bureaucratic complexities of claims validation.[16]

My aversion to constitutionalizing participation in administrative processes, however, is not based primarily on the fear
that constitutionalization may stop innovation that would promote participatory values. It seems to me more likely that the
greater danger lies in the opposite direction; that judicial creativity in a constitutional mode will promote and generalize
innovations that turn out to be dysfunctional. Promoting participation through structural design is a very tricky business.[17]
Many experiments will require anything from minor modification to complete abandonment.

Consider, for example, the sad tale of the Consumer Product
Safety Commission's rulemaking process. The CPSC's organic
legislation was drafted near the peak of public interest in consumer protection and citizen participation and of public distrust
of agency expertise. The statute contains a number of apparently good ideas for increasing the responsiveness of the new
agency to external priorities and external information.[18] Two
are of particular significance. Under Section 10 of the Act any
person may petition the agency for a rule setting product safety
standards. The agency must respond to such petitions within

16. *See, e.g.,* J. MASHAW, BUREAUCRATIC JUSTICE 200–02 (1983); Popkin, *Effect of Representation on a Claimant's Success Rate,* 31 AD. L. REV. 449 (1979); J. THIBAUT & L. WALKER, PROCEDURAL JUSTICE 81–96 (1975); Popkin, *Effect of Representation in Nonadversary Proceedings: A Study of Three Disability Programs,* 62 CORNELL L. REV. 989 (1977).
17. *See, e.g.,* Crampton, *The Why, Where and How of Procedural Public Participation in the Administrative Process,* 60 GEORGETOWN L.J. 525 (1972); Gelhorn, *Public Participation in Administrative Proceedings,* 81 YALE L.J. 359 (1972); Hanes, *Citizen Participation and Its Impact on Prompt and Responsible Administrative Action,* 24 Sw. L.J. 731 (1972).
18. It was described in Congressional hearings as "the most advanced congressional thinking on the technique of federal regulation." *Federal Regulation and Regulatory Reform: Hearings Before the Subcomm. on Oversight and Investigation of the House Comm. on Interstate and Foreign Commerce,* Vol. 4, 94th Cong., 2d Sess. 195 (1976). [hereinafter cited as *Regulatory Reform Hearings*].

120 days. If it grants the petition it must initiate a rulemaking process that has its own statutory time limits and a required oral hearing. If the commission denies a petition for a rule, its reasons must be published in the Federal Register and the decision is subject to review by a trial de novo in a district court.

Within the rulemaking process itself, Section 7 of the CPSCA further establishes what is known as an "offeror process." Whenever the commission proposes to initiate a rulemaking proceeding it must invite persons or groups outside the agency to develop the product standard. If offerors come forward, one of them must be given the assignment, provided the agency determines that it is competent to develop the standard. Standards developed by offerors may not be modified by the agency except through the full rulemaking process, including the offeror process.

These statutory provisions play out a logic of openness and participatory equality that could as easily have been concocted by a court implementing the participatory ideal through due process adjudication. How simple it might seem to determine that due process in a modern administrative state, which is also committed to democratic participatory values, demands agency responsiveness to citizen interests and the inclusion within even technical regulatory processes of those who can make a competent contribution to the policy dialogue. How easy to imagine further that these basic participatory rights require protection from the ordinary and often disappointing politics of administrative regulation by the addition of barriers to facile rejection of external requests for submissions. Those impediments would doubtless take the usual legal forms of strict procedural requirements and cautious judicial review. And, if a modern vision of due process required these things for the CPSC, it would surely view similar, perhaps all, agency functions as similarly burdened.

The progressive logic of participation would thus become the progressive logic of disaster. That is certainly a reasonable description of CPSC regulation. Petitions for rules have swamped the agency in unproductive investigation of useless subjects and destroyed its capacity to set a reasonable agenda for regulation.[19] The offeror process has produced inordinate delay and has made the commission the virtual captive of the industries it was meant to regulate.[20] In 1981, recognizing a disaster when it saw one, the Congress repealed[21] Sections 7 and 10 of the CPSCA and, thereby, abandoned the attempt to "maximize public participation"[22] begun in 1972.

Although the CPSC story is an unhappy one, it is made less tragic by the fact that experiment, assessment, and retreat were engaged in as a part of an ongoing process of political experimentation, not as logical deductions from supposed constitutional principles. Surely the *Vermont Yankee* decision was wise in its belief that judicial review—and a fortiori constitutional adjudication—is too clumsy a technique for the concocting of administrative experiments in participatory governance. In all likelihood it will be too slow to respond initially, too uninformed to be apt, and too slow again to make changes or adjustments.

But my central point is not that constitutional adjudication is necessarily an incompetent way to promote appropriate forms of participation; it is instead that we presently possess the legal means to empower ourselves. The opportunity to affirm our self-worth through acts of public citizenship is ubiquitous in American life. We may lack civic virtue. The will to *be* a public citizen may be in short supply.[23] But if that is the problem, it is a situation that implicitly criticizes neither the efforts of our legislative and administrative institutions to provide access, nor the conception of constitutional due process that has been offered in these pages. Calls to action may be in order, but the action

19. *See, e.g., Regulatory Reform Hearings, supra* at 13, 170; M. LERNER, THE CONSUMER PRODUCT SAFETY COMMISSION 108 (1981); GENERAL ACCOUNTING OFFICE REPORT B–139319: THE CPSC NEEDS TO ISSUE SAFETY STANDARDS FASTER (Dec. 12, 1977).

20. *See generally* Pittle, *The Restricted Regulator*, 12 TRIAL 18 (1976). *See also Regulatory Reform Hearings, supra* at 35.

21. Consumer Product Safety Act Amendments of 1981, Pub. L. No. 97–35, § 1210, 95 Stat. 703.

22. H.R. REP. No. 1153, 92d Cong., 2d Sess. 14 (1972).

23. *See, e.g.,* H. ARENDT, CRISES OF THE REPUBLIC 201–23 (1972); B. BARBER, SUPERMAN AND COMMON MEN 98–125 (1971); for a discussion of the increase in voter apathy, see K. PHILLIPS & P. BLACKMAN, ELECTORAL REFORM AND VOTER PARTICIPATION 1–22 (1975).

needed is not constitutional adjudication to increase participatory opportunity.

DEFENDING WELFARE STATE ENTITLEMENTS

Not since *Goldberg v. Kelly* has the Supreme Court been willing to model the due process hearing rights deemed essential to security of welfare state entitlements explicitly and extensively on the elements of civil trial.[24] When requiring hearings in subsequent cases the Court has left their contours purposefully vague.[25] More often still it merely approves of processes that diverge radically from the trial model with genuflections to the expertise and integrity of the deciders or the complexity of the administrative system.[26] Indeed, as we observed in chapter 3,[27] the whole notion of welfare state entitlements as property has been rendered problematic by the Court's repeated dalliance with a narrowly positivist analytic rigor.

Lawyers alert to the potential that hearing rights have to insinuate outsiders into bureaucratic organizations, to force the development of comprehensible and uniform policy, and to provide some sense of power to the welfare state supplicant, rightly may feel anxious. Failure to press forward the trend toward judicialization that reached its apex in *Goldberg* could in the end permit the development of a Kafkaesque welfare state monster that is the antithesis of the liberal ideal. In our darkest moments we might even imagine that substantive judicial review of entitlements judgments might be foreclosed, and that lawyers will be barred from representing claimants within the administrative process.

Indeed, such an administrative welfare system already exists. It dispenses tens of billions of dollars per year to tens of millions of Americans. Its processes are almost wholly informal, nonadversary, and insulated from the courts and the private bar.[28]

24. *See* Van Alstyne, *Cracks in "The New Property": Adjudicative Due Process in the Administrative State*, 62 CORNELL L. REV. 445, 457–70 (1977).
25. *See, e.g.,* Goss v. Lopez, 419 U.S. 565, 577–84 (1975); Califano v. Yamasaki, 442 U.S. 682, 693–97 (1979).
26. *See* Mathews v. Eldridge, 424 U.S. 319, 343–49 (1976).
27. *Supra* at 151, note 86.
28. *See* Veterans' Benefits, Title 38 U.S.C. (1976 & Supp. V 1981); Veterans

Frederick Davis, one of our leading authorities on state administrative law, calls it "Henry VIII in America."[29] Its more prosaic title is the Veterans Administration. Goaded by Davis's hyperbole, I will call it the most competent and humane social services agency since King Solomon sat to dispense charity and justice to his adoring subjects. A monstrous bureaucracy the VA may be; but it is more like Puff the Magic Dragon than Frankenstein.

I cannot make good on this claim in a few sentences—perhaps not in a few thousand. But consider in brief outline how the Congress and the agency have structured the dispensing of veterans benefits to maximize the claimants' understanding, participation, and security of entitlement. First, far from a regime of personal discretion, the system employs a massive set of regulations and instructions that constrains the subjectivity of individual adjudications.[30] Those rules are backed by a sophisticated quality assurance system[31] and by multiple levels of individual appeals.[32]

In the applications process participation by claimants is both fostered and reinforced. A claimant may have personal access to the adjudicator responsible for his or her claim at any time and on any issue. Any final disagreement between claimant and decider is recorded in an explanatory statement of the case, which then follows the claim to the next level of decision making. Claimants may be assisted, and most are, by specialized claims representatives employed by a variety of veterans organizations, the Red Cross, and state offices of veterans affairs. Those representatives are given access to every item of information collected in relation to a claim. This combination of participation, infor-

Administration, 38 C.F.R. ch. 1 (1982); *See also* P. STARR, THE DISCARDED ARMY: VETERANS AFTER VIETNAM (1973); S. LEVITAN & K. CLEARY, OLD WARS REMAIN UNFINISHED: THE VETERANS BENEFITS SYSTEM (1973).

29. Davis, *Veterans' Benefits, Judicial Review, and the Constitutional Problems of "Positive" Government*, 39 IND. L.J. 183, 185 (1964).

30. Schedule for Rating Disabilities, 38 C.F.R. § 4.1–.150; VETERANS ADMINISTRATION, DEP'T OF MEDICINE AND SURGERY, PHYSICIAN'S GUIDE, VA PAMPHLET IB 11–56 (Washington, 1976).

31. *See* VETERANS ADMINISTRATION, COMPENSATION AND PENSION SERVICE, PAMPHLET M21–4 (Washington, 1977).

32. Board of Veterans' Appeals, 38 U.S.C. § 4001–4009 (1976 & Supp. V 1981), 38 C.F.R. § 19.1–.156 (1982).

mation, representation, and counseling reduces appeals at the final Appeals Board stage to a miniscule 1 to 2 percent of disappointed applicants.[33]

In addition, VA claims examiners are bound to obtain for the veterans every benefit to which they are entitled, not only those for which application is initially made.[34] Outreach programs begin before service personnel leave active duty and continue through multiple media and institutions to alert needy veterans to their potential rights.[35] Congressional oversight is active and congressional casework ubiquitous. Both are overwhelmingly directed at ensuring that reasonable expectations of assistance are not disappointed.[36]

This Panglossian description can surely be disputed.[37] The perfect bureaucracy has never existed and the VA surely has its blind spots. (Some may wonder, moreover, whether I have just been explaining more about the inexorable growth of defense-related public expenditures than about the human realities of obtaining veterans' benefits.) But if the reports of most serious students of VA operations are to be believed, there is surely something interesting going on here. The VA bureaucracy is orderly, humane, comprehensible, and supportive. It has achieved these characteristics without constitutional due process adjudication, indeed within a statutory scheme that proscribes judicial review and fends off the bar by limiting its fees to $10 per case.[38] A generous positive law of welfare state entitlements implemented through a massive bureaucracy is not just a pipe dream. It has been constructed in the VA program through political will and administrative organization. When realized this way, welfare state entitlements achieve their greatest security.

33. Whereas approximately three million claims are filed each year, the Board of Veterans' Appeals received only thirty to thirty-four thousand appeals in fiscal years 80 and 81. VETERANS ADMINISTRATION, ANN. REP. 119 (1981).
34. *See* Veterans Administration, 38 C.F.R. § 3.102. § 3.103(a); *See also* P. STARR, *supra* note 28; S. LEVITAN & K. CLEARY, *supra* note 28.
35. *See* Veterans' Benefits, 38 U.S.C. § 241–243.
36. *See* Klonoff, *The Congressman as Mediator between Citizens and Government Agencies: Problems and Prospects*, 16 HARV. J. LEGIS. 701 (1979).
37. *See* Rabin, *Preclusion of Judicial Review in the Processing of Claims for Veterans' Benefits: A Preliminary Analysis*, 27 STAN. L. REV. 905 (1975).
38. *See* Veterans' Benefits, 38 U.S.C. § 3404(c)(2); Hines v. Lowrey, 305 U.S. 85 (1938).

I will not go further to claim that it is precisely the exclusion of lawyer advocates, courts, and most legal formality that makes the administration of VA benefits a success. Nor do I claim that all other welfare bureaucracies have similar ideals, dedicated and imaginative managers, or benign political environments. The point is more limited: whereas the genuflections of the post-*Goldberg* entitlements jurisprudence to administrative expertise, integrity, and complexity represent to some merely the prudential mask of an authoritarian ideology,[39] a more optimistic interpretation of the jurisprudence can describe the Court as responding to a dimly perceived and badly explained truth about the capacities and the virtues of coordinate institutions. And, whatever one's view of the constitutional jurisprudence, the capacities and virtues are real.

THE DICTATORSHIP OF RULES

In the closing paragraph of *The Ages of American Law*, Grant Gilmore wrote, "In Heaven there will be no law, and the lion will lie down with the lamb. . . . In Hell there will be nothing but law, and due process will be meticulously observed."[40] For many, the administrative state is moving us inexorably toward Gilmore's hell as agency piles upon agency, rule piles upon rule. Administration is almost synonymous with bureaucracy; bureaucracy with red tape; and the red tape of rules with the imprisonment of those human spirits struggling in frustration for freedom from its clinging coils.

Yet I have equated administration, at least bureaucratic rationality, with the liberal ideal; have urged the impersonality of rules as a safeguard against domination, as a means for maintaining the social preconditions of individual moral agency. Instead of urging ever greater use of contextualized adjudicatory process in administrative institutions, I have urged that constitutional due process adjudication make rule-bound bureaucracy one of its primary heuristics for establishing a presumption of constitutional legitimacy. What can explain my lemming-like

39. *See* Burt, *The Constitution of the Family*, 1979 Sup. Ct. Rev. 329 (1979).
40. G. Gilmore, The Ages of American Law 111 (1977).

rush, not just to any shore, but if Gilmore is correct, to the River Styx?

The reasons are straightforward. The first is trite, but bears repeating. Our society does not seem headed for Gilmore's heaven. And, as the government interposes itself between lions and lambs in countless contexts, both of these species will surely be better off if there are some rules interposed between them and the functionaries who would regulate their affairs. To have an administrative state without rules is to have not due process, but *Der Prozess.*[41]

If we would know who wants more rules, we might interview the owner of the Sun Ray Drive-In Dairy, Inc., a convenience food store that applied to the Oregon Liquor Control Commission for a license to sell beer. The Oregon Court of Appeals' description of the applicant's highly personalized treatment at the hands of the commission's employees is both succinct and revealing.

> Petitioner appeals from an order of the Oregon Liquor Control Commission denying its application for a Class B Package Store liquor license for its store in Ontario, Oregon. The commission based its refusal on ORS 471.295(1) which provides that the commission may refuse to license an applicant if it has reasonable ground to believe that there are "sufficient licensed premises in the locality" or that the granting of the license is "not demanded by public interest or convenience." . . .
>
> Various persons employed by the licensing division of the commission testified at the hearing on petitioner's application. Mr. William Alexander, a liquor control officer, . . . initially testified that he recommended refusal of petitioner's application because of (1) objections of area residents; (2) the large number of existing outlets; and (3) the fact that petitioner's store did not have a broad inventory of groceries. However, he subsequently abandoned the last ground. He testified that even if the petitioner's store had been a Safeway, he would have recommended refusal because of the number of outlets already in the area. . . .
>
> Mr. Alexander's . . . direct superior, Mr. Charles Miller, . . . testified that he reviewed Mr. Alexander's report and agreed that the application should be denied. Mr. Miller's reasons . . . [were the

41. DER PROZESS is the original title of F. KAFKA, THE TRIAL (W. Muir & E. Muir trans. 1937).

same as] Mr. Alexander's. . . . Mr. Miller testified that he had no "yardstick" to go by, and that his recommendation was based on his "past experience and judgment."

Mr. Miller's recommendation was . . . passed on to Mr. Don Church, the commission's director of licensing. Mr. Church testified that the number of other licensees in a particular area was not a factor in deciding whether to issue a license. . . . Mr. Church stated that if a store is deemed by the commission to be a "legitimate grocery store," the commission's policy is to grant the store a Class B Package Store license, regardless of how many other licensees are in the immediate area. The reason for his recommendation of denial to the commission, Mr. Church said, was that petitioner's store had been represented to him in the reports from his subordinates as a "gasoline station with dairy products." Mr. Church concluded from the evidence he heard at the hearing that petitioner's store more closely approximated a "legitimate grocery store" than he had supposed, but that there would have to be still greater expansion of the scope of petitioner's inventory and the number of items of each type before he would recommend approval. Mr. Church expressed concern, for example, that the store's inventory listed only three packages of Birdseye creamed peas. . . .

Petitioner gave evidence that several similar businesses in the Ontario area and neighboring cities, some with significantly smaller grocery inventories and one that appears to be an ordinary gas station, had package licenses.

Petitioner asks that we reverse the findings of fact, contending that the proof of each ultimate fact was otherwise. We are unable to review for substantial evidence because we are unable to ascertain the issues or the standards against which the evidence is to be measured. How many licensed premises are "sufficient" in the "locality"? Is sufficiency to be measured by population density, supply and demand, geographical area to be covered, other factors, or a combination of factors? How are public objections to be weighed? What ratio of acceptability should be required? Within what area of the license applicant? Finally, are all grocery stores entitled to a package license? If so, how is "grocery store" defined?[12]

After noting that without published rules there can be no public knowledge of policy, private planning, democratic control, meaningful license hearings, or judicial review of orders,

42. Sun Ray Drive-In Dairy v. Or. Liquor Control Comm'n, 517 P.2d 289, 290–92 (1973).

the court reversed the order of denial and ordered the commission to process no more licenses until it adopted and published some rules.[43] Litigants clamor for rules without seeing all the advantages ascribed to them by the Oregon Court of Appeals. Private parties demand rules as well as assail them,[44] for without rules they cannot plan their lives; they are at the mercy of the petty official, who may be corrupt, incompetent, or merely confused. To be sure dependence on rules can go too far. How far is far enough is a question of extraordinary difficulty.[45] I am therefore also convinced that the courts should neither demand nor proscribe rules except in extreme cases. And I am tempted to say to those who decry the incapacity of rule-bound administration to contextualize cases, that they forget that statutory and administrative rules are themselves contextualized. They are shaped by history, experience, research, public participation, and political oversight, as well as by bureaucratic convenience. This broader context is the reality of the administrative state. Upon sustained examination from this perspective the rules which sometimes frustrate us in individual cases often appear reasonable—all things considered.

Thus, in the end, my argument comes to this: A liberal, constitutional jurisprudence of administrative due process—one that relies on fundamental principles of individual autonomy as the foundation for the recognition of rights—is consistent with the liberal reformist impulse to make our administrative institutions more effective, more responsive, and more humane. Such a jurisprudence does not strip courts of their power (through statutory interpretation and administrative common law) to goad legislators and administrators to experiment with new structures and processes that might better realize our ideals. In-

43. *See* Sun Ray Drive-In Dairy v. Or. Liquor Control Comm'n, 517 P.2d 289, 294 (1973).
44. *See, e.g.*, Holmes v. N.Y. Hous. Auth., 398 F.2d 262 (2d Cir. 1968); NLRB v. Wyman-Gordon, 394 U.S. 759 (1969).
45. *See, e.g.*, J. Mashaw, Bureaucratic Justice 106–23 (1983); Ehrlich & Posner, *An Economic Analysis of Legal Rulemaking*, 3 J. Legal Stud. 257 (1974).

stead it is a jurisprudence that should constantly remind us that the dialogue of constitutional adjudication can be but one of the many conversations through which we shape our public lives and protect our private ones.

Index

Abstraction, 58; as weakness of appropriateness model, 87–93, 99. *See also* Formalism

Accuracy, 102, 108, 112, 156, 254; as goal of due process, 103–04; as social value, 107, 173; costs of, 118–40 (*see also* Social costs); in post-*Goldberg* jurisprudence, 154; misdirects due process analysis, 165; in administrative processes, 202; in prudential model, 204; in dignitary process, 212

Adjective law, 105

Adjudication, 246; of value conflicts, 230–31; as decision model, 232; tension with administration, 233; shift away from, 239

Administration: as process of realizing values, 230; as decision model, 232; tension with adjudication, 233; shift toward, 239; exclusion from zone of privacy, 246

Administrative costs: of AFDC, 117; of DI, 117. *See also* Social costs

Administrative discretion. *See* Discretion, administrative

Administrative due process, 4, 270. *See also* Due process; Administration; Administrative state

Administrative law: history of, 15; phases, 24–25; in interest representation model, 161

Administrative legitimacy, 31, 169, 173; transmission belt model, 16–18, 29–30; expertise model, 18–22, 29; participation model, 22–24, 29

Administrative Powers over Persons and Property (Freund), 77

Administrative Procedure Act (APA), 26, 27, 235, 256, 259

Administrative state, 12, 19, 35, 247, 262; constitutionality of, 4; overintrusiveness, 33, 41; underprotectiveness, 33, 40–41; symbolic appropriateness, 41–43; functional adequacy, 41–43; in instrumental rationality paradigm, 101, 102; legitimacy of, 169; rules application in, 225–27, 267–71

AFDC. *See* Aid to Families with Dependent Children

Aid to Families with Dependent Children, 206, 213, 252; in *Goldberg*, 113–15; costs, 117, 118–24; social welfare, analysis of, 128–30

Alienation, 176, 226

Analogy. *See* Method of analogy

APA. *See* Administrative Procedure Act

Appropriateness model. *See* Model of appropriateness

Appropriate process, 51–53, 103, 170, 232, 239. *See also* Model of appropriateness

Arendt, H., 169

Associational values. *See* Communitarian values

273

274 / Index